*"Human beings draw close to one another by their common nature,
but habits and customs keep them apart"*
—*(Ancient Confucian Saying)*

OPENING DOORS:

SELLING TO MULTICULTURAL REAL ESTATE CLIENTS

The Real Estate Agent's
Guide to Understanding
Culturally Diverse Home
Buyers and Sellers

Michael D. Lee, CRS, GRI

This publication is designed to provide accurate and authoritative information in regard to the subject matter covered. It is sold with the understanding that the publisher is not engaged in rendering legal, accounting, or other professional service. If legal advice or other expert assistance is required, the services of a competent professional person should be sought. *From a Declaration of Principles jointly adopted by a committee of the American Bar Association and a committee of Publishers.*

10   9   8   7   6   5   4   3   2   1

Library of Congress Cataloging in Publication Data

Lee, Michael D. 1950-
    Opening doors: selling to multicultural real estate clients / Michael D. Lee.
        p. cm.
    "The real estate agent's guide to understanding culturally diverse home buyers and sellers."
    Includes bibliographical references and index.
    ISBN 1-886939-32-2
    1. House selling--United States. 2. Minorities--United States. 3. Real estate agents--United States. I. Title.
HD1375 .L44 1999
333.33'3'0973--dc21

                                                                99-050372
                                                                CIP

Oakhill Press
461 Layside Drive
Winchester, Virginia 22602
800-32-Books
Printed in the United States of America

Dedication

This book is dedicated to my parents, John and Ruth Wong, who taught me the importance of valuing our differences. They also showed me by example the importance of never giving up—even against seemingly impossible odds.

This book is also dedicated to the hundreds of real estate agents and clients who took time to share their cultural beliefs with me. There were far too many to list so as not to omit anyone from the list I dedicate this book to you. It is really you, not me, who wrote this book.

Contents

MAP OF THE WORLD:
PETERS PROJECTION

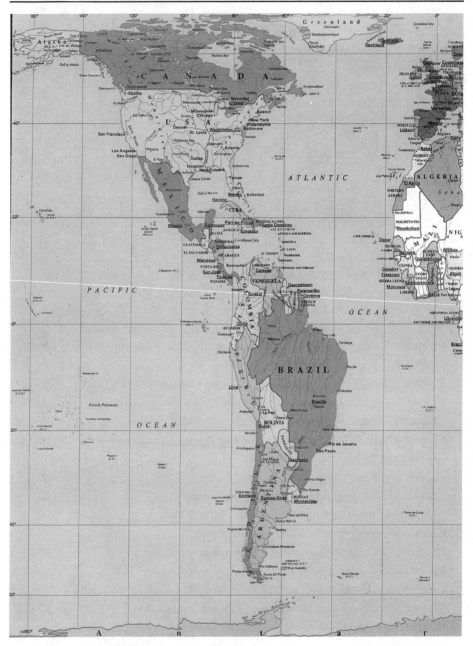

The map which represents countries accurately according to their surface areas.

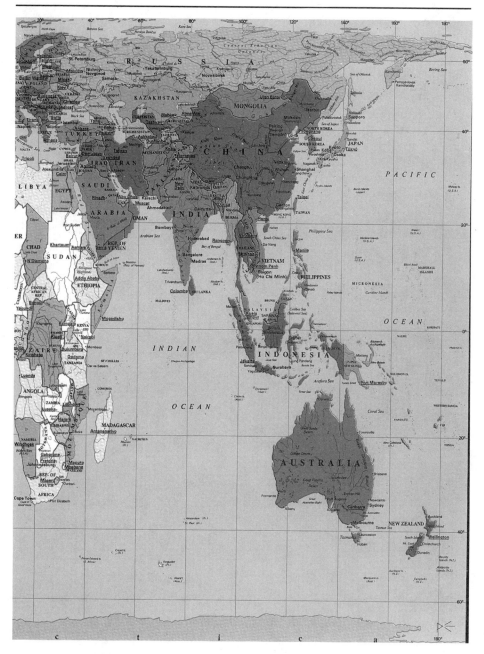

Foreword

I am proud to say that I am the granddaughter of immigrant grandparents—on both sides of the family. Dad's parents—the Barretts—came over on the boat from County Cork, Ireland. Mom's folks—the Dolces—immigrated to the United States from Naples, Italy. When both couples arrived in the United States in the early 1900s, they were young, afraid, and uneducated in the American way.

The Dolces could hardly read or write. When my mother was fourteen years old, she wrote a letter to President Franklin D. Roosevelt on my grandparents' behalf. They were about to lose their home and my mother pled their case. Her letter influenced the passage of new financial legislation—the Federal Housing Administration, thus the FHA loan—that saved them from losing their home. This new loan enabled my grandparents to pay off the private individual who tried to foreclose on them because of one late payment.

What does my family history have to do with Michael Lee's much needed book, *Opening Doors*? His book is about people like my grandparents who come to this country looking for the same opportunities you and I have. Many of you reading this foreword perhaps have immigrant grandparents who opened doors for your family—in ways you will never be able to repay. I have inherited a sound work ethic and a deep, abiding attitude of gratitude from my grandparents. My guess is that many of you now reading Mike's book have inherited these traits, too.

When I became a Realtor®, much of my success was the result of the compassion and instincts I inherited from my grandparents. For example, a couple explained to me that they could not purchase the home of their dreams until I investigated whether or not anyone had died in that home. I did not question their concern because I respected their beliefs and customs. So I abided by their wishes and researched the answer they needed to make a decision. When another buyer insisted that his home face a certain direction, I made sure we previewed property that fit his specific request.

During my last 20 years plus of teaching real estate agents, I have suggested that agents never criticize or make fun of people who do not think or act like everyone else. I have written and produced videos on the subject of understanding multicultural differences. But not until Michael Lee's book have I felt the subject has been properly covered.

So it is with great enthusiasm and admiration that I recommend you not only read, but also practice the strategies presented in *Opening Doors: Selling to Multicultural Real Estate Clients.* Our world is becoming smaller. More people from around the globe are coming together and forming new neighborhoods in America. As we blend with one another, we begin to appreciate our diversity. And in that process we discover how much we really do have in common.

Danielle Kennedy
Sun Valley, Idaho
August 1999

Preface

The real estate profession in the United State is undergoing tremendous change and every time a change occurs opportunities open for those who are ready to embrace it. Today, the *change* is the tremendous number of people from other cultures who have a burning desire to own American real estate. The *opportunity* is to help multicultural people reach their dream of buying property in this county. The obstacles for those who want to open the door to home ownership for multicultural people are differences in beliefs and practices.

The purpose of this book is to help sellers and real estate agents become more aware of the different needs of people from other cultures and to help meet those needs. By meeting those needs, the real estate transaction should be more enjoyable and less frustrating as cultural frictions are reduced.

By learning about long-standing cultural tendencies, those who sell real estate will be able to understand the reasons behind the beliefs and practices of others. However, this book only lays the groundwork for your lifelong journey toward becoming an expert with the cultures you most commonly meet in your practice.

I hope you will find the information in this book helpful in reminding you that people from other cultures are no different from anyone else in this country. We all want to be part of a great country that is the United States. Home ownership is the ultimate sign of loyalty and commitment anyone can make to a country.

Approach

There is precious little data available on the subject of how cultural beliefs impact the purchase and sale of real estate.

Therefore, the author primarily relied on hundreds of interviews with real estate agents and clients during a period of ten years to determine common cultural tendencies. No information has been placed in this book unless it was verified by at least two reliable sources.

In addition, the author has gleaned information from literally thousands of obscure written resources that may have tangentially touched on the subject. A representative sample of these sources is listed in the back of this book.

In spite of how carefully this information was assembled there will be those who disagree with some of the statements made herein. Recognize that culture is handed down from generation to generation, mostly by actions and word-of-mouth. As a result, there may be wide variations within cultures regarding beliefs and practices. Ultimately, the only way *to know* what any real estate clients believes is *to ask* them and then to do your best *to respect* their wishes.

Goal

The goal of this book is to encourage you to look at the process of learning about cultural differences as interesting and educational—not something to be feared. If this work does nothing more than that it will have achieved its goal.

1

Introduction

Whether you are a real estate professional or an owner trying to sell your own house, you are likely to meet people from other cultures as potential clients. If you do, you may be frustrated by some of the myriad cultural differences that can present themselves in a real estate transaction.

Massive immigration into the United States, the greatest part of it from Latin America, the Pacific Rim, and the Middle East, is unprecedented in history. In 1996, the Bureau of the Census reported that 21.8 million Americans age eighteen and over were foreign-born. America allows more legal immigration than the rest of the countries of the world combined. Adding to the increasing multiculturalism of the country is the fact that this influx will have such far-reaching effects that the Census Bureau predicts that 25 percent of all Americans will be Spanish-speaking at the turn of the century. In 1995, non-Hispanic whites accounted for 73.6 percent of the total population of the United States but will be only 52.8 percent by the year 2050.

When they first come to America, new immigrants tend to live in large coastal cities. According to the Immigration and Naturalization Service, some 770,000 new arrivals settled in the gateway city of New York from 1990 to 1995. The 505,000 who came to Los Angeles comprised the second largest group to enter the country. The next largest destination was Chicago, with 245,000, followed by Miami's 240,000. Washington, D.C. follows with 199,500.

Fortunately for the real estate industry, these new arrivals exhibit a greater desire to own their own homes than the balance of the population. Statistics from the Federal National Mortgage Association (FNMA) indicate promisingly that immigrants who rent are three times as likely to have home buying as their number one priority as are other long-time Americans.

The numbers are even more startling in other areas. In southern California, 74 percent of Japanese and 60 percent of Chinese Americans now own their homes. In line with the trend, 57 percent of Koreans and 33 percent of Vietnamese are home owners. For new immigrants, owning a home in America demonstrates to friends and family more than any other symbol that they have achieved success in their new country. Thus, the coming decade will witness a sales boom for those who have the necessary knowledge for enjoying success in this market.

The reason the term *multicultural* is in such common use today is that new immigrants bring their own cultures from their home countries. Soon after arrival, most attach it to that of their new home, the United States. Nevertheless, they exhibit at least one characteristic of earlier immigrants to America: the willingness to save to reach their goals. Culturally diverse people also exhibit a special eagerness to work hard to turn their dreams of home ownership into a reality. The average American family puts away only 2 to 4 percent of its gross income in savings. Many new arrivals come with a long-held tradition of saving 25 percent or more of their income. While a forty-hour work week serves to satisfy most of us, our foreign-born counterparts commonly put in sixty to eighty hours. The most casual glance at these figures makes it clear: the combination of higher savings plus dedicated hard work and a greater desire to buy real estate will make home ownership a reality in the near future for many, if not most, of this dedicated wave of new residents.

These facts foretell tremendous opportunity for professionals in real estate. Equally, related fields like mortgage lending, escrow and title companies, new home construction, and real estate law and insurance can expect to enjoy their share of the new prosperity. People in all of these industries can look forward to the benefits of doing business with new immigrant home buyers.

However, every culture, including our own American culture, is unique. Significant differences in language, dress, food preference, work habits, and attitudes about time can result in frustration for any American who is not well prepared. Success in relationships with people from other cultures means learning the specialized ways of doing business with them.

Anyone who tries to transact real estate with people from other than the American culture will likely become frustrated by multicultural clients who act according to seemingly inconsistent and incomprehensible cultural practices and beliefs. They may have concerns about which direction a home faces or the numbers in the address. Some have an irresistible need to negotiate, and perhaps the habit of talking in their native language in front of others. They may continue to negotiate the terms of the contract after it has been signed. If any of the above are your reasons for purchasing this book, then congratulations—it was written to help you understand the practices of people from other cultures, to help you bridge the gap to rapport and building rewarding lifetime relationships with all your clients.

Stereotypes of Americans

Believe it or not, people outside the United States have stereotypical beliefs about Americans! True or false, these impressions affect their dealings with people here just as stereotypes of multicultural clients impact our dealings with them.

The first belief that others hold is that Americans are always in a hurry. As a result, they think we do not take the time to develop deep, meaningful relationships. They also believe that we make rash decisions because of the pressures of time.

The second stereotype that outsiders sometime hold is that Americans only think in the short term. While relationships may last a lifetime in many other counties, they see American business and personal relationships continuing only for a few years, if that. In fact, some believe that once a contract in the United States has been completed, that is the end of business dealings. Sadly, this is too often the case.

The third stereotype about Americans is that we are somewhat brusque in our business dealings. This may be the result of our incessant need to "get down to business." Outside this country there is usually a lot more "small talk" before business is begun.

The fourth stereotype about Americans is that many of us are overly materialistic. Who could blame others for thinking this after seeing television programs like "Lifestyles of the Rich and Famous?" Remember, just as we stereotype people from other cultures in our media, the media stereotypes Americans in other countries as preoccupied with money, sex, violence, and material possessions.

The fifth stereotype is that we are ethnocentric. Many of us believe that the American culture, the English language, and the Christian religion are the best. Others also see people in the United States as knowing or caring little about world geography, cultures, or religions.

While these stereotypes are certainly not true of all Americans, I think we would agree that there are valid reasons others may draw these conclusions. Just as we would not like to be stereotyped, let us not be guilty of the same crime when it comes to people from other countries.

Americans and Asians: The Widest Gulf

Because of vastly different communication styles, Americans and Asians have the greatest potential for misunderstandings in real estate transactions. To illustrate, people acculturated in the United States place more importance on the speaker than on the listener. On the other hand, people from China, Japan, and India view communication as a process of cooperation between the parties in which speaker and receiver work together toward eventual understanding.

Asians also have a different view of legal contracts. Americans put everything they want in a contract. Signing it brings negotiations and their relationship with the other party, to an end, except for delivery of the promised goods. On the other hand, Asians put only the essentials into written agreements and leave the details for "later," which could turn out to be long after the actual written contract is signed, sealed, and delivered. For this group, signing a contract is just the beginning of a long-term relationship.

Some people in this country think that some practices common to Asian cultures are unethical. As an example, Americans believe that jobs should be given based on merit. Confucian beliefs, however, lead some Asians to hire members of their own family over more qualified strangers, a practice that we disdainfully call nepotism. Indeed, given our cultural viewpoint, it is. According to their beliefs, though, *our* practices are mistaken.

Americans believe in "speaking one's mind" while Asians

believe that a show of emotion is neither acceptable nor well-mannered. People here commonly express the wish to "know where they stand," whereas most Asians have learned to go out of their way to avoid confrontation.

Because of these differences and the beliefs that many Asians hold, this book will devote the largest amount of space helping real estate agents and affiliated professionals understand their Asian clients. However, answers that may have eluded you about Hispanics, African Americans, Middle Easterners, Native Americans, Germans, French, or others will also be given. If any question remains, the final chapter will help you discover your own answers about everything you want to know about these clients.

Becoming successful in business dealings with people from other cultures requires thinking of business relationships in a totally new way. Consider these relationships to be partnerships in which you help your clients understand the real estate process and, in exchange, they teach you about their native language, culture, and customs.

Most agents simply ignore the fact that their clients are from another culture and try to treat them like everyone else. While admirable, this ineffective tactic leads to miscommunication and frustration. Both you and your clients know they are different. Trying to hide this obvious fact creates tension that can pervade an entire real estate transaction and prevent the rapport essential to success from ever developing.

Others protest that fairness requires them to treat everyone exactly the same. They are not concerned with the client's cultural background, they say, and don't understand why anyone would be. I congratulate them on their attempt at impartiality, but the fact is that they are missing the opportunity to fit their presentations and practices to the special needs of special clients. As you will see, there are important differences that your clients would prefer that you not ignore.

In fact, the law requires that you treat all clients fairly—not necessarily the same. For instance, would you treat a client with a hearing or sight impairment the same as everyone else? No—you would try to adapt to his or her needs. In the same way, we should customize each relationship to meet the unique needs of each person with whom we choose to work.

The successful agent acknowledges cultural differences and sets out to bridge the gulf that can result by taking a genuine interest in the client's culture. People love to share their food, beliefs, and language with anyone who shows an interest. The result is that everyone wins. By helping to educate the agent as the agent does them, multicultural people take an active part in their own home purchase. This helps them feel much more comfortable with the process.

Making the effort to learn about other cultures, customs, and languages makes each of us better able to communicate. This kind of cultural exchange provides us with a round-the-world tour without the hassles of lost luggage, seasickness, and expense. It can be a fascinating and enlightening trip for those who are ready and willing to take the first step.

One barrier to understanding is that people in United States tend to see the world from the viewpoint of their unique American culture. In this country, as in others, most of us believe that our culture is the best culture and our way of doing things the most effective. We trace our values, customs, and beliefs back to English common law, Protestant religious ideas, and a fiercely individualistic American heritage. Americans believe that we alone are responsible for our own success or failure. But many other cultures steadfastly hold that a higher being is responsible for the bounty of life and that one must simply accept whatever it provides.

The religious beliefs of Asian immigrants run a complex gamut through Shinto, Buddhism, Taoism, Brahamanism, Hinduism, and Confucianism, each possessing its own special point of view. Customary methods of negotiation are different, legal systems (or lack thereof) are diverse, and language and accents are unlike what we are used to. As horrific as it seems to many Americans, Asians may value group success over individual achievement.

Another barrier to understanding between differing cultures is the impressions Americans develop from common media-borne stereotypes. On television and in films most minority groups are portrayed in less-than-positive roles, such as criminals, gang members, or just incomprehensible foreigners. As a former actor in major motion pictures, the author is painfully aware that although usually unconscious and unwitting, many of these negative images can create confusion, even fear, in people who don't know they are simply Hollywood stereotypes.

Becoming more successful with immigrant cultures calls for setting aside those comfortable, fixed ideas and opening up to other people's way of life. Pigeonholing and stereotyping others' beliefs and behaviors in our own terms of what is correct or incorrect is counterproductive. While someone else's customs may be different to us, they are perfectly appropriate in another culture. Indeed, they may have been the difference between success and failure, or survival and starvation, where they came from.

This book is written to help anyone who is transacting real estate to effectively manage cultural differences. It has little or nothing to do with race, however. While the dominant racial group in the United States is European, there are significant differences between Americans of European heritage and recently arrived Europeans. An Asian whose family came here five or six generations ago to build the railroads that opened up the American West acts more like a second-generation Swede than a newly arrived Chinese immigrant. Hispanic Americans would readily tell you they have little in common with newly arrived immigrants from Mexico.

Culture is acquired and learned through life experience; it influences one's outlook on life and other people. Race, on the other hand, is biological and has little genuine effect beyond one's physical appearance.

Even within the United States, numerous, distinct subcultures exist in the southern, eastern, and western states. Culturally sensitive real estate agents know that it may be more comfortable to speak more slowly than usual and be more relaxed in business manners in dealing with people from the South. Easterners generally feel more at home speaking quickly and getting down to business right away. Those who live in the West are used to easy, friendly mannerisms. Those who come from cultures outside this country seem to exhibit pronounced differences simply because we are not used to them.

To restate a vital point: the simple difference between race and culture is that culture is learned, while color is inherited. Most people would agree that African Americans, while racially similar to people in Africa, are vastly different in culture. Children of fifth- and sixth- generation families whose ancestors came from China, Sweden, or Patagonia are as American as baseball and apple pie. Looking different is not the test. If there is a test to quantify all cultural differences, I haven't seen it, and I have looked. The things that separate us are subtle and individual, but they definitely exist.

All that said, some will ask, "Cultural differences! What do you mean, cultural differences?" They assume that because we live in the same country we can't really be so different. And it's surely true in more ways than not. We all think, behave, and view the world from our own perspective. The longer someone lives in the United States, the fewer cultural differences will be apparent and the more "mainstream" they become.

Generational Differences

Generational differences are widely recognized, not just by sociologists, but by new immigrants themselves. The Chinese refer to themselves in terms of the length of time the family has been here. New immigrants are first generation and harbor the most unfamiliar beliefs and customs that may affect real estate dealings with American agents and sellers. They are the least comfortable with American culture and language. As a result, this group can only work long hours at menial jobs to survive and prosper. Their children, the second generation, learn to study hard in school to succeed in this country. The dark side to this admirable trait is that there is tremendous family and peer pressures to do well. The suicide rate among Asian school age children is high.

The third generation of Chinese heritage retains little of the language skills and cultural awareness of their forebears although their handling of real estate can still be greatly affected by beliefs of their parents and grandparents. It is a shame to lose your cultural heritage in the proud Chinese culture. It is an even bigger shame to be unable to speak Chinese. In fact, the Chinese have a special term for those who cannot communicate in this proud language—*jook sing*, meaning "empty head."

The Japanese also specifically recognize generational differences. They call their first generation in this country *issei*, the second *nisei* and the third *sansei*. In keeping with the simplicity of their traditions, these terms literally mean first, second, and third. The three generations show virtually the same characteristics of change as the Chinese. So do Germans, Swiss, Italians, and nearly all new immigrants.

The generational difference is one of the reasons why there are so few minorities in the real estate profession. First-generation Asians, for example, are very uncomfortable with the English language and the American culture and so must rely primarily on manual labor to make a living here. The second generation gets an education and strives for "traditional jobs" where the path to success is well defined, such as in engineering, accounting, and medicine. The third generation and beyond are the first ones to consider nontraditional careers in sales and the arts, where success is not so clearly defined.

Almost all immigrant cultures are aware of these seemingly inescapable differences. You can always break the ice with multicultural clients by asking where their ancestors came from and how many generations have lived in the United States.

The second important step in breaking down cultural barriers is to know that the new immigrants cannot easily be lumped together into neatly defined groups. Many American real estate agents wrongly assume that all Asians belong to one big happy family with identical beliefs, languages, and customs. Since they think Asians look alike, they must be alike. Nothing could be further from the truth.

> *"People from other cultures present a tremendous opportunity for real estate agents who take the time to understand the differences."*

2

Background
Information

Before we can begin to open the doors of home ownership, we need to look at the background of the various
cultural groups.

The United States

To put the issue of multiculturalism in perspective, it is important to look at some facts that not all North Americans
may be completely familiar with. The United States is the
fourth largest country in terms of land mass and the third most
highly populated country in the world (behind China and
India, respectively). It is one of the youngest countries being
only a little over two hundred years old compared to other
cultures that have been in existence for thousands of years.

There are approximately 270 million Americans, of which over 80 percent are comprised of people of Anglo-European descent. The country's ethnic composition, however, is undergoing rapid change, which is one of the reasons for this book. African Americans currently make up the largest minority group, followed by Hispanics and Asians, who are the fastest-growing minorities.

The United States was founded on Judeo-Christian principles and values. Most Anglo-European Americans are Protestants or Catholics. One of the major principles is individualism—we control our own futures. One of the popular sayings that reflects this belief is that "God only helps those who help themselves."

American English is the official language of the United States but hundreds of other languages are regularly spoken. In some states multicultural people are having a strong impact. For instance, in California more people speak Spanish than English.

American family names reflect the multicultural matrix that makes up the country. It's not unusual to look in the telephone book of any major city and see English, German, French, Chinese, Japanese, Korean, Indian, Pakistani, Pacific Island, Middle Eastern, and other surnames represented. In the United States, children tend to take the family names of their father and a given name precedes it. Some women keep their maiden name even though married and others will add the surname of their husband, using a hyphen, such as "Jane Smith-White." In this example, "Jane" is the given name of a woman from the Smith family who has married a man named White. As you will discover, this is not necessarily the convention followed by families around the world. Knowing the difference will not only help you avoid embarrassment but legal entanglements as well.

Americans value time as a scarce resource. Being punctual and prompt in both social and business settings is expected. People in the United States are extremely competitive. Rewards are an important reflection of individual achievement. Strong eye contact and hand shakes are a sign of honesty and sincerity. Anything less is looked upon with great suspicion. Americans have numerous beliefs: the number thirteen is unlucky, black cats crossing one's path can bring bad luck as can walking under a ladder. Good luck can be the number seven, four-leaf clovers, or a rabbit's foot. People in the United States tend to associate the color white with happy events such as weddings and black with sad occasions like funerals. Red is the traditional color used for Valentine's Day and romance.

African Americans

While African Americans are certainly Americans, they are also a distinct cultural group in America. They are a blended culture whose roots can be not only be from Africa but also Egypt, Puerto Rico, Jamaica, Cuba, or any number of other countries. Anthropologists estimate that nearly 95 percent of African Americans are of mixed ancestry.

African Americans have been a part of the country since they were first abducted from Africa and brought here as slaves in the seventeenth century. During slavery days, families were split apart to enable their masters to control them more effectively. Selected slaves were used to breed other slaves in the same way that cattle and horses were bred. Females who nursed and raised the children of their masters and frequently bore children by them were often treated more kindly by their masters. It has only recently come to light, for instance, that some of the descendants of Thomas Jefferson are part African American.

The freeing of the slaves after the Civil War did little to integrate African Americans into American society. At the end of the war, 91 percent of the African Americans in the United States lived in the South. Most had obtained few useful skills and it was hard for them to find gainful employment, especially in the cities. As a result, the Caucasian majority began to think of this minority as a lazy, shiftless people with no sense of responsibility.

Laws in the United States have consistently been used against African Americans. For decades, they were effectively denied the right to vote, especially in the South, by the imposition of laws requiring literacy, property ownership, and other qualifications. "Jim Crow" laws enforced segregation in almost every aspect of life in the South, from buses to restaurants to hotels. The testimony of an African American against a Caucasian person was ruled unworthy in a court of law. Miscegenation was a law that prohibited sexual relations between African American men and white women although the union between white men and African American women was not banned. When African American behavior was within the law but disliked by whites, lynching was a common solution.

In 1880, the industrial revolution encouraged many African Americans to move into northern cities. The two periods of largest migration were between 1916 and 1919 and between 1921 and 1924, primarily driven by labor shortages as a result of World War I.

By 1929, African Americans were an integral part of the American labor force, primarily in the steel industry, mining, railroad, shipping, automobiles, and meat-packing. They were almost always restricted to jobs requiring unskilled labor and banned from joining labor unions.

In 1954, the United States Supreme Court ruled that racial segregation of public schools was unconstitutional. The result was riots throughout several southern states by white protesters. It took National Guard troops to clear the way for African American students to attend previously all-white schools.

In 1963, Dr. Martin Luther King, Jr. led two hundred thousand people to Washington, D.C., to support civil rights for African Americans. As a result of this visibility and other pressures, Congress drafted and President Lyndon Johnson signed into law the Civil Rights Act of 1964. It provided federal funds to ensure African Americans the right to vote, to speed school segregation, and to eliminate discriminatory employment practices.

Today, African Americans are only really beginning to achieve equality in the United States. They still lag far behind whites in terms of income, home ownership rates, and almost any other measure of parity. There is currently a large migration of African Americans to the southern states due to increased opportunities in jobs and housing.

The church is an integral part of the life of many African Americans, most of whom are Baptist, Methodist, or Episcopal. Practicing the Christian religion was one of the few comforts they were allowed during the slavery period and its fervor has not slacked to this day. Some African Americans have joined the Black Muslim church, which advocates the creation of a separate state for their group.

Much of the African American language dialect is a direct result of hearing the King James Bible read aloud since they weren't allowed to attend school throughout their early history in the United States. Music is also an important part of the culture since it was one of the few forms of expression that was permitted when they first arrived here.

Historically, African Americans have experienced widespread discrimination, including segregation, lack of voting rights, and refusal to sell or rent housing to them. This has resulted in one of the lowest rates of home ownership of any cultural group in the country in spite of the fact that studies place the purchasing power of African Americans between $450 and $533 billion.

There is a strong sense of pride in the African American heritage and in their cultural uniqueness. There is also a strong sense of loyalty to the extended family, which may include blood relatives and others on whom the family can rely. This can certainly include real estate professionals if you demonstrate that you can be trusted and that you care more about them than about your commission. African Americans tend to value the importance of family over individual success. It is expected that those individuals who do achieve success will share with the larger community.

African Americans tend to be more tactile and touch each other more than European Americans during conversation. Interrupting two people from this culture who are talking can be considered offensive. Conversations between African Americans can be interpreted as dramatic by outsiders because of the common use of large gestures. Like most Americans, African Americans tend to like strong eye contact when they are speaking to you. On the other hand, they may give you less eye contact when listening than when talking. This is thought to be the result of historical master-slave communication styles during slavery. Also, names given to African Americans are extremely important. Be sure to ask them what they would like to be called instead of assuming. Never call any African American by the first name without permission as it could be taken as a sign of disrespect. Always address them as "Mr.," "Mrs.," or "Ms."

Caribbean Islanders

The Caribbeans are a group of islands scattered across 100,000 square miles of the southwest Atlantic Ocean. It is a mixture of races, languages, and cultures consisting of independent countries as well as territories. Languages spoken include English as well as Spanish, French, and Dutch.

Jamaica is the Caribbean's third largest island with long, beautiful beaches surrounded by lush green mountains ringed by cane fields and coconut and banana plantations. It is the largest English-speaking island, with a population of 25 million. Tourism is the main industry in this country that is about the size of Connecticut. While English is the official language, many Jamaicans also speak "Patois" (pronounced *Pa-twa*), which is a mix of Creole English and West African. The two most popular sayings on the island are "no problem" (don't worry) and "walk good" (be well).

Most Jamaicans are of Black African descent with a minority of Afro-Europeans and Afro-East Indians. So many Jamaicans have left the country to live in England and the eastern United States that the numbers who live on the island are about the same as those who live off the island. The majority of Jamaicans are Christians, primarily of the Anglican and Protestant faith. Many other beliefs are practiced in the country, including Roman Catholicism.

There are 2 million Puerto Ricans living in the United States, making up 10.5 percent of the Hispanic population in this country. This island nation is about the size of Rhode Island and Delaware combined. It was a Spanish colony for four hundred years; shortly after 1900, it became an American affiliate. Don't forget that its residents are American citizens since it has been an U.S. Commonwealth for over eighty years. Therefore, immigrants from Puerto Rico are familiar with the American legal system and the home ownership process. There are two official languages in Puerto Rico, Spanish and English. As a result many people speak "Spanglish," which is a combination of the two languages.

In 1950, some Puerto Ricans began emigrating to this country. Their first stop was New York City, where most initially settled. Puerto Ricans have larger households than most families here, 37 percent of which are headed by women. Puerto Ricans are also a hard-working and well-educated people. They have the sixth highest rate of number of people in college in the world.

The Dominican Republican is about twice the size of Utah and consists of the eastern two-thirds of the island of Hispaniola. The remainder of the island is the country of Haiti. Today, there are over a half million people from the Dominican Republic living in the United States. This island nation is only fifteen minutes' flying time from Puerto Rico, and Dominicans usually have a close relationship with people from this neighboring island.

Spanish is the official language of the Dominican Republic but is heavily influenced by Caribbean phrases and accents. Many people in the Dominican Republic also speak English. The word *confianza,* meaning "trust," is often used in this country and is a status that must be earned by outsiders.

Over a million Dominicans live either part- or full-time in New York City and are known as "Dominican Yorks." While Dominicans are considered Hispanic, Haitians are usually included in the black population count. Most Dominicans profess to be of the Catholic faith. Dominican family names run the gamut of popular Hispanic names. The surname that is most unique to the Dominican Republic is "Delmonte."

Dominican men usually wear business suits or the traditional *chacabana* (white shirt worn over dark pants) while women often wear blouses and skirts. Many people from this country try to emulate New York fashions.

The Republic of Haiti is about the size of Connecticut and Hawaii combined. It occupies one-third of the island of Hispaniola and several other islands. It is a mountainous country with about 40 percent of its land area above 1,600 feet. It is the only French-speaking nation in the Americas. Nearly all Haitians are of African lineage, having descended from 480,000 slaves who were freed when Haiti gained independence in 1804. There are a very small minority of mulattoes and whites on the island. While Haiti's major religion is Roman Catholicism, voodoo is still widely practiced. The official languages are Haitian Creole and French. Haiti is the poorest country in the Americas. As a result, many of its residents suffer from deplorable heath conditions, including malnutrition, tuberculosis, and malaria.

To the west of the Dominican Republic and only ninety miles south of Florida is the Republic of Cuba, which few people know actually consists of two islands—Cuba and Isla de la Juventud. The island of Cuba is the largest island in the West Indies being about the size of Tennessee.

Most Cubans are of Spanish ancestry while some 12 percent have Black African roots and 20 percent are of mixed backgrounds. The official language of Cuba is Spanish but English is spoken by many inhabitants.

Due to communist influence, it is the least religious of all Latin American countries. Even so, the most common religion practiced is Catholicism but it has become mixed with African ideas to the religion known as "Santeria." Other beliefs such as witchcraft and communicating with the dead are still practiced today.

Cubans are a friendly people who love music and dance. They are very proud of their country despite the attempted influence by the United States to affect their economy and politics. Cubans have the highest literacy rate and lowest infant mortality rate of any country in the Western Hemisphere. Today, our relations with Cuba have warmed to a point where Americans can now own land there. Miami, Florida, is a city comprised mostly of ex-patriot Cubans.

Cubans are the best educated and most affluent Hispanic group, making up 4.7 percent of the Latino population in America, mostly living in Florida. Most have come to the United States since 1960 and there are now over a million Cubans in America. So many Hispanics have settled in Miami that the bodies of unidentified Hispanic men are tagged by police as "Juan Doe." Cuban family names reflect their Spanish heritage. The surnames that are most unique to Cuba are Bautista, Fuentes, Iniguez, Mendieta, Mulanes, Montefus, and Zaldivar.

Aruba is a small island located in the southern Caribbean. It is only twenty miles long and six miles wide. It enjoys sunny days all year round since it is situated outside the hurricane belt that sometimes affects the other islands. It is a popular tourist destination since it is less than three hours' flight time from Miami, Florida.

Barbados is the most eastern of the Caribbean islands. It is only twenty-one miles long and fourteen miles wide but is another popular vacation spot. The population is mostly of

African descent with a large percentage of mestizos.

Bermuda is still a Caribbean island even though it is situated totally outside the Caribbean Sea. This group of three hundred islands is only 650 miles east of Cape Hatteras in North Carolina.

The Cayman Islands are located in the western Caribbean. Making up the Caymans are the coral islands of Grand Cayman, Cayman Broc, and Little Cayman. They are conveniently located just fifty miles south of Miami.

Other islands in the Caribbean include the Bahamas, consisting of Grand Bahama, Providence, and Paradise Islands; Barbados; the U.S. Virgin Islands, consisting of St. Croix, St. John, and St. Thomas; the British Virgin Islands, consisting of Peter Island and Virgin Gorda; and Curacao.

Religious beliefs in the Caribbean range from old tribal religions with different degrees of Christian influence to completely Christian churches. In Haiti and the Dominican Republic voodoo is sometimes still practiced today. In Grenada, Trinidad, and St. Lucia, religions combine both African and Catholic elements.

Hispanics and Latinos

There are around 40 million Hispanics living in the United States with a combined estimated purchasing power of between $300 and $387 billion. The term *Hispanic* tends to refer to people who were born or whose background is from one of the Spanish-speaking Latin American countries, Spain, or Mexico. It may also be used by people who come from Caribbean countries such as Puerto Rico and Cuba. Some people from Spanish-language backgrounds may not like the term *Hispanic* due to negative stereotypes portrayed in the media. These individuals may prefer the term *Latin* or *Latino*. "Hispanic" is not a race of people because many Hispanics are a mix of races. Most are mestizo, being of both Spanish and Indian backgrounds.

Many Hispanics are religious, primarily Catholic. For these people the church and their beliefs play an important role in their lives. Be aware that many Hispanics, particularly those of Mexican descent, have lived in the United States for several generations. These may prefer to call themselves Americans as opposed to any other cultural-specific title. The family is important to most Hispanics. The extended family may include grandparents and godparents. The father is usually considered the head of the household and he may make decisions about the purchase or sale of the home without consulting his wife. Hispanics tend to be less individualistic and competitive than Americans. They generally emphasize group cooperation and achievement.

Some members of this group may avoid eye contact as a sign of respect for authority, while others demand strong visual contact. Gestures when talking may be more broad than Americans are comfortable with. Time is more flexible among Hispanics than Americans. Appointments may not be kept as precisely as people in the United States are used to. The exception is people from the former British Honduras, now called Belize, who are usually very punctual.

Hispanics are the fastest-growing group of minorities in America but they are also not a homogenous people. While most in this country come from Mexico (61 percent), 1993 U.S. Census Bureau figures show that some 12 percent come from Puerto Rico, 11 percent are from Central and South America, 5 percent come from Cuba, 4 percent hail from Spain. Again, many do not want to be called Hispanic, preferring the term *Latin* or *Latino*. Further complicating the issue, all do not speak Spanish. Remember, too, that when speaking about "North America" Mexico is also included in this area.

Mexicans

Mexico is one-fifth the size of the United States and is the bridge between our country and South America. It has twenty-nine states, two territories, and the Federal District of Mexico City. It has experienced political unrest and economic instability since the beginning of the twentieth century, although recent reforms have quieted things down.

Mexican Americans tend to be fiercely proud of their cultural heritage, which is a combination of Spanish, Mayan, and Aztec backgrounds. The original inhabitants of Mexico were ancient Indian civilizations, including the Olmec's, dating back to 2000 B.C. The Mayan Empire ruled from about A.D. 300 until the time of the Aztecs, who built elaborate cities with complex canal systems in Mexico from 1168 until being crushed by the Spanish conqueror Cortéz in 1519. As a result, the religious beliefs of Mexicans blend Catholicism with ancient Indian practices.

The majority of Mexicans are mestizos and about 30 percent of the rest are descendants of Mayan and Aztec Indians. Mexico City, the capital of Mexico, has about 25 million people, making it one of the largest cities in the world. Descendants of the Aztecs are particularly numerous in and around the capital.

The official language of Mexico is Spanish, although it is a bit different from that spoken in other parts of the world. Other languages spoken in the country include the twenty-seven Mayan and numerous Aztec Indian dialects. Mayans are mostly found on the Yucatan Peninsula and many speak Mayathan. Aztecs who mostly come from around the Mexico City area speak the Aztec-Nahuatl language. English is commonly spoken in the larger cities due to the large tourist trade from the United States.

Family names in Mexico can be confusing. One reason is the fact that many Hispanic women do not change their family name when they get married. These women simply add the husband's name as a middle name. Another reason for the complexity of Hispanic surnames is the addition of a *y* (pronounced *ee*) between the father's and mother's name. Yet another complication is the use of *de* (pronounced *day*) before the family name to indicate nobility. Family names commonly found in Mexico include Beltran, Bustamonte, Calles, Camacho, Castillo, Chavez, de la Cruz, de la Rosa, de Souza, Fuentes, Hidalgo, Huerta, Ignacio, Maldonado, Najera, Orozco, and Pavon.

Almost 90 percent of Mexicans are Roman Catholic. This religion has a tremendous influence on the Mexican culture and beliefs. The patron saint of Mexico is the Virgin of Guadalupe and she is a national symbol. Various other saints are honored throughout the year, including St. Anthony's Day on January 17, when children take their pets to church to be blessed.

The 1,800-mile border between the United States and Mexico sees thousands of Hispanics cross each year, both legally and illegally. The subject of immigration and legal status is generally a touchy subject for most people from Mexico.

Land is an important asset in Mexico since the value of money has been extremely unstable throughout recent history. This explains, to some degree, the importance Mexicans place on home ownership when they come to the United States.

Thirteen million Hispanics in America are Mexican Americans. They have the lowest educational level of any minority group, with only 44 percent receiving high school diplomas and 6 percent earning college degrees. One of the primary reasons for this disparity is that while schooling is important, family is a higher priority and it is the duty of older children to support the family, even if it means dropping out of school.

South Americans

South America accounts for 5 percent of the Hispanic American population. One-third come from Colombia and the rest are from Ecuador, Peru, Argentina, and Chile. There are over 1,500 different languages spoken in South America besides Spanish so do not assume that just because someone is from that country she or he necessarily speaks Spanish. Also do not assume that what you understand about Mexico applies to South America. For example, tortillas and tacos are a uniquely North American food and there are no such dishes found in South America.

Argentina is the eighth largest country in the world, being one-third the size of the United States. It is the second largest South American country and occupies most of the southern portion of South America. The official language of Argentina is Spanish, but people can speak with recognizable regional accents. Probably the most distinctive is "Porteno," spoken primarily in Buenos Aires and which has been influenced by Italian. Prominent surnames for Argentines are Carcano, Codovilla, Drago, Echeverria, Irigoyen, Larreta, Marmal, and Torcuato. Unlike most other Latin American countries, Argentina has a relatively small population of mestizos. The majority of Argentines are of European descent. Most people in the country practice Roman Catholicism while there is a substantial number of adherents of other religions, such as Christians, Buddhists, and Jews. Argentines are a proud people who tend to dress fairly conservatively. Older women rarely wear pants, which are believed to be masculine, although younger women from this country may do so.

Bolivia is the fifth largest country in South America about the size of California and Texas combined. It has some of the highest Andean mountain peaks on the continent. In fact, the Bolivian Plateau, which rises some 13,000 feet, is one of the highest inhabited places on earth. The majority of Bolivians are descended from the Incas, speaking only their own dialects of Quechua or Aymara'. The largest minority are mestizos and the rest are mostly of Spanish blood.

Brazil is the fifth largest country in the world, covering an area larger than the United States. It occupies almost half the area of South America and is so big that it has a border with every country in South America except Chile and Ecuador. Brazil has some twenty-two states. To get a conversation started, you might ask your Brazilian clients, "What state are you from?"

Brazil's people are young, with almost half under age twenty. Its official language is Portuguese, which is only slightly different from that spoken in Portugal; however German and Italian are spoken by many of its people. Common Brazilian surnames include Cabral, Castro, Emanuel, Mendez, Salvador, Torres and Vera Cruz. Most people profess the Roman Catholic religion although there are many minority Christian churches. The majority of people in Brazil are of European descent, with mostly German, Italian, Portuguese, Russian, and Spanish origins. The next largest groups are mulattoes and mestizos.

Brazilians are a fun-loving people who enjoy combining work and play. They are fashion-conscious and value well-polished shoes and manicured fingernails on both men and women. One of the most recognizable features of Brazil are the *gauchos* or Brazilian cowboys.

Chile is a long country of 2,670 miles which is extremely narrow with an average width of around 110 miles and an area a bit larger than that of Texas. It is the longest country in the world running north-to-south and as a result it has many different climates and regions, from deserts to swamps to mountains to seashore.

The official language of Chile is "Castellano," which is a form of Spanish. While similar to Spanish it has its own uniqueness. Most people are mestizos. Minority groups include Germans, Austrians, Italians, French, Swiss, English, and Middle Easterners. Like other South Americans, most Chileans are Christians of the Roman Catholic faith. Popular family names include Arboleda, Balmaceda, Bulnes, Davila, de Heridia, Solar, and Vicuna. People from Chile tend to be shy and have a great sense of humor. They take great pride in wearing stylish clothing. Even lower-income Chileans consider sloppy attire to be in poor taste.

Colombia is the fourth largest South American country and is about the size of Texas and California combined. It is located in the northwestern part of the continent between

Central and South America, with much of the southeast covered by jungle, so most Colombians live in the west.

Most people from Colombia speak Spanish, the official language, but there are also some forty other languages spoken by natives. The purest Spanish in South America is spoken in the capital city of Bogota. Most Colombians are mestizos and there is a larger minority of Caucasians. Indians are a small percentage of the population. The primary religion is Roman Catholicism. Like many other South Americans, Colombians are proud of their *rumbero* spirit—the ability to work hard while playing hard. They tend to be suspicious of people from outside their culture, but once they get to know you they will treat you like family. People in Colombia pride themselves in being clean and well dressed. Men usually wear suits and women wear dresses. Many Colombians have the last name Abadia, de Caldas, Cordoba, Flores, Gomez, Lleras, Narino, Obando, Olaya, de Paula, Reyes, Robledo, Sanclemente, Torres, and Zea.

Ecuador is a small country about the size of Nevada located directly on the equator (for which it is named). Spanish is the official language although "Quichua," the original language of the Incas, is spoken by highland Indian groups. Many people of Ecuador bear the family name Basquerizo, Icaza, Morino or Rocafuerte. Most Ecuadorians are of the Catholic faith. Most of its people are either pure Indian or of mestizo descent. There are two main regions that influence attitude: highland people are known as "Serranos," who tend to be more formal and reserved than their coastal counterparts, the "Costenos," who are considered more cosmopolitan and sophisticated. Serranos often prefer to wear clothing of blue, brown, and black, while Costenos seek to like brighter colors such as white, yellow, and red.

Paraguay is a landlocked country around the size of California located in the heart of South America. Most of its occupants are mestizo although there are some Asians and Middle Easterners as well. Paraguay is a bilingual country with two official languages—Spanish and "Guarani," the language of the original Indian tribe who occupied the country. The dialect of Spanish spoken in Paraguay is Castilian, which is somewhat different than that spoken in the rest of South America. Most Paraguayans are Catholic with a minority of other religions, primarily Mennonites. Western-style clothing is commonly worn and women usually wear dresses. The most common family names in Paraguay are Balbuena, Pintos, Salinas, Solano, Sosa, and Xuares.

Peru is the third largest country in South America, about three times the size of California. Most of its residents are descendants of the Incas, with the next largest group being mestizos. Peru has two official languages—Spanish and Quechua, the native Indian language. Most residents are Catholic although both Protestant and Evangelical churches are prevalent. The most popular surnames that are unique to Peru are Ambrossiani, Balta, Caceres, Castilla, Gamarra, Orbegozo, Pardo, Peirola, and Salcedo.

Uruguay is the smallest country in South America, about the size of Washington State, and sits on the Atlantic Ocean. Its people are mostly of a Spanish and Italian mix. The most unique family name in Uruguay is de Ibarbourou. Spanish is the official language of Uruguay. A combination of Spanish and Portuguese, known as "Portunal," is also spoken in the north. Uruguay is probably the least religious country in South America, with no official religion, although most belong to the Catholic Church. The symbol of Uruguay is the cowboy or *gaucho*. Uruguayans have a very flexible view of time. They often arrive late for meetings with friends unless it is a formal occasion.

Venezuela, located in northern South America, is about the size of Texas and Oklahoma combined. It is the most urbanized of all South American countries, with over 90 percent of the population living in the cities. Most people of Venezuela are mestizos with a minority of Europeans. Most people practice the Roman Catholic religion. Spanish is the official language of Venezuela, although some speak Portuguese. Venezuelans are known for their colloquialisms and my friends from there tell me that if you want to be liked by them you should use them frequently. For example, *chevere* means "very well" and *estar limpio* means "to be broke." The unique surnames found in Venezuela are Fombona, de Miranda, Monagas, Vallenilla, and Yanes.

Venezuelans are proud of their country and their liberator Simon Bolivar. They may regularly be late for appointments since the needs of people are more important than schedules. They are also very fashion-conscious and often wear the latest European styles.

Central Americans

Latinos from Central America comprise 6 percent of Hispanic Americans. Half come from El Salvador, while 20 percent are from Guatemala and 15 percent hail from Nicaragua.

Belize is a small country in Central America about the size of Massachusetts; it was formerly known as British Honduras when it was a crown colony of the United Kingdom. It has a wide mix of peoples, ranging from aborigines to Creoles to mestizos. English is the official language of Belize and most people also speak Creole. Most Belizeans belong to the Catholic Church but there are strong influences from the Anglican and Protestant religions.

El Salvador is the smallest and most densely populated republic in Central America. This coastal country is approximately the size of Massachusetts. It is called "Land of the Volcanoes" since over two hundred extinct volcanoes dot the landscape. Most of its people are a mix of Spanish and Native Americans known as "mestizos". El Salvador's official language is Spanish and most of its residents are Catholics. They pride themselves in being clean and well-groomed.

Nicaragua is roughly the size of Iowa and mostly populated by mestizo people. Spanish is the official language of Nicaragua although English is often spoken along with many Indian languages. Most Nicaraguans are Catholic but other Christian religions are also practiced. They place a great deal of importance on personal appearance. The uniquely Nicaraguan surnames include Sarmiento, Zavala, and Zelaya.

Guatemala is slightly larger than Ohio and is bounded on the north by Mexico, on the south by El Salvador and Honduras, on the east by Belize and the Caribbean Sea, and on the west by the Pacific Ocean. It is two-thirds covered by mountains. Do not assume that all Guatemalans speak Spanish. Almost 60 percent are of Indian background and may speak one of eighteen native dialects. Catholicism is the primary religion but the Indians still practice the worship of ancient tribal gods. The family name that is probably most unique to Guatemala is Carrera. People from Guatemala usually come to America for to improve themselves economically so they work extremely hard, even at menial jobs.

Asians

While Asians comprise a relatively small proportion of the U.S. population (less than 5 percent), research puts their purchasing power somewhere between $100 and $188 billion. Some of the Asian cultures are over four thousand years old, such as the Chinese, Korean, and Vietnamese. As a result, there tends to be a heavy emphasis on tradition and history. Learning something about Asian history goes a long way toward building rapport.

The family is extremely important to most Asians. This might include the extended family, with several generations living in the same household. Elders are highly respected for their wisdom and knowledge. Many Asians greatly respect education. They see it as a way to advance in this country. Asian parents may place a great deal of pressure on their children to do well in school. The suicide rate among Asian school age children is high.

"Saving face" or avoiding embarrassment is extremely important to many Asians. Some would rather die than lose face. Direct eye contact may be considered rude or intrusive. Also, keeping one's composure is important because "control over the body is control over the mind." Many Asians will ask what Americans may consider to be very personal questions when they first meet. Such queries as, "How old are you?" "Are you married?" or "How much do you earn?" are not intended to be offensive but are used to determine the status of the person to whom they are talking. Asians tend to be restrained in their public communications. Rarely is there any touching or use of large gestures when talking.

The 1990 Census shows that the majority of Asians in the United States were Chinese at 24 percent, the Filipinos next largest at 20 percent, Southeast Asians like the Vietnamese were 16 percent, Japanese and Asian Indians and Koreans each represented 12 percent, and Pacific Islanders were around 4 percent. It is predicted that immigration patterns will change these numbers, making Filipinos the largest group, the Chinese second, and Vietnamese third by the turn of the century.

Unlike Caucasians, most Asians are unusually adept at distinguishing among the facial characteristics of Koreans, Japanese, Chinese, Vietnamese, Hawaiians, Filipinos, and the like. When the author was growing up he learned very quickly that his parents did not want him to bring Japanese friends home because of the centuries-long animosity between the two cultures. Korea has also mistrusted the Japanese since that country was invaded and subjugated by them in 1910.

Contrary to a common impression, Asian languages are vastly dissimilar. Koreans uniformly speak the Han'gul tongue while the Chinese might speak any one of a hundred dialects. Although Chinese, Japanese, and Korean writing appear similar, they are easily distinguished.

Many Asians practice Buddhism, with the chances of having a higher station in the next life after reincarnation, which is determined by the number of good deeds done during the present life. There are two main types of Buddhism: "Theravata" Buddhism, which is practiced mainly in Burma, Cambodia, Laos, Sri Lanka, and Thailand, and "Mahayana" Buddhism, followed by the inhabitants of China, Japan, Korea, Mongolia, Tibet, and Vietnam. Theravada Buddhism is different from Mahayana in that it deemphasizes the importance of becoming fully enlightened Buddhas and adherents do not accept the Mahayana scriptures.

Buddhism has also played a major role in the development of the culture of India for fifteen centuries. Buddhists believe in "karma" in which your fate is determined by what happened in a previous life. This can cause some to be fatalistic when it comes to buying or selling a home.

Other Asians may follow Confucianism, which is very different from Buddhism. It emphasizes the welfare of the family over individual interests. It also stresses acceptance of authority. Confucianism is practiced mainly by Asians in China, Japan, and Vietnam.

In addition, Hinduism and Jainism are also important religions. Jainism is the belief that every living being, including insects, have an indestructible, immortal, and immaterial soul. Because of the passions of desire and hatred, the soul is rendered vulnerable to karma, which forces it to suffer until it is purified. The majority of the over 500 million Hindus live in India. Closely related to the Hindu religion is the caste system, which says that social status is determined at birth.

Chinese

Even among the Chinese there are enormous differences in politics and economics. Mainland China, exclusively socialist until recently, is just beginning to make use of some capitalistic ideas. Hong Kong consists of two main islands (Hong Kong and Lantau), two hundred smaller islands, and 420 square miles on the south coast of China. The actual island of Hong Kong is just off the coast of the mainland of

China is but slightly smaller than Los Angeles. Its bustling 6.3 million people are among the most entrepreneurial of Chinese anywhere in the world.

Hong Kong was originally acquired by Great Britain in three stages: the main islands were obtained in the Opium War of 1840–1842; the Kowloon Peninsula was annexed by the Convention of Peking in 1860; and in 1898 it was granted a ninety-nine-year lease on the mainland north of Kowloon plus the adjoining islands. England wanted the natural harbor of Hong Kong for trade between the West and China because it was the only suitable seaport between Shanghai and Indochina.

When the British ninety-nine-year lease on the island expired in July 1997, the colony returned to Chinese ownership and control. As much as twenty years before the event, fear of coming effects caused many Hong Kong residents to sell their real estate holdings to buy property in the United States. Seeming to validate their fears, the People's Republic of China (PRC) wrote a new constitution before taking over, canceling many of Hong Kong's civil rights and most of its democratic laws. The huge buying spree has slowed only recently.

Today, Hong Kong's official language is Chinese but prior to the return to Mainland Chinese English was the official language so most people speak English. The primary religions are Taoism and Confucianism although Buddhism is also practiced. Ancestor worship is followed by many.

The island of Taiwan (previously Formosa) has 21 million Chinese people living under a more democratic regime, known as the Republic of China (ROC). It has grown into the thirteenth largest economy in the world and is the third largest supplier of computer hardware. Most people on Taiwan are of Chinese descent although there are many Japanese and some aborigines. The official language of Taiwan is Mandarin Chinese, but most residents also speak Taiwanese, a unique dialect of Chinese. Most Taiwanese people practice Buddhism, Taoism, or Confucianism.

Mainland China (PRC) has made threats to take over Taiwan for years. It would be a gross error to confuse the ROC with the PRC in conversation with either nations' citizens because relations between the two are controversial. In 1954, the United States agreed to protect Taiwan if it was ever threatened by the Mainland. However, in 1971 Mainland China was admitted to the United Nations in place of Taiwan. In 1979, the United States ended diplomatic relations with Taiwan in favor of the People's Republic. However, the United States still unofficially continues trade relations with Taiwan.

The People's Republic of China is the most populous place on earth and second only in area to the former Soviet Union. It boasts one of the oldest continuous civilizations in the world, being around five thousand years old. It is the largest socialist country in the world but is becoming increasingly capitalistic. Most of the residents of China are Han Chinese with over fifty-five minority groups. The Hans were a proud dynasty that ruled China from 202 B.C. to A.D. 220. The official language is Mandarin Chinese with each of the fifty five minority groups speaking their own dialects. While officially atheist, the Buddhist, Taoist, Muslim, and Christian religions are practiced.

Buddha accepted the Hindu philosophy that life is cyclical, with death followed by rebirth in accordance with the law of Karma. Karma is the principle that the nature of one's existence today is determined as a reward or punishment for one's deeds in past lives. The heart of the Buddha's teaching is the four Noble Truths: (1) life is essentially painful; (2) all suffering is the result of ignorance and desire; (3) beyond suffering is a heavenly state called "Nirvana"; and (4) the path to Nirvana is reached through perfection of wisdom, morality, and meditation.

In most Asian countries the group is more important than the individual, so the family name traditionally comes before the given name. The priority of groups over individuals was so important that the order of family name first was decreed by law in 2852 B.C. Chinese Americans will commonly adopt the Western practice of putting the given name first, so be sure to ask Asians which is their "family" name.

In spite of the differences noted above, one thing that Chinese around the world do share in common is surnames. All family names come from the poem, Po-Chia-Hsing, meaning the "Hundred Clan Names." In 201 B.C. every family was required to adopt a name from the poem. Today, one-quarter of all Chinese families are named Chang, Wong, or Li (Lee). In fact, so large is the group of people named Chang around the world that they now outnumber all the people in Great Britain and Canada combined. Other common Chinese surnames include Chu, Dong, Fong, Hu, Jang, Kong, Liu, Ong, Tse, Tao, and Wu.

The Chinese language is based on single-syllable words, which each can stand for several other words. Some words can have many meanings, depending on whether they are spoken with a rising or falling tone, giving Chinese a somewhat "singsong" sound. While there are hundreds of different dialects of Chinese, the five major dialects are Mandarin, Wu, Min, Hakka, and Cantonese. The latter three are the most common languages of Chinese Americans due to emigration patterns in the mid-1800s. Chinese writing is not alphabetical but in "pictographs." Each character can represent one or more words.

The Republic of Indonesia is a group of some 13,600 islands sitting on the equator between the southeastern tip of Asia and Australia covering an area three times the size of Texas. Most of its people practice the Muslim religion. Most of the people of Indonesia are of mixed Malaysian backgrounds. The most common language spoken is Indonesian, otherwise known as Malay. There are some sixty other languages spoken throughout the country. The majority of Indonesians are Muslims although there are many Christians and

Buddhists. One of the most common Indonesian family names is Fitriyanti, along with other traditional Chinese surnames.

Japanese

Japan is actually four main islands, not just one (which most Americans believe). You can demonstrate your geographic knowledge by asking Japanese clients, "Which island do you come from?" Honshu is the largest island, also known as the mainland where Tokyo is located; Hokkaido is northernmost, where the city of Sapporo is situated; there is Shikoku; and Kyushu is farthest south. These islands combined form a land mass around the size of Montana.

Japan is known as *Nihon Koku*, literally, "The Land of the Rising Sun." It is one of the most densely populated places in the world where land is at a premium. For example, land in downtown Tokyo has been sold for as much as $1 million *a square foot*!

Most of the people of Japan are ethnic Japanese with a small minority of Koreans and Chinese. The official language of Japan is Japanese, which is totally unlike Chinese although their written language (Kanji) is historically similar to Chinese pictographs. English is often spoken in business so many Japanese are somewhat conversant in this language. The Japanese language is rather vague and imprecise compared to others. Speakers prefer not to be direct or blunt and may go to great lengths to avoid a specific answer like "no." This can be very frustrating to American real estate agents when trying to get a commitment from a Japanese.

Like most Asians, the Japanese also usually place their family names before their given names. Common Japanese surnames include Adachi, Chiyo, Chuman, Dobashi, Doi, Goto, Otsuji, Nanbu, Takeda, Yamane, Yamashita, and Zakohi.

Most Japanese follow the Shinto religion. Shinto principles honor ancestors and respect nature. Its name comes from the

Chinese words *shin tao*, or "way of the gods." Shinto ceremonies take place at predetermined times during the year and
are aimed at pleasing the Kami, the powers of nature that provide and protect followers. These are mysterious forces that
inhabit holy places such as mountains, cliffs, caves, springs,
trees, and stones. Buddhism was introduced to this country in
the eighth century.

Koreans

Korea is about the size of Indiana and Mississippi combined.
It was divided into South Korea (The Republic of Korea) and
North Korea (The Democratic People's Republic of Korea)
following World War II. South Korea has grown in just three
decades from a primarily farming country to the world's
eleventh largest economy.

In 1950, the North Korean army invaded South Korea,
drawing the United States and the United Nations into a
three-year war. In 1953, a truce was signed but a formal
peace pact was never signed. The subject of unification is
still fairly controversial with Koreans, even today. About 99
percent of all Korea's residents are Korean with only a few
Chinese minorities. Most Koreans are Confucian and many
believe in Shamanism. This is a system of beliefs in good
and bad luck where a practitioner or "shaman" acts as the intermediary with the spirit world.

Chances are better than 50/50 that your Korean real estate
clients will bear the last name "Kim" or "Park" since they are
by far the most popular surnames. Less well-known are the Korean family names An, Cha, Cho, Ko, Min, Pak, Shin, and Yi.

The Republic of Singapore is a densely populated island in
the South China Sea. Most of its people are Chinese with
some Malay and a few of Indian descent. The official languages of Singapore are English, Chinese, and Tamil. Family
names in Singapore tend to be those most common among
Chinese. The majority of people practice the Buddhist or

Taoist religion but most of the major religions are also followed, including Christianity, Islam, Hinduism, and Judaism. Taoists seek access to the Tao as the supreme reality and consequent immortality through meditational, liturgical, and alchemical means.

Filipinos

The Philippines are officially known as The Republic of the Philippines. They are a group of over 7,100 islands covering an area of some 300,000 square kilometers. If you want to demonstrate your knowledge of geography to Filipino clients, you can ask, "What island are you from?" Luzon, which houses the capital city of Manila, and Mindanao are the largest. Depending on which island the client is from, it can indicate level of sophistication. Luzon is well developed, with high-rise buildings and freeways, while smaller outlying islands may still have people who live in thatched huts.

The Malay people first colonized and ruled the Philippines in the thirteenth century until Ferdinand Magellan claimed it for Spain in 1521. The Philippines was under Spanish influence until 1899, when Spain turned control over to the United States. Japan held the islands from 1941 until the end of World War II, when it returned to U.S. rule. On July 4, 1996, the Philippines became an independent republic but America has maintained a military presence up until today.

Spain not only influenced the economic and political life of the Philippines for over four hundred years, but it also influenced family names. Most Filipinos have Hispanic surnames although some may not be found in other Hispanic areas since they are Filipino personal names. Some of the more popular Filipino family names are Aglipay, Battung, Bumanglag, Butay, Comilang, Delacruz, Dugay, Escosio, Gabay, Gatan, Hipolito, Honorato, Ibason, Layugan, Macapuguay, Magwili, Mata, Penaranda, Quezon, Reyes, Santos, Tubilang, and Villaflor.

Filipinos are mostly descended from Malaysians with a small minority of Chinese. The official languages of the Philippines are English and Tagalog (pronounced *tah-gah-log*). The Philippines is the only Christian country in Asia, with over 80 percent belonging to the Roman Catholic Church due to the previous influence of Spain. Inhabitants there also practice the Muslim faith as well as other religions. There is also a sizable group that are members of the Philippine Independent Church or Aglipayans.

Pacific Islanders

The Pacific Islands are comprised of twenty-two countries and territories of the South Pacific in three major areas: Polynesia, Micronesia, and Melanesia. There are only around 5 million people in all of the Pacific Islands but many are immigrating to the U.S. mainland. Sixty percent of its inhabitants live in New Guinea while three-quarters of the rest live in Fiji, the Solomon Islands, French Polynesia, New Caledonia, Western Samoa, and Vanautu (formerly New Hebrides). Each island in the Pacific has its own unique culture and language. Don't assume they are all the same.

Polynesia includes the islands of Hawaii, Samoa, Tahiti, New Zealand, and Tonga. Most immigrants coming to America are currently from Hawaii, Samoa, and Tonga. While 58 percent of the 365,000 Pacific Islanders in this country come from Hawaii, about 17 percent have come from Samoa and 14 percent are from Guam. Don't forget that Hawaii is already part of the United States and people there refer to our part of the country as "The Mainland." There are 35,000 Samoans living in American Samoa and 65,000 living in the United States, including Hawaii. The people of the Hawaiian Islands have been heavily influenced by the Chinese, Japanese, Filipino, and Korean cultures.

Melanesia includes the Solomons, Fiji, New Hebrides, and New Caledonia islands. Micronesia encompasses the Guam,

Mariana, Marshall, Palau, Caroline Gilbert and Ellice islands. Guam is the most highly populated island in Micronesia, with over ninety thousand people. Guam is the largest and most southern island in the Marianas. It is a territory of the United States and follows many American rules, laws, and conventions.

There are over 1,200 languages spoken in the Pacific Islands, including Hawaiian, Samoan, Fijian, and Tahitian. The religions in these islands can be just as diverse, ranging from Christianity to Balinese and Javanese.

The residents of American Samoa are mostly Polynesians. The Samoan language is believed to be the oldest Polynesian language. Samoa is divided into the U.S. possession of American Samoa and Western Samoa. American Samoa consists of the Tutuila, the Manua group, Aunuie, Rose Island, and Swains Island. Western Samoa consists of two large islands and seven small islands. Most Samoans carry Polynesian-derived surnames such as Ala'ilema, Faiiae, or Leoso.

While Hawaii is a state, it is actually eight major islands and over a hundred minor islands. It has been a state since 1959 and using phrasing like "we in the United States" when speaking to these fellow Americans would be extremely culturally insensitive. Most Hawaiians are as proud to be Americans as anyone on the "Mainland." To build rapport you can ask Hawaiians, "What island are you from?" The main islands, in descending size, are Hawaii, Maui, Oahu, Kauai, Molokai, Lanai, Niihau, and Kahoolawe.

Hawaii is a true cultural melting pot with a population that is one-quarter Caucasian and one-quarter Japanese; the rest are Chinese, Filipino, Korean, and native Hawaiians. The official language is English but Hawaiians' native language is a dialect derived from Tahitian and Polynesian languages. There is also a contrived dialect of "Pidgin," which is a combination of English and Hawaiian. In it, the word *bra* is not a piece of women's apparel but the friendly term for "brother" as in, "Hey, bra, come here." Christianity is the most widely practiced religion in Hawaii. Almost every other belief in the world is probably also represented somewhere in the islands.

Hawaiian family names are derived from Polynesian roots although many have "haole" (non-Portuguese European) names. Popular Hawaiian surnames include Aloalo, Hakuole, Holokai, Keoloha, Kaalakea, Kahaialii, Kane, Kekoa, Kimo, Lanakila, Lei, Makakoa, Napua, Pililani, Pono, Uakea, and Wehilani.

Southeast Asians

People in America tend to think of people in Southeast Asia as a homogeneous group. But this is not at all the case. There are many different peoples, languages, and cultures.

Vietnam is officially known as The Socialist Republic of Vietnam and is the size of New Mexico and Connecticut combined. It is primarily an agricultural country with 55 million people. It is located on the western shore of the South China Sea. Most Vietnamese are Annamites—a Mongolian people whose language and culture are Chinese in origin. Chinese are the largest minority; in addition, there are Thai, Hmong, Man, Meo, Indonesians, and Moi. Vietnamese is the official language with English, Khmer, and Thai spoken to some degree throughout the country.

Vietnam was a French colony in the late 1880s and then occupied by Japan during World War II. After Japan was defeated, the Allies divided Vietnam into North and South. In 1956, the southern Communists were joined by the northern Communists to form the "Viet Cong," who rose up to challenge the ruling government. The Soviet Union and China supported the northern group while the United States supported the South Vietnamese.

The United States withdrew its troops in 1972 and the country fell to the Communists in 1975. Thousands of refugees left the country at this time and eventually found their way to America and other countries. In 1976, the North and South were rejoined under the name the "Socialist Republic of Vietnam." In 1978, Vietnam invaded Cambodia but withdrew in 1989. In 1994, the United States lifted the trade embargo it had instituted in 1976. Since that time many Vietnamese have immigrated to this country. The early refugees in the 1960s were middle- and upper-class people who had the financial resources to leave before the communist takeover. Today, more middle-class Vietnamese are immigrating to the United States.

Most Vietnamese practice Buddhism while a smaller number believe in Taoism and Catholicism. Ancestor worship is an important part of most Vietnamese belief. There is a particular enmity between the Vietnamese and the Chinese and Japanese due to the occupation by both of these countries.

Vietnamese follow the Asian tradition of placing the family name before the given name. The most common Vietnamese surname is Nguyen with others being An, Bui, Chau, Dao, Diep, Dinh, Duong, Hoa, Huynh, Ky, Le, Ly, Minh, Ngo, Nhu, Pham, Phat, Phung, Thang, Thuc, Tran, Trinh, Trung, Van, Vu, and Xuan.

Laos is officially called the Lao People's Democratic Republic. It is a small mountainous country in Southeast Asia about the size of Minnesota and New Jersey combined, occupied by 3 million people. It is landlocked and bordered by the People's Republic of China to the north, Vietnam to the east, Cambodia to the south, and Thailand to the west. It is well known for its summer monsoons.

Laos became a French colony toward the end of the 1800s. During World War II the Japanese occupied the country, but after the war it was returned to French rule. Laos became involved in the Vietnam War in the mid-1960s and was extensively bombed by the United States during the early 1970s. Today, the relationship between Laos and the United States is tenuous.

The Laotians are mostly Siamese in origin and there are small but important groups of Indonesian and Chinese tribesmen who live in the mountains. The official language of Laos is "Lao," with Hmong spoken as well. The Laotian culture has a distinctly Indian influence and is divided into two groups. The northern Laotians speak a language related to Burmese while the eastern Laotians speak a language that is more related to Thai.

Some Laotians speak French due to the long-standing influence of France. Lao family names usually precede personal names and can indicate members of the royal family. Common Laotian surnames are Baravong, Champassak (royalty), Chounramany (royalty), Lamphouthakoul, Luangpraseut, Pathammauong, Phouma (royalty), Sasority, Soukbandith, Vathanatham, Vatthana (royalty), Vongsok, and Voravong (royalty).

Most of those coming to America today are Hmong (pronounced *Mong*), one of the largest hill tribes from the northern part of the country. They had a strictly oral form of communication with no writing until missionaries introduced it to them in 1960. Many in this group have a strong belief in evil spirits.

Most Laotians follow the Hinayana form of Buddhism and some still practice animism, which reveres all living things. Hinayana Buddhists aspire to attaining the enlightenment of the Arahat rather than to the complete and perfect enlightenment of a Buddha. An Arahat does not believe in the karmic cycle of death and rebirth. There has also been a Hindu influence in Laos.

There are around 160,000 Laotians living in the United States today. Around one third of those live in California. Many of the others live in Oregon or Minnesota. Most Laotians were farmers living in remote villages. Living here in America is quite a culture shock to this group, and many find it difficult to assimilate.

Cambodians are from a small agricultural country in Southeast Asia about the size of Missouri with 7 million people. Most were farmers in their homeland with limited educational opportunities.

Cambodia was founded by Indians almost two thousand years ago and then colonized by France from the 1860s until independence in 1953. In 1978, Vietnam invaded Cambodia. The country was wracked by war between government forces, invaders, and guerrilla groups until recent times, which has seen democratic elections.

The majority of Cambodians are Khmer, one of the original groups who have inhabited the country since around the ninth century. These people tend to mostly speak the official Khmer language of "Paali," which is similar to Thai or Laotian. Minority groups in Cambodia include Vietnamese, Chinese, Chams, and Europeans. French is also widely spoken due to that country's early influences on the country.

Cambodians place their family names ahead of personal names. Some of the more popular Cambodian surnames include Ang, Chak, Chanthora, Chea, Dap, Haing, In, Ith, Khreu, Long, Men, Mit, Pen, Pok, Sak, Sreu, Sirik (royalty), Sisowath (royalty), Ta, Tep, Vorn, and Yun.

The Kingdom of Thailand is an odd-shaped country about the size of California and Virginia combined located in the center of Southeast Asia. It is bulbous at the northern end with a "boot" like Italy at the southern border. It was originally called Siam and its history extends back some four thousand years. Japan occupied Thailand during World War II and its alliance with the United States during the war made it an important base for military action during the Vietnam War.

From 1975 Thailand became a refuge for many people fleeing the war. Most of the occupants of this primarily agricultural country are of Thai background with a minority of Lao people. The official language of Thailand is Thai although other dialects are spoken in addition to Lao, Khmer,

Chinese, and Malay. Buddhism is the established religion of Thailand. Other religions that are practiced include Muslim, Christianity, and Hindu.

Thais put their family name first and personal name last. Popular Thai family names are Chira, Chula, Dhamsong, Khamsing, Khuang, Luan, Pantum, Phao, Prayad, Puey, Rajadhon, Sanet, Sarit, Seni, Sombhund, Sumon, Thawat, Tongkum, and Yupho.

Burma is a mountainous country situated in the northwest portion of the Indochinese peninsula about the size of Texas. Most of its people are Burman who are racially related to the Tibetans and the Chinese. Minority groups include Indians and Chinese. The bulk of Burman people are Hinayana Buddhists. Other religions practiced in Burma are Christianity, Islam, Hinduism, and Animism.

Asian Indians and Pakistanis

Many people in this country mistakenly lump Indians and Pakistanis together as one group. Nothing could be further from the truth. There has been a great deal of animosity and outright war between the countries for over half a century due to religious and political differences.

While Asian Indians sometimes consider themselves Asian they are ethnically Caucasian. Nearly three-quarters of the people are Indo-Aryans, with most of the rest being Dravidians. About half of the residents of the island of Fiji are Indian.

India is officially called The Republic of India and is one of the largest countries in the world with over 3,000,000 square kilometers—about one third the size of the United States. It is one of the world's oldest continuous civilizations with a history that can be traced back some five thousand years. The official languages are English and Hindi, plus another fourteen unofficial languages, including Punjabi and Urdu. In India over fifteen major languages are spoken along with over eight hundred dialects. India has the world's largest

English-speaking workforce outside the United States. If there is one city in India you should be familiar with it is Nilgiris where the famous Taj Mahal is located.

Most of the people of India practice the Hindu religion that has no official supreme being but has a rather rigid caste system that has been legally abolished but is still practiced. Hinduism says that in order to leave life on earth to attain a better existence you must work your way through various castes or levels of life. At the lower level is the laborer, above that is the farmer and merchant, and then there is the intellectual or leader caste. People have an opportunity to improve their lot in life as they are reincarnated after death.

In the United States are large communities of people who practice the Sikh (pronounced *sick*) religion. It combines tenets of both Hinduism and Islam and its followers can be readily identified by the colorful turbans on their heads. This headwear can be up to forty feet long and must be rolled daily, which can take as long as twenty to thirty minutes. Sikhs celebrate three important festivals each year: Baisakhi is the New Year festival, which is in April; Davali is the Festival of Lights celebrated in October or November; and Hola Mohalla is held the day after the Hindu Holi celebration in February or March. The date April 13, 1699 is important to Sikhs because it marked the official beginning of their religion.

One of the most often-asked questions the author receives about the Indian people is, "What does the red dot on the forehead mean?" The answer is that Hindu women may put a red dot or *bindi* on the forehead, which traditionally symbolized femininity, grace, and even marital status. Today in America it has lost much of its significance to the point where the color may even be only important because it complements the outfit being worn.

Many Indians came to the United States in the 1950s while a wave of professionals arrived during the 1970s. There is a strong emphasis on technology today in India so recent immigrants to this country will likely be mathematically and technologically oriented. They tend to prefer to see computer printouts to handwritten calculations.

Indian family names are usually derived from caste and subcaste names or show descendants. For example, the name "Kali" means goddess; "Sadhana" is devotion; "Sumati" means unity; "Takabri" is starlight; and "Vayu" means goddess of the word.

Pakistan is officially called The Islamic Republic of Pakistan and is situated to the west of India and is about the size of Texas and Tennessee combined. This, mostly mountainous country, was originally inhabited by Muslims until the 1800s, when the East India Trading Company from England basically controlled the country until Britain granted independence in 1947.

Most Pakistanis are ethnically Punjabi with minorities of Baluchi, Mahajir from India, Pashtuns, and Sindhi. It is an ethnically diverse country whose residents can range from light-skinned people with blue eyes to dark-skinned people with brown eyes. The official languages of Pakistan are English and Urdu.

Most people in Pakistan are Muslim (97 percent). The majority are Sunni Muslims with the rest Shi'ite Muslims. Sunnis follow the code of behavior as outlined in the Holy Koran while the Shi'ites follow the authority of the Imam leader. Minority religions include Hinduism and Christianity.

Like their Indian neighbors, Pakistani family names are usually derived caste and subcaste names or show descendants. The most common name in Pakistan is "Khan," meaning "lord," which is the name of the highest caste.

Middle Easterners

The Middle East encompasses a large area about the size of the United States and includes Israel, Iraq, Iran, Saudi Arabia, Jordan, Kuwait, Egypt, Turkey, Sudan, and the United Arab Emirates. The largest group in the Middle East is the Arabs.

Most people immigrating into the United States are Arabs.

One would imagine that the Middle East presents a unified front to the world, but this is, again, not the case. The Arab world contains twenty-two separate countries that have substantial disagreements, ranging from economics to matters of religious interpretation. Nearly 20 percent of all Arabs are Muslims who follow the religion of Islam. Islam is the second largest religion in the world and is the Arabic word for "submission" because its followers surrender themselves to the divine will of God. The largest Muslim country in the world is Indonesia with large groups of followers in Asia and Africa.

Muslims believe that Allah (God) gave the rules for proper conduct in the sacred book of Islam, the Koran. Devout Muslims do not drink alcohol and may not eat beef or pork. They are required by their religion to face Mecca and pray five times daily—at sunrise, three times during the day, and at sunset. While most Muslims do not believe in divorce, some may practice polygamy as the Koran allows a male follower to be married to four wives at the same time as long as he treats them all equally.

The Koran is the scripture of Islam as the Bible is to Christians. Muslims believe that Allah has revealed himself throughout history through prophets, including Moses and Jesus. They accept Jesus as a prophet, like Muhammad, but not as the Son of God since Allah does not have children. Muslims believe that God's final revelation was delivered to Muhammad in the form of the Koran, making him the last and greatest of the prophets. Like Christians, Muslims believe in life after death.

The Islam religion makes no distinction between religious life and all other facets of human activity. The official day of worship is Friday, which is a day of prayer. Keep this in mind when you are planning to show property to Muslims.

Most Arabic countries do not use family names. Men's names list their genealogy, as in *ibn* which means "son of."

It's a little-known fact that "Hajji" is not a name but is added to the name of any man who has been to Mecca. Therefore, Hajji Asad is not "Mr. Asad" but a man with the given name of Asad who has been to Mecca. "Sharif" is a title for any Arabic man who is a descendant of the Prophet. Thus, the movie actor Omar Sharif should not have been addressed as "Mr. Sharif" but his name meant that his given name was Omar and he was descended from the Prophet. Common female Arabic names are Bahaar, Faaria, Fatima, Huda, Jamila, Kamala, Layla, Saleema, and Yasmine. Popular male Arabic names are Anwar, Asad, Faheem, Ghaazee, Hadi, Hassan, Jalaal, Jamil, Nasir, Omar, Raashid, and Sayyid.

Turks, Persians, and other Eastern Muslims tend to use names with "al-din," "ed-din," or ud-din," meaning "the faith" (referring to Islam). Examples would be Hadi-al-din, Jalaal-el-din, and Omar-ud-din.

Saudi Arabia, officially known as "The Kingdom of Saudi Arabia," is the largest country on the Arabian Peninsula at about one-quarter the size of the United States. It is comprised mostly of deserts and plains bounded by steep mountains.

Most Saudis are Arabs with a small minority of Afro-Asians. The official language is Arabic while English is used for business transactions. Arabic originated on the Arabian Peninsula and remained there until the seventh century, when Arab armies spread the Islamic religion and the Arab culture to Afghanistan, North Africa, Persia, Spain, and beyond.

Today, the state religion of Saudi Arabia is still Islam. It is said that this country is the birthplace of the sacred prophet Muhammad. Most of the people of Saudi Arabia practice the Sunni Muslim religion and there is a minority of those who follow the Shi'ite Muslim religion. Shi'ites believe in a strict interpretation of the Koran. Sunnis consider the Koran to be more of a guide which is shaped by daily events and circumstances. They follow Imam, or worthy descendants of Muhammad.

Saudi Arabians can greet each other with elaborate rituals. They may also give expensive gifts to real estate agents. This is one of the most restrictive countries for women in the world.

Egypt is about the size of Texas and New Mexico combined and is comprised mostly of deserts. The Nile River spans the country, running from south to north, and most of Egypt's major cities are located along its banks. The Nile Valley includes both Egypt and Sudan. Over the past half century Egypt has been at war with Israel.

The majority of Egyptians are descended from both native Egyptians and Arabs who subjugated the country in the seventh century. About 5 percent are Copts, who are direct lineal descendants of the ancient Egyptians. Today, Arabic is the official language of Egypt while English and French are used in business settings.

Syria is officially known as "The Syrian Arab Republic" and is about the size of Illinois and Indiana combined. While it borders on the Mediterranean Sea, it is mainly desert in the east. It also has had wars with Israel for over half a century and as recently as 1973.

The majority of Syrians are Arabs with minorities being Kurds, Armenians, Turks, and Assyrians. The official language of Syria is Arabic, although Kurdish and Armenian are also commonly spoken. Syria is officially a non religious country but the majority of its citizens are Sunni Muslims. Other religions regularly practiced include Armenian Orthodox, Greek Orthodox, Syrian Orthodox, and Syrian Catholic.

The United Arab Emirates (UAE) consists of seven Shaikhdoms on the south shore of the Arabian Gulf covering an area of about 84,000 square kilometers. The leaders of the seven states form the Supreme Council that governs the UAE. Most of its inhabitants are people who have fled from other countries, the majority of which are Asian Indian. Others include Iranians and those from other Arab countries. The minority of local people are primarily Arabs or Persians.

Tribes are important in the life of the people of the UAE. If you have clients from this country, you might ask, "Did you belong to a tribe?"

The official language of the UAE is Arabic although English is used for business activities. Persian and Urdu are also spoken in various parts of the country. The state religion of the UAE is Islam and the use of alcohol is prohibited for all Muslim residents.

Iran, where many of our new immigrant real estate clients come from, is not considered an Arab country because its people speak the Persian or Farsi language. Iran is officially known as "The Islamic Republic of Iran" and is about the size of Alaska. This country, formerly known as Persia, consists of both mountains and deserts. There are over 67 million people in the country, with nearly 10 percent of these living in the capital city of Tehran.

The official language of Iran is Persian Farsi with numerous other languages spoken, including Turkic, Kurdish, Baluchi, and Arabic. Persian is part of the Indo-European languages. It has different origins than Arabic or Turkish. The state religion for centuries has been Shi'ite Islam with nearly all Iranians following this belief and a small minority belonging to the Sunnis.

Afghanistan is about the size of Texas at 650,000 square kilometers in size. The official languages of this primarily mountainous country are Persian and Pashto (an Iranian branch of the Indo-European family of languages); some Turkic and Mongolian dialects are also spoken. Most of the people of Afghanistan are from the Durani tribe, who are said to be descended from the Jews. The official religion is Islam. Most residents of Afghanistan practice the Sunni Muslim religion along with a minority of Shi'ites.

Algeria is a desert country with over 90 percent in the Sahara Desert covering some 2,380,000 square kilometers. Its original inhabitants were Berber people, who were native, non-Arabic tribes that inhabited larger areas of North Africa.

The official religion of Algeria is Islam. Most of its practitioners are Sunni Muslims. There are some Christian churches in the country. The official language of Algeria is Arabic although Berber and French are spoken in many quarters. It's interesting to note that while most people think that the Sahara is the largest desert in the world, technically it's actually Antarctica where the humidity is less than that of the Sahara and annual snowfall in the interior of Antarctica is less than two inches.

Bahrain is a tiny island country of only 680 square kilometers about twenty miles off the coast of Arabia. Today it is a major banking and telecommunications center. The official language of Bahrain is Arabic, but English is commonly spoken throughout the country.

Iraq is officially called "The Iraqi Republic" and is nearly 450,000 square kilometers in size. Most of its people are Arabs with the largest minority group being Kurds. Other groups include Jews, Turks, and Iranians. The official language of the country is Arabic although some Kurdish, Persian, and Turkic is spoken by its residents. Most people are either Sunni or Shi'ite Muslims.

Israel is 20,000 square kilometers, or about the size of New Jersey, with a long and storied past. Also known as "The Holy Land," it was believed to have been established by the twelve tribes of Israel that left Egypt with Moses in Biblical times.

It is a country comprised of many peoples, the majority of which are of the Jewish faith. The word *Jewish* is not a cultural designator but describes a religion, a culture, and a nation. Israelis are citizens of Israel so although you might be an Israeli you are not necessarily Jewish.

The official language of Israel is Hebrew, although Arabic is spoken and taught in schools. English is often spoken during business transactions. The official religion of Israel is Judaism, which has its Sabbath from sundown on Friday to sundown on Saturday. The next largest religious group is the Muslims, while Christianity is also practiced.

Israeli family names are often based on Old Testament names. "Ben" signifies an original immigrant family of Israel. Common surnames in Israel include Ben-Hama, Cohen, Eckstein, Fraenkel, Gerstein, Giron, Hertzig, Kahn, Katz, Kohen, Levi, Mann, Morris, Rosentzwig, Rothschild, Sheinfeld, Steiner, Wingarten, and Zakai.

Jordan, officially called "The Hashimite Kingdom of Jordan," is about 100,000 square kilometers in size. It is a monarchy whose official language is Arabic; English is spoken as a second language. Most Jordanians are Arabs with a minority of nomadic Bedouins. Its residents are primarily Sunni Muslims and a small percentage are Christians.

The State of Kuwait is a small country of about 18,000 square kilometers. Like Jordan, it is a monarchy with Arabic as its official language. English is widely spoken throughout the country. Most of the people in Kuwait are Sunni Muslims and about 30 percent are Shi'ites.

The Republic of Lebanon is a small country of only 10,000 square kilometers. Arabic is the main language spoken along with French and Lebanese. Most residents are Shi'ite Muslims while a third are Sunnis. There is a large Christian population in Lebanon as well, mostly Maronite, Greek Orthodox, and Greek Catholics.

The Great Libyan Jamahiriyya is about the same size as Kuwait. Most Libyans are Berbers with minorities of Arabs and Africans. The main language, as in most Middle Eastern countries, is Arabic, although English, Berber, and Italian are also spoken by many people. The state religion is Islam and most of the occupants of Libya are practicing Sunni Muslims.

The Sultanate of Oman is a country consisting of about 300,000 square kilometers. While Arabic is mainly spoken, English is also commonly heard across the country. Nearly three-quarters of the people of Oman follow the Ibadi Muslim religion while the rest are mostly Sunnis.

The State of Qatar is only slightly larger than Lebanon. Most of its residents speak Arabic and it is another country where English is widely spoken. The majority of its people are Sunni Muslims.

The Republic of Tunisia is about 150,000 square kilometers in size. Most of its people are Arabs and Berbers. The majority of its people speak Arabic and French along with some Berber dialects. Most of the residents of Tunisia are Sunni Muslims with a minority of Jews and Christians.

The Turkish Republic is some 780,000 square kilometers in size. Most of its people are Turkish, with Kurdish, Arabian, Greek, and Armenian minorities. The official language is Turkish while some Greek and Armenian is spoken in parts of the country. The majority of the residents of Turkey are Sunni Muslims along with a small number of Christians and Jews.

Palestinians lost their home at the end of the Arab-Israeli war in 1948. Most have since settled on the East Bank of the Jordan River. There are large populations of Palestinians living in Syria, Lebanon, and Kuwait, with small groups residing in Saudi Arabia, Egypt, Iraq, Qatar, the UAE, Oman, and Cypress.

Native Americans

Most of the 2 million Native Americans live in the western United States with the highest concentrations in Arizona, New Mexico, Washington, Montana, South Dakota, North Dakota, Nebraska, and Kansas. Contrary to media stereotypes, only about 20 percent of American Indians live on reservations. Yet, only one-third own a home—the lowest ownership rate of any American minority group.

Native Americans are also called "Indians" because that what Christopher Columbus named them when he arrived here and thought he was in Asia. Anthropologists believe that Indians were originally Mongoloid people who began migrating to the Western Hemisphere from northern Asia in about 20,000 B.C.

Historically, Native American families have been male-dominated although women have had well-defined rights. While not allowed to participate in some tribal activities and ceremonies, women had custody of the children and owned all of the property with the exception of weapons and horses.

Native Americans respect animals, plants and all objects of nature. Some of these were believed to be especially powerful particularly the sun, fire, water, buffalo, eagles, rattlesnakes, cottonwood, corn, tobacco, and mescal, which could be made into alcohol or chewed as a narcotic stimulant.

In the early 1900s most Native Americans lived quiet existences on reservations until 1922, when Congress tried to pass the Pueblo Land Bill. This would have taken valuable land and water rights away from the Pueblo tribe, but public outcry was so strong it was defeated.

As a result of the heightened public awareness of the plight of Indians, Congress passed a bill in 1924 granting full citizenship to all Native Americans in the United States. At the same time, the Institute for Government Research conducted a study of the condition of Native Americans in the United States and found the following: per capita income under $500 a year; 10 percent had tuberculosis; high infant mortality; inadequate schools; and hospitals, and living conditions well below the standards of even the poorest whites. From 1953 to 1954, Congress enacted a series of laws designed to transfer the administration of Indian affairs from the federal government to the states. Persistent poverty and discrimination have made it difficult for Native Americans to buy real estate.

The U.S. government has always treated Native Americans as a simple and backward people who need to be cared for. Just one example—in the early 1900s, members of the Pueblo tribe legally challenged Congress's control over their affairs. In a ruling that went all the way to the U.S. Supreme Court, it said, "Always living in separate and isolated communities, adhering to primitive modes of life, largely influenced by superstition and fetishism and chiefly governed according to crude customs inherited from their ancestors, (the Pueblo) are essentially a simple, uninformed and inferior people. . . . As a superior and civilized nation (the U.S. government has both) the power and the duty of exercising a fostering care and protection over all dependent Indian communities within its borders,." (*United States v. Sandoval* 1913).

Many Native Americans do not believe in the private ownership of land. Many grew up in tribes or clans that consider themselves the caretakers of land, not the owners. Most have a great respect for the land.

The family is more important to Native Americans than any material possession. Each family member is expected to support others in the family. They do not believe strongly in accepting help from outside the family. Try to refrain from complimenting Native American children as it draws harmful attention to them. Many people from this group do not believe in standing out from the crowd and may even actively avoid competition. Harmony among individuals, society, and nature is important. Native Americans often avoid direct eye contact as a sign of respect. They may take a long time before answering a question in order to give it the consideration it deserves.

Many people think that Native Americans are passive because of their belief in "taking life as it comes." There can also be a great number of beliefs that can affect the purchase and sale of real estate. Much of this relates to the harmonization of the house to the land. Also, certain pictures, dolls, or animals may be believed to cause bad luck. The only way to know is to ask.

Religious beliefs of Native Americans can range from Roman Catholicism to Indian beliefs. The Protestants also had an influence when they built missions on reservations. One of the basic beliefs of Native Americans is the existence of two souls in every person. One is a "free soul" which is able to leave the body during dreams or vision states. The other is a "life" soul which leaves the body permanently when the breath is gone.

Traditional Native Americans have names that tend to be related to nature. Family names were originally nonexistent since people could be named using descriptive adjectives such as "Falling Leaf" or "Sitting Bull," or "Red Hair" or "Tall Woman." Today, they've been forced to adopt the practice of using family names and as a result some of the most common Native American surnames are Bark, Bean, Bigfeather, Bigfoot, Brown, Cree, Eagle, Flowers, Green, Horn, Irons, Lightfoot, Shadow, Shell, Thorn, Water, and Wolf.

Native Americans tend to experience contradictory feelings when it comes to buying real estate. On the one hand, ancient Indian philosophy dictates that no one owns land but rather simply uses it to sustain oneself without harming it. On the other hand, Indians know that American law encourages the private ownership of land.

One of the problems that Native Americans have when they want to sell reservation land that they own is called "fractionation." In 1887, Congress passed the General Allotment Act, which divided reservation land into 160-acre parcels that were then given to the heads of Indian families. Fractionation then further subdivided these parcels in order to make the rent payments to its owners smaller and, thus, more affordable to tenants. However, this practice clouds the ownership of land. If you run into this process, contact the Bureau of Indian Affairs in Washington, D.C.

In Alaska, there are three types of native peoples—Eskimos, Indians and Aleuts. The Eskimo or Inuit settlements are scattered along the coast of the Bering Sea, on the Yukon delta, the Kuskokwim river, and Bristol Bay. The Indians settled along the rivers of central Alaska as well as in the rain forests and along Prince William Sound. The Aleuts were maritime people who lived in the Aleutian Islands, the Alaska Peninsula, the Kodiak archipelago, the Pribilof Islands in the Bering Sea and along the Kenai Peninsula and Prince William Sound.

Europeans

While currently not the largest immigrant groups, Europeans from England, France, and Germany have had a significant impact on real estate in America for several decades. In fact, while the Japanese bought high-profile buildings in New York and Los Angeles during the 1970s and 1980s, the English actually were the largest foreign purchasers of American real estate.

Generally, Europeans are a visually oriented people (just think of the influence of the visual arts on Europe). If you have difficulty communicating with a European client, try drawing a picture, which is much easier for them to grasp than verbal sales pitches. Europeans also tend to judge people by how they dress and the quality of brochures and other materials. Be sure to dress impeccably and use high-quality printing on any marketing materials aimed at this group. Remember: even though the majority of people in the United States are of European descent, there are vast differences among the respective cultures.

England is also known as the "United Kingdom" and is about the size of New York. Sometimes called Great Britain, England is actually only part of the island that also holds Scotland and Wales. The United Kingdom is actually comprised of England and Northern Ireland.

While most people in England are Caucasian there is also a small but rich mix of other groups, including Indians, Africans, and Asians. The official language of England is British English which, as anyone knows who's been there, is not the same as American English. England's official religion is

Anglican as espoused by the Church of England. Anglicanism contains elements of both the Catholic and Protestant religions. In addition, there are large groups of traditional Catholics, Methodists, Presbyterians, and Jews.

The "Brits" are a reserved and conservative people. It's always best to err on the side of formality as they tend to view Americans as too casual. Titles such as "doctor" or "professor" are preferred to "Mr." or "Ms."

English family names come from all over Europe. The most common surnames in England are Brown, Davies, Evans, Johnson, Jones, Roberts, Smith, Taylor, Thomas, and Williams. Some English men and women will use hyphenated surnames such as Marilyn Ashley-Cooper. The name Ashley is the mother's family name and Cooper is the father's.

The ideal English home is a house with a garden. The majority of people in England own a home and densely populated condominiums, townhouses, or cooperatives tend to be the last choice in real estate.

France is a country the size of Texas bounded by Germany, Italy, and Spain. Its occupants are mostly of Celtic heritage mixed with other European groups. There are highly segregated minority groups of Algerians, Tunisians, Moroccans, West Africans, Caribbeans, and Asians.

French is the official language of France although English is often studied in school. The French people are extremely proud of their language and culture. Most people in France are Roman Catholics while there are a few Christian, Jewish, and Islamic churches throughout the country. These are a polite, reserved, and private people who consider Americans to be somewhat pushy and unsophisticated.

French family names are obviously French and sometimes are names after saints. Some of the more usual French surnames you may run across are Sainte-Beuve, de-Saint Maure, Saint-Simon, d'Amboise, Barbier, Bataille, Gaumont, LeForce, Lemieux, Marchand, Mercier, Radisson, Robidoux, and Rochette.

Most people in France live in the urban areas so they are used to city living and are much more accepting than the English of living in condominiums, townhouses and cooperatives. Pets are extremely popular with the French.

Germany is about the size of Montana and its people are of two Caucasian races. Alpine Germans are usually dark-haired with brown eyes while Teutonic Germans are often blue-eyed blondes and taller than the Alpines. Its minority groups include Turks, Italians, Greeks, and Poles.

German is the official language with different dialects reflecting varying locales throughout the country. English is required to be studied in school as a second language. Most Germans are Christians, the majority of whom are split evenly between the Catholics and Protestants. Quite a few other Christian churches are well established across Germany along with a few Muslim sects.

German family names are mostly derived from the Germanic language. The prefix *von* in front of a surname indicates some level of nobility although the Germans are fond of taking titles, no matter how distant the relationship. More common German family names of your clients might be Ackermann, Ayrer, von Bader, Baumgarten, Baur, Becker, Blum, Brandt, von Bruhl, Dalman, Deterich, von Dingelstedt, Distler, Eichler, Fried, von Furth, von Balen, Gerhardt, Haas, Hauptmann, von Neuhof, Oberhoffer, von Papen, Reinecke, von Schwartzenberg, Stein, or Vogel.

The German people like buying American real estate because it is relatively inexpensive compared to that in Germany. Land is at such a premium that many Germans will buy or rent small pieces of land for gardens.

Germans generally value orderliness, cleanliness, and punctuality. If you really want to turn off potential German clients, show up fifteen minutes late with a dirty car and wearing a wrinkled shirt!

Canadians

Canada is the second largest country in the world and it shares with the United States one of the longest borders in the world. It has ten provinces: Prince Edward Island, Newfoundland, Nova Scotia, New Brunswick, Quebec, Ontario, Manitoba, Saskatchewan, Alberta, and British Columbia. Canada contains more lakes and inland waters than any other country in the world. There are some 30 million people in this rather sparsely populated country. Over two-thirds of Canadians live within a hundred miles of the U.S. border. The official languages of Canada are English and French although most people mainly speak English. French is the primary language of the province of Quebec.

While Canada is our neighbor to the north, its culture can be as different as that of Asians. It's important not to assume that because Canada is so close that its people are the same as Americans. Most of the residents of Canada are of European descent. There are strong minority populations such as in Vancouver, where many Asians have settled. There are also large groups of Native Americans in Canada, mostly of the Algonquin tribe.

Roman Catholics are the largest religious denomination in Canada, most of whom live in Quebec. Other religions are Protestants, Anglicans, Presbyterians, Baptists, Lutherans, Greek Catholics, Jews, and Greek Orthodox.

In this book we will discuss general characteristics of some, but not all people from outside the United States as well as multicultural Americans. You are encouraged to bear in mind that it is important to treat every potential client as an individual, just as you would like to be treated.

As you can see, if we want to be successful with new immigrants we cannot just lump them together into neat packages that the average agent would designate as Hispanic, Asian, or Middle Eastern. Probably the most important rule in successful multicultural relations is a corollary of the Golden Rule: "Treat Every Client as an Individual," as you would have them treat you. Follow this advice and you won't make the mistake of insulting your Chinese or Korean buyers by talking about your Japanese clients' preferences or assuming that all Hispanics come from Mexico.

Out of necessity, this book will make some generalizations about cultural "tendencies." However, readers are urged to see that each client, of whatever cultural background, is unique. Some you will meet will not practice the beliefs outlined here or may have an unexpected and unique personal set of traditions. The only way to know for certain what beliefs your client holds to ask.

Take interest in your clients as individuals and genuinely desire to know more about them. You will not only be more successful selling to multicultural clients but you will learn more about other peoples' cultures than any round-the-world trip could ever teach you.

> *"Take an interest in other peoples' cultures—*
> *you will find it fascinating and profitable."*

3

Becoming Aware
of Differences

It's perfectly acceptable to ask where people are from. Better than to assume and be wrong. One simple way to show interest in your client's culture background is to ask straightforwardly, "Where are your ancestors from?" Notice that the identical question can apply to someone of Irish or German descent, and with equally interesting results. If you practice real estate in an area with a significant number of new immigrants or multicultural Americans, you will want to make this as much a part of your usual questions as "How many bedrooms and bathrooms do you need?"

For example, Australians and New Zealanders are from very different countries although their accents may sound similar to the untrained ear. Australians have a more pronounced and "singsong" accent while New Zealand speech is much more flat with less inflections. Australia is much more cosmopolitan and New Zealanders like to consider themselves more "folksy." People from these areas compare Australia to New York and New Zealand to California.

Similarly, Canadians do not like to be called "Americans" even though they do indeed live in North America. They want to be differentiated from people from the United States. Simply call them "Canadians."

Pursuing an interest in your client's culture may teach you that, for some, gifts and colors carry meanings that others find quite incomprehensible. In Germany, a gift of red roses expresses love and romance. This is hardly a fitting present for one's lawyer or mortgage lender, even if female. Here in America, red roses denote the same thought in affectionate relationships, yet are acceptable in most other cases simply because they are beautiful and fragrant.

Persons from some parts of Mexico could imagine themselves insulted or even threatened by a yellow gift because many in that culture associate the color yellow with death. The Chinese traditionally wear black at weddings and white at funerals, the opposite of the European and American traditions.

Nearly everywhere, including here in America, numbers often carry connotations of good or bad luck. We hear people saying, "That's my lucky number!" While seven is often believed to bring good fortune in the West, people from abroad cannot understand why so many of our buildings lack a thirteenth floor. In much of Asia, four is a bad omen and the number eight is lucky. Woe to the real estate agent who expects a newly arrived Asian family that believes in numerology to buy a house with an address like 4444 Fourth Street.

We notice that other cultures have beliefs they rely on to guide them, yet so have we. Theirs are just different. As you will see, your new immigrant clients are not really inscrutable and incomprehensible, but may hold unfamiliar and confusing (to us) views. Those differences can be frustrating or fascinating, may help or hinder your efforts, depending on how you choose to approach them.

These facts about numerology, food, and colors are certainly interesting, but what do they have to do with the real estate industry and related fields? Do they have a place in your practice? Absolutely! Culture affects property transactions in more ways than uninitiated Americans might imagine. No region of our country will long remain unaffected by the historic influx of new arrivals. Everyone knows that the states of California and New York have historically had high percentages of new immigrants because they arrive through the gateway cities of San Francisco, Los Angeles, and New York. Surprisingly, though, some of the fastest growing multicultural populations are in North Carolina, Georgia, and Florida.

Thus, no one in the real estate profession can expect to succeed in this multicultural marketplace without being aware and putting that awareness to work. Size, color, appointments, and location are significant. But the layout of the kitchen may be the deal-maker or deal-breaker for Hispanic buyers. Asian Indians often want a separate room facing the east for prayer. Almost without exception, clients from the Middle East look for one-story homes. Such preferences may never be directly communicated, so if the agent is not aware from the beginning, the client might give up and go elsewhere without a word of explanation.

Home builders can make their products attractive to discrete markets by providing special amenities and color schemes. Floor plans can be designed to satisfy special cultural expectations. There is a thin line between the person and the culture; each assumes equal importance. As much may depend on what the client is used to, as upon what tradition dictates. The basis of many traditional beliefs has become lost over time. Few Americans know the history of our most common architectural styles, yet they usually have a specific preference. The same is true for non-Americans; they might not fully realize why, but they expect certain things in the homes they buy.

Loan officers, real estate agents, and brokers must be careful how they broach the subject of credit with new immigrants. Buying on credit is not widely available outside North America and Europe. A number of cultures consider owing money a disgrace. In others, merely asking how much is available for the down payment could threaten the client's life. Some ethnic groups pool their resources to help each other buy property.

In more than a few places, banks are subject to general mistrust. That view is common in countries where they have a reputation for instability. Not every government protects consumers through bank regulation. Worse and all too often, bankers have simply absconded with depositors' life savings. These and other issues may need to be addressed in the earliest stages of an agent's relationship with new arrivals if you want a smooth transaction.

Foreign nationals rarely know much about the real estate profession. The idea of a professional whose job is seeking out prospective homes, showing them to prospects, and negotiating the conditions of purchase is quite novel to most immigrants. In some cultures, the principals handle everything between themselves. In others, lawyers take care of one part of the transaction, accountants another, and the buyer and seller get together for the rest. In still other places, the buyer may have no part in the process until it is time to write the check. Real estate professionals must take time to explain exactly what they do, the benefits to the client, how they are paid, and, most important, why this laborious process is necessary in the first place.

Real estate developers and salespeople must educate themselves about the features that may be of interest to certain cultural groups. Asian cultures may prefer a certain compass direction for the front door or give critical significance to the number of steps leading to the front door or the sleeping quarters. African Americans may want their house to look different from other properties on the street.

Many Asians favor curved walkways, spiral staircases, and round windows because they consider straight lines unlucky. Hispanic buyers favor stucco and rough-textured plaster in preference to wood. Anyone who visits Mexico or the American Southwest will note the predominance of adobe buildings in those parts.

Unfamiliarity with standard building practices and habits of usage can affect the choice of a home. People who come from the Middle East have little interest in basements because they are rare, if they exist at all, in their part of the world. It would make no sense to build a basement in sandy soil, after all.

Agents and others in related fields who ignore cultural differences will find themselves wasting a lot of time and could eventually—and foolishly—decide that it's simply not worth the trouble trying to deal with unreasonable people who see things from strange viewpoints. An "irrelevant" question like "Has anyone died in this house?" may confuse and irritate the agent who doesn't know the reason behind it. Yet the answer needs to be known. You might have to be prepared to lose the sale if a death has occurred in the house. In fact, many longtime American residents would be averse to buying a home where a murder had taken place.

Better to do the research and know if death in the home is a material fact for this client. If the buyer doesn't find out until after the purchase, a lawsuit is a distinct possibility. The author has appeared as an expert witness in several such court cases. In each case, certain deaths and other sad events could be enough to cause the buyers to back out. Oddly enough, similar events could be good luck to other cultures. You can only know the difference by asking the right questions about the property before the subject comes up.

Since the American tradition of attaching great importance

to private property is not common to all lands, neither are the mechanisms we use to protect it. The agent using an escrow company and title insurance needs to explain the importance of these entities to new immigrants. Having one or both sides pay money to a neutral intermediary to collect the money, deeds, and other necessary documents, see that the contracts are adhered to, and then transfer title, is confusing enough to Americans. If they sometimes think, "Here's another middleman looking for a fee without providing legitimate service," then you had better carefully explain it to people from very different traditions. Becoming familiar with the nuts and bolts of this important function would serve many real estate agents well. The real estate professional who involves an attorney must constantly be ready to explain the lawyer's role. Attorneys may meet with suspicion from immigrants from the many countries where the legal profession is often corrupt or incompetent. In others, it serves only those who wield power over the ordinary citizen. (In a more than few places, it is still possible to become a lawyer simply by calling oneself a lawyer!)

With that kind of fear or suspicion present, even the faint prospect of a lawsuit can bring everything to a grinding and permanent halt. At the other end of the spectrum are societies where the legal systems are so impotent that the threat of a lawsuit brings only laughter in response. In any case, everyone needs to understand that the attorney's role is that of a fellow professional whose services protect everyone.

The legal concept of "material fact," once fairly clear, has been muddied by various court rulings—what is material in one cultural tradition may not matter in another. More confusion ensues from the traditional Asian practice of seeming to negotiate endlessly after the contract is signed. An informed real estate professional prepares for this common stumbling block by handling the problem solidly and firmly with the client before it arises.

Obtaining inspections for pest control, roofs, and septic

tanks can be another area impacted by culturally based mis-understandings. The services such companies perform are more common here than elsewhere. Hence, immigrant buyers may have trouble accepting that they are necessary. Professionals in these fields often become fodder for continued negotiation, or are thought of as superfluous. If the inspections are explained and justified at the contract signing, an excess of difficulties can be defused in advance. But as you explain, it is vitally important to understand the point from which the client views them.

The author no longer tries to count the number of times he has heard, "Why don't these people get it? They're in America. They ought to do as we do here!" This is particularly ironic because when people from this country travel abroad we are called "Ugly Americans." When we, with our two hundred-year-old culture, travel to other countries many of us are offended to find that people whose background may incorporate thousands of years of history don't speak English and behave like us.

Likewise, it is even more difficult for immigrants from cultures with millennia of history to leave all their behaviors and beliefs behind. No culture is universal and no practice common to all. Many immigrants struggle to change cultural behavior developed over hundreds of lifetimes. Visit any English-language adult night course and you will see new immigrants trying to learn the language and culture of America.

Plenty of people make a conscious effort to deal equally with everyone. Admirable as this objective is, today, treating everyone the same is seldom enough. Success with the tidal wave of new immigrants demands that we be proactive and learn to appreciate and adapt to their way of thinking. This book is about those individual variations in attitudes toward life that make us who we are and how they affect real estate transactions. Moreover, it is about respecting the cultures of others and working harmoniously with people who don't always do things as we're used to.

Meeting all the unique needs of clients, regardless of culture, is the basis for providing exceptional client service in today's new multicultural marketplace. By satisfying their needs, we will achieve the success to which we all aspire.

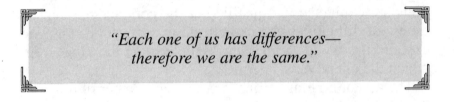

"Each one of us has differences—
therefore we are the same."

4

The Opportunity for Real Estate Professionals

Every year over a million new immigrants enter the United States. This influx from other cultures has fueled a boom in home ownership. These immigrants hold better jobs and have more advanced degrees than in the past, giving them greater purchasing power than any previous group. Immigrants tend to have a strong faith in an improved future. Buying a house is an expression of that faith. According to the Fannie Mae Foundation, immigrants accounted for 47 percent of U.S. home owners in 1990, up from 22 percent in 1980. As a result, minority households now account for nearly one-third of all new home owners.

A Harvard University study shows that 4 million minority and immigrant households became home owners between 1994 and 1997. During the same time, minorities accounted for 42 percent of the growth in American home ownership. In addition, Fleet Mortgage Group estimates that 80 percent of all first-time home buyers in 2010 will be immigrants.

The most spectacular growth is in Hispanic households, which grew 16.3 percent from 1995 through 1997. During the same period, U.S. residents from Mexico, Puerto Rico, Cuba, and South America numbered around 28 million. At the same time, other minority groups like African Americans and Asians also experienced substantial increases. From 1980 to 1990, people of Asian and Pacific Island descent (Hawaiians, Samoans, Filipinos, etc.) increased their numbers from 3.8 million to over 7.3 million.

A burgeoning rate of immigration is the main reason for this growth. It began when the Immigration and Nationality Act replaced the restrictive national origins quota system in 1965. With that change, the former trickle of new immigrants began expanding into a flood of people from other cultures seeking opportunity in America.

The million immigrants who enter the United States every year will increase the "minority" portion of the American population from 24 percent (1990) to 32 percent by 2010. Minorities will account for over 75 percent of total population growth during this time.

Immigration aside, an increasing birth rate is another reason for the growth in home ownership by multicultural clients. While the Caucasian population in America is expected to grow at a rate of less than one-quarter of one percent annually after 2000, far greater numbers are projected for minorities. The Census Bureau anticipates that minorities in America will grow by 74 percent from 1995 to 2010. The Caucasian population will grow by 26 percent in the same period. Latino immigration adds 325,000, with 550,000 Latino births adding up to a total of 900,000 for this cultural group alone each year. As a example of the impact of Hispanics on the United States, in California and Texas the most popular baby boy's name is no longer John, James, Michael, or David. It's Jose.

As can be seen, immigrants are entering the country in record numbers. In 1996, 27.2 percent of the influx came from Mexico, 26.7 percent from Asia, and 6.9 percent from Europe. South and Central America account for another 11.9 percent, while 10.5 percent arrived from the Caribbean Islands.

Every state, county, and city will feel to some degree, the effect of this tidal wave. None will remain unaffected. According to 1997 Census Bureau figures, some 9.6 percent of U.S. residents were born elsewhere. This is the greatest number since six decades ago, when 11.6 percent of U.S. residents in 1930 were natives of other countries. At that time, the new arrivals were mostly from Europe.

The same Census Bureau figures show that California is attracting a strong plurality, 24.9 percent of the state's residents being foreign-born. New York holds second place with 19.6 percent, followed by Florida at 16.4 percent; 15.4 percent of New Jersey residents were from abroad. The Texas figure stood at 11.3 percent. Again, although most of these new Americans are from Latin America and Asia, the effects are different on every state.

Even within a given state there are marked differences in the makeup of immigrant groups. California's city of San Francisco attracts so many Chinese that it now has the largest population of Asian groups outside China. In southern California, Hispanics coming from Mexico and Latin America predominate. Florida cities like Orlando draw Puerto Rican and Caribbean Island immigrants, while Miami attracts more Cubans because of its close proximity to that island country and its long-established Cuban community.

In the southern states, where many mistakenly think there is little cultural diversity, Asians and a number of other non-native groups are growing rapidly. By Census Bureau statistics, Asian population in the South rose 45 percent from 1990 to 1996. The largest increase unexpcctedly took place in Georgia, where the Asian population exploded by 70 percent. North Carolina was next, with a 62 percent increase. Florida experienced 57 percent, while Asians in Texas grew by 50 percent and those in Tennessee soared 49 percent.

These increases brought the total number of Asians in the South to 1.67 million people. Compared to an overall Asian heritage growth of 45 percent, the population of African Americans in the southern states grew by 13 percent while Caucasian growth was proceeding at a comparatively low 8 percent. By the year 2010, 80 percent of all first-time home buyers will be immigrants.

Once these new Americans are here long enough to become acclimated, they spread out across the country. For instance, Vietnamese are moving in great numbers to Minnesota. East Indians are now moving into Michigan, Maryland, New York, and Los Angeles. Mexicans keep moving farther north and are now going into Idaho, Oregon, and Washington.

No matter where you practice real estate, doing business in or near a major metropolitan city means that you will experience the impact of multicultural home buyers and sellers. Prepare yourself now for working with these new Americans, or you may have to find a different line of work.

Nevertheless, it would be wise to remember that the forebears of many new immigrants have been in this country since pioneer days, or even before. The author is a fifth-generation Chinese American whose grandmother came into the world in Monterey, California, in 1869.

Multicultural clients who are born in the United States should receive the same treatment as any other American. Anything that you wouldn't say to another American is something you wouldn't say to an Asian American, African American, Hispanic American, Middle Eastern American, or any other. Saying "You really speak English well" to anyone whose family has been here for generations is both insulting and incomprehensible.

There is a story about Eleanor Roosevelt, who sat through an official luncheon next to a Chinese official she hadn't met before. Although he was well dressed and obviously of some importance, he never spoke. The First Lady therefore assumed his English must be poor. Finally, she thought to begin the conversation by talking about the meal. Mrs. Roosevelt asked, "Likee soupee?" The gentleman nodded and smiled graciously.

Minutes later, the same gentleman rose to give the keynote speech of the day in perfect English. Returning to his seat, China's Ambassador to the United States and graduate of Harvard Law School, Wellington Koo smiled broadly at the red-faced Mrs. Roosevelt and asked, "Likee speechee?" Readers are strongly advised not to make similar assumptions to avoid such embarrassments.

So, how do you know if your clients are new immigrants or natives of the United States? Just remember to ask, "Where are your ancestors from?" or "Where did your family move here from?" If the answer is Omaha, Topeka, or San Francisco, you are obviously dealing with someone who didn't get here last year.

Remember: the longer an immigrant family resides in this country, the less strongly they tend to hold to the belief system of their mother country. However, cultural ties are incredibly strong and even a family that has been in America for over a hundred years may still exhibit a few of the traits of the traditional culture.

African Americans now number over 30 million or 13 percent of the U.S. population. The majority are found in North Carolina, South Carolina, Georgia, Alabama, and Louisiana. Today, a large number are moving to the North Carolina metro markets of Raleigh-Durham and Charlotte. While they are not recent immigrants, most consider themselves a distinct cultural group in the United States, one with specific housing wants and needs. Of all the major cultural groups in America, African Americans have the lowest household income due to various well-documented forms of historic discrimination. As a result, they have had the most difficulty in affording home ownership, with only a 45 percent rate compared to white Americans' nearly 70 percent. Only recently have significant numbers of this group been able to own property.

This low home ownership rate among African Americans means real estate agents must spend a little more time than usual explaining the process to members of this group. Not only are they first-time home buyers, but they may not have any friends or family who own homes from whom they can learn about the process.

Native Americans, also not new to the United States, are a significant home buying force in many parts of the country. The 2 million members of this unique group are most prevalent in the states of Arizona, New Mexico, Washington, Montana, South Dakota, North Dakota, Nebraska, and Kansas. While many Americans think that most of the original occupants of this country live on reservations, only 20 percent actually do and that number appears to be dwindling.

Many people also mistakenly believe that all Native Americans are alike. Native American reservations comprise 308 sovereign nations within the United States. Each has its own territory, governmental structure, and laws. The largest tribes are the Cherokee, numbering around three hundred thousand, with the Navajo second in size. The third largest are the Chippewa and Sioux, with approximately one hundred thousand members each. There are hundreds of tribes with less than a thousand members.

As the above facts illustrate, every person is an individual, regardless of cultural background. Traits that are mentioned here may not apply to your clients. Always treat clients individually, never assuming they will behave in certain ways or that they believe in particular systems of ideas. This book is a guidebook to general traits which provides a partial explanation for why some people do as they do.

This book also intends to show the many ways people are similar. We are made of the same material; we have many of the same goals for happiness and fulfillment and the natural desire to avoid unpleasantness. Once we recognize and get past the differences we can look for commonalities on which to build long-term relationships.

For example, ego is an important factor in American culture, although it is certainly not ours exclusively. To many, the term signifies personal pride or honor. The seemingly humble Asians have an ego as well, called face. The Hispanic cultural equivalent is machismo. African Americans recognize the concept as respect. Those in Jordan call it pride. When dealing with these groups we must take this issue into account so they don't lose face, have their machismo offended, be disrespected, or have their pride hurt. Every culture has some similar concept and some have specific mechanisms in place to acknowledge such a quality.

Some aspects of culture are deeply rooted in the subconscious. Culture is a shared system of beliefs, values, and customs that explains and simplifies basic aspects of living in society. It tells us how to behave and function within our own group. The danger may come when two dissimilar cultures interact. Since they may see things from different viewpoints yet not know the reasons for the difference, there is potential for misunderstanding and conflict.

"High context" cultures make greater distinctions between insiders and outsiders of their group than "low context" cultures. Sociologists say that context is one reason why it may take longer to develop rapport with the high context Asians and Hispanics than with other cultures.

Before trying to relate to others, it's important to realize how most in the American culture view the world. Those who study such things say there are two major types of cultures in the world, "individualistic" and "collectivistic."

(This is a postulated, not political, definition.) In individual-istic countries like the United States and most of Europe, "average" people are encouraged to stand out from the crowd. Here, the individual is supreme. Most of our social perceptions and value judgments proceed from that view-point. To members of this group it would be perfectly ac-ceptable to discuss the unique amenities or distinctive design of a home.

On the other hand, group identity is most influential in "collectivist" countries. In these, one's prosperity and sur-vival are secondary to and depend on those of clan, race, family, religion, or employment. Good illustrations include China, Japan, Pakistan, Taiwan, Peru, Argentina, Brazil, Sweden, Norway, Saudi Arabia, India, Korea, Mexico, Egypt, and Guatemala. To buyers from these countries you would emphasize traditional floor plans and how the archi-tecture conforms with its surroundings.

A significant problem occurs when people of one type of culture use their values and standards in attempts to under-stand others. The individualist view insists that the same eth-ical and social criteria ought to apply to everyone. Our polit-ical and legal systems reflect this assumption.

The collective view tends to apply different values and stan-dards to different group members. Thus collective societies are likely to have caste systems and permanent classes that few can find their way out of. A massive failure of communication occurs when either view is applied without a grasp of the other. When one or both recognize the source of the potential problem, though, it is less likely to develop into one.

In America we believe in equality of the sexes and express that belief through laws and public policies. Other cultures, like that of the Middle East, find this idea offensive. In such countries women may not vote or ride with a man in the cab of a truck. The picture of a woman walking three feet behind her husband is a reality in much of the world. We need not accept or even agree with the point of view that holds this custom to be proper. Nevertheless, good manners and good business remind us to allow others to live in the ways they choose.

Americans admit to being materialistic and judge people by what they own ("Keeping up with the Joneses"). South American cultures share material possessions for the benefit of all. While we compete zealously for prizes and awards, people who live in Japan give credence to the principle of harmony. Americans are strongly future-oriented while Filipinos, Mexicans, and Latin Americans tend to place the most importance to now and today. At the other end of the spectrum, people in China and Japan place great stock in past events and the traditions that come from them.

The notion of truth also differs from one culture to another. Nearly all Americans believe in the saying "Honesty is the best policy," while Hispanics may alter facts slightly to protect the other person's feelings. The Japanese often nod their heads to mean "I hear what you are saying," not necessarily "I agree." Americans who interpret this gesture as agreement wonder why those "inscrutable Japanese" seem to change their minds so often.

Culture gives us expectations that confuse and disorient us when they are not realized. Communicating with other cultures calls for expecting this and trying to resolve the unease we may feel. Focusing on learning from them reduces the discomfort. Expecting people from other cultures to be different means you will only perceive differences. Look for similarities and you will see them.

Working with multicultural clients brings a tremendous opportunity to learn about other peoples and cultures around the world. However, you must be willing to expend time and energy. It takes work in this phase as in all others to become more successful in your real estate career.

We must forget fixed ideas and be accepting of other people's differences. Beneath all of the dissimilarities, all home buyers want to own a nice home, raise their families in safety, and own the American dream.

> *"People from other cultures want the same thing Americans want—a nice home, safe neighborhood, good schools for their children, and a chance to achieve the American dream."*

5

How People from Other Cultures Choose an Agent

Multicultural home buyers and sellers do not necessarily seek out real estate professionals from their own cultural background. In truth, few care about a Realtor's®[1] culture as much as they do about the qualities of trust, patience, and personal interest. This is evidenced by the thousands of American agents with whom the author has spoken who are totally baffled and befuddled by their multicultural clients.

Chinese clients often prefer agents who are specifically not Chinese because they fear that someone from their own culture might disclose their personal financial information to others in their community. People of Brazilian heritage may not want a Brazilian agent because they want to avoid the

---

1. *Realtor* is a registered trademark of The National Association of Realtors.

high taxes that government imposes. They prefer that their U.S. property dealings not be known. Although both of these concerns are generally groundless, an agent can do little to alter a client's fears.

In fact, a multicultural client wanting to hire an agent from the same ethnic background might be hard pressed to find one. National Association of Realtors (NAR) 1996 statistics show that only 4 percent of its members were Latino or Hispanic, 2 percent Asian, and 2 percent Black. Therefore, the Caucasians who comprise ninety two out of every a hundred agents had better learn to work with diverse clients, and soon!

One belief about real estate held by people of all cultures in America is the misconception that real estate agents and brokers do virtually nothing to earn ridiculously high incomes. The average person thinks that an agent shows a few homes, meanders over to the escrow company or attorney's office, and collects a big, fat check. This myth leads real estate clients to be less than loyal to their agents. They know nothing of the hundreds of actions required to successfully transfer property from buyer to seller. Such activities may include writing the purchase agreement, negotiating the purchase, and locating a suitable loan.

Depending on local laws and customs, they may also have to conduct title searches, arrange for inspections, contract for repairs of items disclosed by inspections, arrange insurance, and more. Imagine the confusion of a person from a culture where few of these jobs are done by anyone.

The following is a list of just some of the things that the author does to help clients buy real estate:

1. Explain the benefits of a buyer-broker agreement to clients.
2. Determine the approximate price range for which the buyer can qualify.
3. Describe the services that lenders and loan brokers perform.

4. Explain the benefits and drawbacks of various types of home financing.
5. Explain loan fees and their relationship to interest rates.
6. Provide ideas for alternative methods of finance for purchase.
7. Explain the use and benefit of a lender pre-qualification letter.
8. Explain the use and benefit of a lender pre-approval letter.
9. Provide a list of several lenders or loan brokers.
10. Review clients' financial and personal plans as they relate to real estate.
11. Make sure clients are buying a home that meets their needs.
12. Provide clients with an "agency disclosure statement."
13. Explain the agency disclosure statement.
14. Assist in developing a prioritized list of home selection criteria.
15. Keep track of those criteria when analyzing various properties.
16. Inform clients of possible tax benefits in purchasing real estate.
17. Explain some of the drawbacks of real estate ownership.
18. Explain how the structure of the clients' purchase can affect them financially.
19. Help determine the most advantageous time to make an offer.
20. Help determine the most advantageous time to close the escrow.
21. Provide a sample copy of the purchase agreement for clients to study.
22. Provide a list of appropriate neighborhoods in the clients' price range.
23. Provide rating data about local schools.
24. Provide locations and characteristics of shopping areas.

25. Provide information about local and regional transportation systems.
26. Share information about recreational facilities.
27. Explain sports facilities and programs that exist locally.
28. Provide information on various churches and religious institutions.
29. Give facts and resources on any native aspect of the local area.
30. Explain how the Realtor® multiple listing service (MLS) works.
31. Search the MLS for appropriate properties.
32. Examine local newspapers for appropriate homes.
33. Check real estate magazines for properties that meet the client's parameters.
34. Review a personal list of homes that might be available.
35. Check for-sale-by-owner properties that may suit the clients' needs.
36. Contact owners of property to arrange to show homes to clients.
37. Share personal knowledge about local history, weather, political activity, or other factors that may affect the clients' purchasing decision.
38. Explain real estate terminology used throughout the home buying process.
39. Discuss the benefits and drawbacks of various styles of homes.
40. Discuss the pros and cons of various building materials.
41. Describe how the orientation of the home affects its comfort.
42. Show clients how to add value to a home that may not be perfect, but has most of the features they require.
43. Act as a "sounding board" in the clients' decision-making process.
44. Provide information about the seller's motivation for selling.
45. Provide a "comparative market analysis" to determine

appropriate offering price that will best meet the clients' needs and protect their interests.

46. Explain the significance of various clauses in the purchase agreement.
47. Explain the lender's appraisal process.
48. Make sure that the events and conditions agreed upon in the contract can be realistically performed within time limits provided.
49. Provide a written estimate of the costs to close the escrow, including down payment and the monthly payment under the terms of the clients'.
50. Explain how offers to purchase property are presented.
51. Make an appointment to present the offer that meets everyone's schedule.
52. Present the offer to the seller in a professional manner.
53. Add credibility to the clients' offer by confirming their ability to perform under the terms of the agreement.
54. Negotiate the areas of objection with the seller.
55. Explain the possibility of multiple offers in the clients' purchase.
56. Structure the clients' offer for maximum impact in multiple-offer situations.
57. Respond to seller objections with minor modifications that allow the seller to accept while not significantly altering the clients' position.
58. Recalculate costs and monthly payments in the event of a counteroffer from the seller.
59. Verify all representations by the seller.
60. Help remove negotiating obstacles before they arise by knowing the financing in escrow process.
61. Provide a list of reputable companies for home inspection.
62. Provide a list of reputable companies for pool inspection.
63. Provide a list of reputable companies for pest control inspection.
64. Provide a list of respected well inspectors and testing companies, when appropriate.

65. Provide a list of respected septic inspectors, when appropriate.
66. Provide a list of reputable companies for chimney inspection.
67. Provide a list of reputable companies for roof inspection.
68. If requested, provide a list of reputable companies for environmental inspection.
69. If requested, provide a list of reputable companies for lead inspection.
70. Make arrangements for the various inspections, as required.
71. Be present if possible when inspections are conducted to add clarity to written reports.
72. Help interpret which report items are relatively minor and which require further clarification.
73. Assist in finding the least costly solutions to problems in reports.
74. Renegotiate with seller to pay for items that are important or a matter of health and safety.
75. Arrange as requested to have another expert give an opinion in cases where experts express differing opinions.
76. Arrange for repairs as necessary.
77. Provide a transfer disclosure statement from the seller.
78. Rewrite the contract as needed.
79. Provide seismic hazard report, as applicable.
80. Provide flood zone information, as applicable.
81. Provide smoke detector information, as applicable.
82. Provide Foreign Investment in Real Property Tax Act disclosure to seller.
83. Give the buyer a choice of title or escrow company.
84. Open escrow.
85. Deposit earnest money.
86. Review terms, price, and projected closing date with escrow officer.
87. Inform the officer of all parties to the transaction and how to contact them.

88. Provide the officer with conditions and data needed to order payoff demand from existing lender.
89. Order a preliminary title report.
90. Explain title insurance and any exceptions to it.
91. Review preliminary title report for any "clouds on title," unforeseen liens, easements. or encroachments that could delay closing.
92. Explain any covenants, conditions, or restrictions, as appropriate.
93. Make sure that pending sale has been reported to MLS.
94. Closely follow deadlines listed in the contract, as errors in timing can nullify the agreement.
95. Work with lender to provide information and approvals, as stipulated.
96. Provide weekly updates on escrow progress to buyer.
97. Arrange for buyers to inspect the property again, as needed.
98. Explain the protections offered by a home warranty plan.
99. Order a home warranty plan, as requested.
100. Explain home owner's insurance requirements.
101. Assist in arranging for home owner's insurance, as requested.
102. Provide a list of reputable moving companies, as requested.
103. Provide a list of telephone numbers for the local gas, electric, water, garbage, and cable TV companies.
104. Arrange for a smooth transfer of utility service from seller to buyer.
105. Help buyers locate temporary housing, as needed.
106. Assist buyers in locating reliable child care, as requested.
107. Coordinate the move out by seller and move in by buyer.
108. Negotiate for buyers if the escrow process takes longer than expected.

109. Negotiate an interim occupancy agreement, as required.
110. Draw up a rental agreement if seller needs to stay after close of escrow.
111. Conduct a final "walk-through" inspection of the property to assure that nothing significant has changed since the purchase agreement was signed.
112. Make arrangements to rectify any problems discovered during walk-through.
113. Provide written explanation of the various ways to hold title to real property.
114. Provide the names of at least three attorneys who can explain the income tax and estate tax ramifications of holding title.
115. Review the closing documents for accuracy.
116. Explain closing papers to buyer.
117. Arrange for wire transfer of funds, as necessary.
118. Deliver closing documents to buyer.
119. Deliver any final refund check to buyer.
120. At all times, protect the buyer's interests.

Real estate professionals face a second myth concerning the amount and source of their compensation. Some people believe that agents receive a salary from their brokers. Others believe that all agents receive a part of the commission from any transaction that goes through the office or an office with the same name if a franchise. Many Americans think that the agent takes home around 6 percent of the sales price.

Imagine how much people in your area think you make in real estate. Take an average sales price, multiply that by around 6 percent, and that is the average commission they believe you earn. Next, multiply that by forty or fifty houses a year people think you sell, and you have some idea of what the average person thinks real estate agents make a year. Thus, if your average home price is $100,000, most of your clients believe you bring home between $240,000 and $300,000 annually.

Below is an explanation that the author uses to justify the commission for a real estate agent. Clients seem able to easily grasp it because of its simplicity.

How an Agent Earns His or Her Income

Most people mistakenly believe that real estate agents earn an outrageous amount of money for the work they do. Now that you've seen the list of over one hundred activities agents do to help you purchase the home of your dreams, you can understand that it is a very complex process.

With a hypothetical commission of 6 percent (remember that commissions are negotiable between the listing broker and the seller), the agent who represents the seller usually gets half, leaving only 3 percent to the selling broker who represents the buyer.

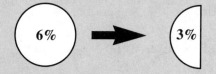

Of the 3 percent left to the selling broker, the broker gets around one-third for rent, utilities, advertising and other costs leaving your agent with 2 percent.

Of the 2 percent left to the selling agent, there are real estate expenses that must be paid in order to earn that income. These costs take about a third of the commission, leaving your agent with only around 1 percent to pay for personal living expenses such as home mortgage, food for the family and children's education.

Some of the business expenses that real estate agents must pay include:

- Automobile maintenance and repair
- Gasoline
- Automobile insurance
- Real estate board dues
- Multiple listing fees
- Advertising
- Signage expenses
- Lock boxes
- Purchasing forms and contracts
- Computer hardware and software
- Computer on-line services
- Computer maintenance
- Professional liability insurance
- Professional education
- License fees
- Income taxes on real estate income
- Self-employment taxes
- Postage
- Copying
- Business entertainment
- Referral fees to other agents
- Cellular telephone/pager
- Business telephone

With myths about rich real estate agents so common among Americans, imagine what people from other countries must think! Obviously, it is doubly important that agents explain their duties and compensation to every client. Do this as soon as possible after rapport is established.

Based on these myths, many Americans think it perfectly reasonable to ask for part of what is in their minds, an exorbitant commission. Without a clear understanding of how hard an agent works and how little he or she actually earns, people from countries where hard negotiation is a given are even more likely to look for a kickback.

If people believe that real estate agents make too much money and don't do much to earn it, is there any wonder why we have trouble getting clients to be loyal to us? They figure because you earn so much if they leave you for another agent you will make it up from some other client.

Few people from immigrant cultures know enough to care about the agent's experience or how many transactions he or she has completed. Most new clients only care about one transaction—their own. People who are new to this country are more concerned that the agent is honest and trustworthy than they are about professional awards and applause. That you are good parent carries more weight than a term as president of your local board or association. Likewise, the belief that you care more about them than you do about your commission outweighs all the professional recognition you have ever received.

Stories demonstrating that you have these qualities should be told, modestly, during the rapport-building stage. Many cultures transmit information from one generation to another through storytelling, called oral tradition. They truly appreciate an agent who uses this method to relate professional qualities. This is far more effective with multicultural people than a canned sales pitch.

People from other cultures take their time choosing a real estate agent. Even Europeans want to have confidence in their agent by getting to know her or him first. People from all cultures expect this to be a long-term relationship with them, their family, and their friends. In America we tend to have many informal personal relationships and only a few deep, lasting friendships. In other cultures friendships are much more permanent. It's probably a good practice for Realtors® to aspire to become clients' agent for life, irrespective of culture.

Filipino clients may prefer an American agent for other reasons. Since the United States ruled their homeland for five decades beginning in 1898, then gave it back as promised, some Filipinos greatly appreciate Americans out of a belief that we are probably worthy and reliable.

Filipinos may trust and believe Americans more than their own cultural brethren. The mistrust some Filipinos have for agents from their own culture comes from the Philippine practice of *la gai,* literally "grease money." Much of Philippine business practices *la gai.* An agent who refers a roofer or other contractor to a client expects a little grease money from the provider. This practice drives up the cost of doing business in direct proportion to the number of providers involved.

La gai will affect real estate transactions when agents fail early in the relationship to teach their Filipino clients how hard they work and how little they really earn. Clients may expect *la gai* from an agent who hasn't informed them about such issues. The client may think that an agent from his own culture receives *la gai* from the seller, driving the price higher. The client may even believe that using an American agent will make the purchase price lower in the absence of *la gai.* In addition, Filipinos may expect their agent to continue serving them after the transaction is complete. It is not unusual for them to ask their agent to help find a roofer or electrician or to help them clean the house years after the close of escrow. If they were never informed, they may think that you are getting *la gai* from other service providers and thus you should continue to help them in exchange. This is why it's important to explain that all your pay comes from the one transaction. Tell them that you will be happy to refer them to appropriate professionals, but only that.

La gai is similar to the Indonesian practice known as *sogok.* This term also translates as "grease money." Educate these clients the same as you would Filipinos. Explain how hard you work and how little money you get in proportion. If you do, demands for *sogok* will be less likely.

China has a related custom called *guanxi* (pronounced *gwan-shee*). Although this is sometimes considered bribery as well, they think of it locally as a referral network system whose function is to locate a trustworthy agent based on the advice of satisfied previous clients.

Similar systems of greasing of the skids are common around the world. In Mexico, petty official bribery is known as *la mordida*. The Arab world knows it as *baksheesh*. Immigrants from these and other areas come here with the expectation of having to deal with it everywhere. Most are quite surprised, and many disbelieving, when they learn that this culture condemns such practices as unethical.

There is no question that clients want to trust and believe in the agent they choose. In the best case, you are referred and introduced by a satisfied client of the same culture. Referrals from other agents are almost as good. Either gives you credibility at the outset. After the introduction, you can help yourself by sharing stories from your personal life that demonstrate the highly valued qualities of openness and honesty.

African Americans present contradictions in choosing an agent. Until as recently as the 1964 Civil Rights Act, there was limited contact between this group and Caucasians. Many believe that racism causes the economic gulf between themselves and the dominant culture. This belief helps perpetuate the ill-feelings some African Americans harbor toward members of the Caucasian race. Buyers who feel this way may be better served by looking to agents from their own culture first.

At the same time, other African Americans have, for a long time, viewed the dominant culture as superior to their own. This misconception may cause them to deliberately seek a Caucasian agent. It's important for non-African Americans to realize that this contradiction can exist and be prepared to deal with it.

About 75 percent of African Americans are active church members. Most are Protestant—11 million Baptists and 6 million Methodists. If your clients from this culture express strong beliefs and you share the same you may wish to mention it. They may also have conflicts with looking at properties on Sunday so you should ask about their availability.

Americans who are the most credible in business demonstrate decisive, unyielding, and confident behavior. The opposite may be true in other cultures. For instance, well-regarded Japanese leaders take great pains to appear indirect, flexible, and humble. It would serve agents well to take a similar approach in dealing with clients from these cultures.

At the other extreme, Middle Eastern men may expect agents to boast openly of how outstanding they are professionally and personally. Bragging in this culture is a high art and you are expected to "Toot Your Own Horn" with directness and enthusiasm. It is considered bad form, however, to do so in an overtly competitive manner. Politeness demands that you meet but not try to "top" another's exploits and accomplishments.

Some Hispanics come from countries where even the best education is not highly valued. Those who come here for purely economic reasons may not be as well schooled in general as those whose driving purpose in immigrating is to get an education. The literacy rate in Mexico is one of the lowest in the world. The most important concern is taking care of the family, even if it means leaving school early. Having little familiarity with the value of education, their vision of the American opportunity may encompass no more than respectable housing and a well-paying job.

This lack of schooling on the part of some Hispanics means that a good agent will carefully and patiently explain such foreign concepts as buying and financing a home, then answer every question until the new ideas are clearly understood. As noted, 70 percent of white households own a home while only 44 percent of Hispanics are as fortunate. As with African Americans, they may know few property owners from whom they could learn about this complex subject.

Remember that lack of knowledge is not the same as stupidity. Demonstrate respect and do your job conscientiously and the Hispanic client will be quite loyal and may provide you with many enthusiastic referrals.

At the other end of the academic spectrum, educated Latin Americans often put their titles and degrees on their business cards. In these cases, take the time to spell out any degrees and professional designations that you may hold, since these are highly prized by those who display their own credentials openly.

In general, however, most new immigrants are not overly impressed by credentials, designations, and degrees. They are more likely to be concerned with the quality of whom they are dealing with. It is most effective for agents to talk about themselves and their own families instead of real estate in the early stages of relationships with multicultural buyers or sellers.

To be successful with people from other cultures, you must possess and display four personal characteristics: sincerity, honesty, integrity, and patience. Sincerity is meaning what you say, keeping your promises, and making a genuine effort to put the client's interests above your own. It is saying what you mean, meaning what you say, and going the extra mile to make your given word a reality in practice. Your clients will be truly appreciative to discover that you intend genuinely to be more of a consultant than just another salesperson. Consultants do not stress making the sale, while salespeople tend to do that and that alone.

The second tenet, honesty, means providing answers to questions if you know them and telling the client when you don't know. And it means the answers are true to the best of your knowledge. Clients seldom expect you to be perfect or to have all the answers at your fingertips. They do want you to find the answers to their questions in a timely fashion.

The third rule, integrity, is being what you represent yourself to be, saying what you are going to do, and doing it.

Consistency is a vital part of integrity. Be sure to write down any promises you make and keep them. Few agents do this or stop to realize how important integrity is to the client.

Finally, patience is being prepared for a seemingly endless list of questions and answering them one by one until the clients understand. Once more, first-time home buyers may not be comfortable with the language, culture, contracts, or complexities of the home buying and selling processes. Your job is to educate them while being fully aware of their discomfort with real estate.

"Multicultural clients are far more interested in the quality of the person who represents them in a real estate transaction than in degrees, designations, or awards."

6

Building Rapport with People from Other Cultures

Culture can have a tremendous impact on the home buying process. Everything is affected from showing the property to negotiations to obtaining the loan—all the way through to the closing. Getting started properly with the client and building a comfortable level of communication is crucial to success with people from other cultures.

Newly arrived in a strange land, multicultural clients strain mightily to cope with customs they find hard to understand. Recognize that they can be just as frustrated by American cultural peculiarities as people in this country are of theirs.

Meeting and Greeting

Both men and women in the United States are used to greeting each other with a smile and firm handshake. However, even among Americans greetings can differ due to long-forgotten cultural influences.

Most African Americans shake hands although some of their greetings can be very ritualistic. It can be another reflection of their desire to express uniqueness. Hispanic Americans may hug friends after shaking hands. Asian Americans may bow slightly while shaking hands. Again, Americans can be quite ethnocentric. It's surprising to people here that most of the world does not greet by shaking hands.

For example, people from Asian cultures generally bow but there are differences between how people bow. For instance, people from Cambodia and Laos will often bow with both hands together in front of the chest as if praying. In Japan, the depth of the bow can signify the level of respect for the other party. Many Koreans feel most comfortable bowing and if they shake hands the right hand is supported at the wrist by the left hand to show respect. People from Taiwan generally nod the head in recognition rather than bow. Thais bow with palms together about chest-high with their fingers outstretched.

Filipinos will commonly greet each other by shaking hands and then touching the shoulder of friends. In addition to shaking hands, people from these islands expect to receive a broad smile from an honest agent. Next, it is customary to offer coffee or tea to show your respect, and do what you can to make them comfortable. A little introductory personal—but not too personal—conversation is fitting.

Native Hawaiians hug each other, exchanging breaths. The custom is called "aha." Their name for a white person is *haole,* meaning "no breath," because we shake hands without further body contact. Ancient Hawaiians, by the way, actually bumped heads together. Just be glad they don't do that today: Real estate already has enough headaches! Burmese show affection at greeting by pressing the mouth and nose on a friend's cheek and inhaling forcefully. Samoans put their noses opposite each other's and smell deeply.

People from Latin America and Mexico hug close friends in what is called an *abrazo*. In Mexico, this *abrazo* is a measure of the friendship; the longer the embrace, the deeper the camaraderie. Latino men commonly hug each other as a sign of friendship. If your Cuban male client kisses you on the cheek, you know you have made it into his circle of friends. Many American real estate agents are not used to men kissing them but be aware that if you turn away, a kiss intended for the cheek could land embarrassingly on your lips!

Immigrant men from the Middle East often shake hands with a slight nod or bow and then exchange kisses on both cheeks. Traditional Muslim men may shake hands and then touch the right palm of their hand to their heart as a sign of friendship. Men from this country generally do not shake hands with women. They often do not introduce women whom they are with nor is it expected that you shake hands with her. Do not attempt to shake hands with a Middle Eastern woman unless she offers her hand first. Simply nod in her direction and say, "Hello."

Traditional Muslim women will usually avoid shaking hands with unfamiliar men or women. You can usually spot them easily because every body part but the hands is covered and all the face but the eyes is veiled. Obviously, you should not try to shake hands with them. Simply nod in their direction to acknowledge their presence.

Following centuries under British rule, mostly Hindu Eastern Indians seem to have adapted quickly to Western habits. Shaking hands is normal behavior for both men and women. If the woman is older, a courteous, respectful nod of the head to acknowledge her presence is better than a handshake, which might be seen as disrespectful. Traditional Indians may greet you with a *namaste,* which is a slight bow with the hands folded prayerfully in front of the chest. Many traditional Indian men do not ordinarily shake hands with women.

Pakistanis simply shake hands with strangers and hug friends. Some men from this country do not shake hands with women. Since Pakistan is a largely Muslim nation bordering on India, people greet each other with *salaam,* which is the equivalent of our "hello." The *salaam* is done by bowing with the palm of the right hand on the forehead. *Salaam* means "peace," or "May peace be with you." Note that it is not the same as the *namaste* greeting of Indians.

Even cultures that do shake hands, such as those in England, France, Germany, and Italy, do not all shake the same way we do here. People in England prefer a brief but firm handshake while those in France have a light grip while sharing one gentle single shake that is quickly withdrawn. Germans will give a very firm shake of the hand with just one "pump" while the French consider such a greeting unmannerly. More than one shake with Germans or French is seen as a sign of aggressiveness. Italians will shake hands and then hug friends or kiss them on both cheeks.

Men in Eastern Europe, Portugal, Spain, and Italy will often kiss male friends on the cheek in greeting. In Greece, and much of Eastern Europe, men meet with an embrace and a hearty pat on the back.

The primary multicultural business rule is: never assume anything! Many real estate agents have been embarrassed by wrongly assuming that a client is more comfortable with a traditional greeting. For example, thinking that an Asian client will bow automatically, they start out in this manner. As they bow, the client, adhering to our American customs as perceived, extends a hand. The embarrassed the agent sees this and quickly straightens up to offer a hand. The client, seeing the agent begin to bow, quickly pulls back and starts to bow at the moment the agent proffers his hand. This dance could go on for quite some time. The longer it continues, the less comfortable the relationship may become. Such a cultural faux pas could taint your entire transaction!

To avoid this embarrassing scene, the agent should begin with a polite word or two such as "Mr. and Mrs. Wong, it's so nice to meet you at last." After that, hesitate for a moment, giving the clients an opportunity to offer the kind of greeting that is most comfortable for them. Then, of course, the agent mirrors that gesture, shaking hands or bowing, as appropriate. It's simple, but you have to be aware of how to properly handle these critical first moves in the relationship.

Speak slowly and clearly to people from other countries who seem to be having difficulty with English. If your clients still do not understand you, try to find another way of explaining yourself. You can illustrate your point as you speak with pictures or diagrams. Many cultures, especially Asians, might appreciate this because their written languages are built on pictures. Remember where the saying, "A picture is worth a thousand words," came from.

Above all, *do not shout*. Clients who don't comprehend your words are not hearing impaired, just unfamiliar with English. By the way, what good does shouting at someone who is deaf do anyway?

There are several words that should be eliminated from our multicultural vocabulary. The first is the word *Oriental*. This now obsolete term implies inscrutability, which in turn means "not knowable." Nobody wants to be thought of as a person whose acquaintance is impossible to make. Likewise the word *Eskimo* is a crude and outmoded term. The currently preferred term is *Inuit*. Similarly, many African Americans today prefer that term to *Black* because they recognize that their culture is unique in more ways than mere color implies. Other races and cultures are not identified by "light brown," "dark brown," "pink," and so forth.

Exchanging Business Cards

Business cards carry more significance in other parts of the world than they do in the United States. Don't be quite as casual as you may be used to when exchanging cards with people from other cultures.

Characteristic of the culture, the Japanese have a whole ceremony, called *meishi*, built around the initial greeting, including a prescribed method for the exchange of business cards. They are proffered with both hands and a slight bow, with the printed words facing them. As the client bows extending a business card, be ready to offer your card with the left hand as you accept her or his with the right.

The hand you use to accept the client's card can be significant, since the left hand is believed to be unclean in much of Asia and the Middle East. Receive the client's card with your right hand; otherwise clients might be highly offended. When in doubt, you can't go wrong if you follow the client's lead.

Next, do something that most real estate professionals rarely do. Let the client see you read the card. Study it as if it were a holy book since that level of significance attaches to business cards in Japan. Do the best you can to pronounce the name phonetically. Japanese names are usually polysyllabic and may be stressed differently from what we are used to, like Ta-KE-da or Ya-MA-shi-ta.

You may wish to ask the client to pronounce the name for you, then write it down phonetically—*but not on the card*. A Japanese would no more write on another person's card than on his or her face. That is the degree of importance that they attach to their business cards.

If the client is new to American business practice, clarify what the term *real estate agent* or *broker* means. Again, they may have no equivalents where they come from. Ask about the Japanese person's business card and any title shown, if appropriate. These indicate the all-important rank and status of the Japanese businessperson. You may also wish to ask how long your potential client has been with the company. Tales are told of the legendary Japanese loyalty, so don't be surprised if this is the only company the Japanese person has worked for in her or his lifetime. Unlike much of American business, loyalty goes with equal vigor from employee to employer and back in Japan.

Bring out your business card from a nice brass card case in your desk, coat pocket, or purse. It's probably best to avoid leather card cases since the cow is sacred in some cultures. Don't pull business cards out of your shirt pocket—body heat dishonors your card. Respectfully place the client's card into your case and back in your coat pocket. Never put a Japanese person's card in a shirt pocket, as subjecting it to body heat and perspiration would be taken as disrespectful to the card and thus to the person.

Men should never put the card in a wallet taken from a pants pocket because such an act would portray one's intention to sit on the client! Nor should a woman ever put the card in her purse and sling it below her waist—again equivalent to sitting on the client. I hope these illustrations will help readers grasp how important the business card is to a Japanese!

Remember: never write on the business card. Also, never ask for another card. To do so would mean you have lost a symbol of your client's identity. For the same reason, do not walk away from a table where you have placed the card because you might forget it. Doing so would be the equivalent of ignoring the client. Finally, put the card away securely and, thus, honor the client.

Agents who work often with other cultures may choose to help make the clients more comfortable by having their business information on the back in the client's language. It's advisable to avoid potential embarrassment by having someone who knows both real estate and the language translate the wording for your card.

When working with a translator, be sure that you know specifically where the majority of your multicultural clients are from. For instance, simplified Chinese is used primarily in mainland China, while traditional Chinese is preferred in Hong Kong and Taiwan.

Type size and all other aspects should be identical on both sides. If your picture is on the English side, it must also be on the Japanese side. Be sure any logo or other artwork also appears on both sides. Color printing on the English side requires using the same color on the foreign-language side. Any difference, even calling the special side "the back," may be heard as a slight to the client, implying that the American culture and English language are superior to the other's. Done incorrectly, it might turn out to be worse than not taking the trouble to print the card in their language at all.

Should you print your home phone number on your business card? Generally, for safety reasons it is best to leave it off your card until you have developed enough of a relationship to provide this information. At this stage you could provide it to your clients but now it seems special—like you are giving it only to them and not just to anyone who has your card. While giving out your home telephone number is not always a good idea, people from India regularly do this. It is taken as a sign of accessibility and caring in that culture.

Names

Surnames can give you a clue about where the client's ancestors came from. Asian names tend to give Americans problems and are the hardest for us to pronounce. Fortunately, Chinese names are usually monosyllabic. Typical Chinese names include Wong, Lee, Fong, and Chin. On the other hand, Japanese surnames are usually polysyllabic like Takeda, Watanabe, and Yamashita. Prevalent Vietnamese names include Nguyen, Tran, and Vu, whereas Koreans' are Kim, Park, and Shin. In Pakistan the name Khan, meaning "lord," is in common use because it once was used to designate people from the upper classes. As a result, a large number of people from that country now use this name.

The thing to do with someone with an unusual name is to have them write it out for you. Most agents feel embarrassed when they can't pronounce a name but better agents make a point to get it right. Ask the client how to say the name, then write it out phonetically. Yamashita might be written out Ya-*mah*-she-tah. You will find that clients really appreciate this effort and the respect it shows.

Next, establish which is the surname. A name like "Lee Wong Kong" can confuse agents who don't know that a lot of Asian cultures place the family name first. To ask, "Which is your last name?" might elicit the response "Kong" because it is written last. But Kong is not necessarily the surname. Calling the person "Mr. Kong" might be the same as calling an American "Mr. Bill." With any group, try asking instead, "Which is your family name?" A properly phrased question like this will help you get it right.

This technique is especially important when dealing with Vietnamese, who often, but not always, place the first name last. Nguyen Van Dong uses Dong as the first name and Nguyen as the surname. Another person might do the opposite. Again, avoid confusion by asking which is the family name.

Vietnamese women may have three or four names, all different from the husband's. When in doubt, you can't go wrong if you are prepared to follow the client's lead. It is common in that country for a woman to retain her family name if there are no sons to carry it on. The grandmother may have passed along another family name as well, hence the fourth name.

This can be likened to practices in the Latino or Hispanic culture, where people have two surnames, one the father's, the other inherited from the mother's side of the family. A married Hispanic woman often keeps both surnames, adding her husband's. In general, only one is used in casual conversation, but the full name comes out in business and other formal settings.

People from Mexico and Latin America may have more than one given name and two surnames such as Juan Jose Martinez Santiago. The first surname (Martinez) comes from the father and the second surname (Santiago) comes from the mother. The father's family name is generally the official surname so the person with the same name as above would be correctly addressed as "Mr. Martinez."

Hispanics should be addressed by "Mr.," "Mrs.," "Ms.," or their title such as "Doctor" followed by their family name. Rank and title is especially important to this group. Always address the oldest Hispanic in a group first as age is also highly respected.

As you introduce yourself to clients from other countries, take your time with your own name. If it is difficult for others to pronounce (you've probably figured out by now), look for a way to make it easier. Some American names are difficult for Asians to pronounce. Because their language has a different set of sounds, the Japanese have difficulty distinguishing the pronunciation of the English letters "L" and "R." Top producing agent Ralph Robert's name might be pronounced as "Lalf Loberts." As a polite gesture, he might have these people call him something that is more easily pronounced.

We in America are relatively informal people and are quick to use each other's first names. However, it is usually safest in business to be more formal. Do not call clients by their first name unless they invite you to do so.

First names are rarely used in Asian cultures. Addressing an older Asian by the first name might be viewed as a high insult. It is usually best to call all of your clients Mr., Mrs., or Ms. unless and until they invite you to call them by their first name.

The Japanese are a formal people who almost never call one another by the given name, even if they have been acquainted for years. They commonly call each other by the last name with the suffix *San,* a respectful non gender specific title roughly equivalent to Mr., Mrs., or Ms. Yamamoto San, then, might refer to any person with the surname Yamamoto.

As a courtesy, it is usually better not to address any client by the first name until invited to do so. French and Germans rarely move to a first-name basis early in a business or personal relationship. Similarly, some African Americans feel disrespected if called by their first name too soon. In fact, some are sufficiently concerned about this issue that they have taken first names like King, Queen, or Duke. That way, even when called by that name, they are given respect.

Language

Learning to deal with other languages is one of the most frustrating parts of working with unfamiliar cultures. On the other hand, once you dig beneath the surface it can be a very enlightening experience.

Because they sound similar to the untrained ear, some people wrongly assume that Asian languages are all the same. Many are surprised to learn that each culture actually has its own distinctive written and spoken language and that they usually cannot be understood by others.

For instance, the "Chinese language" actually consists of many different dialects that are mostly incomprehensible to one another. The language of most Chinese Americans whose ancestors came to America in the 1800s is Cantonese, of which there are several distinct dialects. The lingua franca of China today is Mandarin, which many have learned in addition to their own unique village language. Villagers who cannot speak Mandarin may not be able to communicate with people outside their village except through writing, which has a universal form.

Unlike English, Chinese writing is nonphonetic. It uses ideograms, characters that often look like a whole word or idea, instead of a single letter as in European tongues. There are over forty thousand ideograms in the Chinese language.

The Japanese speak a completely different language from the Chinese. While their writing is similar because it developed from Chinese ideograms, Japanese writing is called *kanji*.

Likewise, Koreans speak a separate language from the Chinese and Japanese. They have their own alphabet called *han'gul*, which consists of forty characters. Of all Asian groups, Koreans are considered the most emotional and can get quite animated in conversation.

The Filipinos speak Tagalog (Ta-GAH-log) which, like most Asian languages, has several different dialects. Their writing, too, is unique and distinct from those of other Asian groups.

The Hawaiian language evolved from several Polynesian languages. Some Hawaiians still speak pidgin, a slang hybrid of English and their own tongue developed to make communication easier for early white settlers.

In the Middle East, Muslims such as Arabs must learn Arabic in order to study the Koran. Arabic is the second most widely used form of writing after the Roman alphabet. Arabic is spoken by over 200 million people. It is a very expressive language in which a spirited conversation can easily be mistaken for an argument by untrained ears.

Another misconception is the common belief that all people with a Latin American heritage speak Spanish. Many Americans do not realize that Brazilians, for example, speak and write Portuguese because explorers from that nation first colonized the country.

While a majority of people from Guatemala speak Spanish, about 53 percent come from a Mayan Indian background. These people may speak any one of twenty native dialects. In India, twenty major languages and hundreds of dialects are spoken. Because of India's history as a British colony until

1980, most are comfortable with speaking English.

India's Pakistani neighbors speak four major languages, each one totally different from the impressive array of tongues spoken in India. However, the national language of Pakistan is Urdu. It is also spoken in the heavily populated northwest part of India.

Eye Contact

Eye contact does not have the same effect in all cultures. In America and Europe, steady eye contact indicates honesty and a sincere interest in the other party. Western society expects the person with whom we are communicating to look us in the eye. It is so ingrained that we are suspicious of anyone who doesn't make direct eye contact with us.

In some cultures, averting the eyes is a display of respect for the speaker. It can be unnerving at first but the best course is to resist the temptation to try gaining eye contact until you know the culture. The impression that you are staring could be taken as rude and intrusive.

Vietnamese and Koreans often avert their eyes to show respect, especially for authority. Japanese feel strongly that prolonged eye contact is threatening, rude, and disrespectful. Some Asian Indians and Pakistanis also eschew direct eye contact as courteous and respectful.

Middle Easterners are quite opposite to these groups. An Arab looks directly into the eyes of the person he speaks with, for what Americans may see as an uncomfortably long time. This practice stems from the belief that looking into the eyes helps one seek out the truthfulness and integrity of the other person. They believe that the eyes are indeed "the windows of the soul." In addition, some gesturing in the Middle Eastern culture is done with the eyes.

African Americans believe that good eye contact shows one's sincerity and honesty. Like most Americans and Europeans, they sense that it indicates honesty and integrity. But agents should be aware that African Americans tend to use more eye contact than Caucasians when speaking, less when they listen.

Hispanic and Latino men tend to prefer direct eye contact, known as *gada a gada,* or face-to-face. Nevertheless, it is considered impolite to look at Hispanic women with long-lasting eye contact. An unwavering gaze can be taken as showing romantic interest, an insult to both the woman and her husband. Instead, cast polite glances of short span in the direction of a Latina, only enough to show you are paying attention.

Many Native American tribes dislike strong eye contact. For instance, Navajos teach their children that a stare is like an "evil eye."

Differences in attitudes toward eye contact can result in unfortunate misunderstandings. In Los Angeles, Korean businesses in African American neighborhoods were targeted for complaints because many residents felt they were disrespected. One reason cited for this impression was the lack of eye contact they got from Korean shopowners. It was generally unknown in the community that Koreans avert their eyes as a sign of respect. But African Americans expect very direct eye contact for the same reason. Is it any wonder this cultural difference led to ill feelings?

Body Language

As Americans we pride ourselves on being casual, friendly people who feel comfortable slouching or leaning while talking to other people. However, these habits may not make people from other cultures comfortable.

Posture is important in any number of cultures. Asians in general believe that control of the body evidences discipline of the mind. Slouching or leaning is taken as a sign of an undisciplined or untrustworthy person. Therefore, do not lean on chairs, tables, or walls when talking to Asians. The Japanese prefer to see a firm, upright posture with both feet firmly planted on the ground. They feel that such a posture exemplifies a solid person.

Americans seem to feel most comfortable sitting with knees crossed. Again, this habit is not universally accepted. Middle Easterners find it offensive to see crossed legs with the bottoms of the feet pointed in their direction. To do so is one of the highest insults in that part of the world because the foot is the lowest part of the body and the sole of the shoe is the dirtiest of the low. They cross their legs as an intentional, overt insult to the other party. Showing someone the bottom of your foot says you are looking for a fight. Many people from Thailand also interpret this action in the same way.

In fact, body language is often different from what Americans expect. Any expressive body language is carefully avoided in most Asian nations, for fear of betraying one's inner feelings. The Chinese do not readily display emotion in public because concealing it is deeply rooted in their culture. The "inscrutable Oriental" myth is rooted in the perceived need for "saving face," or preserving honor. A display of emotions breaches the custom because it disrupts harmony and may cause conflict.

Other cultural groups may also be somewhat reserved in their hand gestures and facial expressions, so watch carefully and take their lead. Be conservative until you are sure you can be more outgoing. Be yourself. But be aware that others may not be used to doing things the way you are.

At the other end of the body language scale, African Americans tend to display more emotion, to be more enthusiastic than white Americans in their demeanor and use of voice. You can usually be less restrained and more demonstrative in your dealings with people from this culture.

Italians, Middle Easterners, and some Hispanics also tend to be much more expressive than European Americans. Some agents here tend to think they are angry when they see the expressiveness of communications from these groups.

Gestures that are seemingly habitual to Americans such as

the raised index finger for "number one," the closed thumb and index finger for "okay," or pointing with the index finger can be perceived as obscene or insulting in other countries. It's best to avoid the use of such gestures.

In Asia, most people point by cupping the hand with the palm up and using it to point. Turning the palm down and pulling the fingers in a "scratching" motion beckons others to come toward you.

Yawning in public without covering one's mouth is universally considered to be impolite. So is the rather unique American habit of chewing gum.

Americans have a large percentage of the population that are naturally left-handed. It is such an accepted fact that there are stores that cater exclusively to "south paws". Left-handed people should, however, minimize the use of this hand in the company of people from other cultures. Eating in front of or accepting a business card with that hand may be considered rude, even outrageous. A great number of people whose background lies outside the United States have learned to believe that the left hand is unclean and usable only for hygienic purposes. The strong proscription against its use leads parents in those countries to wrap and restrict the hand of a child who exhibits a tendency to favor it.

Putting your hands in your pants pockets in the presence of Europeans is considered rude. They prefer to see your hands, especially when conversing.

Attire

It is usually best to dress well when meeting people from other cultures. Latin Americans, Germans, and Japanese in particular look at how you are dressed to determine your level of success. Obviously, if you work in a less formal location like a resort community you should dress appropriately.

Don't forget that if you visit Japanese clients in their home you remove your shoes. It's not something a real estate agent normally thinks about when getting dressed in the morning. However, if you show up with holes in your socks or runs in your stockings they will think you are not successful.

African Americans will often dress formally, especially to attend church. Dress well in your first couple meetings to observe the level of formality they prefer.

Personal Space

Agents should be aware that the personal space we are used to is not the same in all cultures. In America, we are used to shaking hands, dropping them, and then talking, leaving about two-and-a-half to three feet of space between the parties. That distance is comfortable for most business conversations in America. Less distance implies a more intimate discussion while more may denote mistrust or a need for greater psychological distance from the other party.

Hispanics tend to stand more closely in normal conversation than Americans are used to. Standing back displays distaste or distrust. An interesting study of Venezuelans showed that they stand farther apart when speaking English than when conversing in Spanish. In Peru, as in many Latin American countries, people tend to stand very close together when talking.

The Chinese may stand closer than Americans are comfortable because of the crowded spaces in China. Do not back up when clients stand close or they will feel offended.

Some Americans have the impression that people from the Middle East are aggressive because they stand barely a foot away from the person they are speaking with. This is not usually true. In that culture, the operative principle in friendly discussions is "I want to feel your breath on my face."

Americans need to be aware of this difference and not back up when a Middle Easterner, Asian, or Hispanic stands uncomfortably close. It might be especially difficult for female American Realtors® to maintain such close quarters when talking to an Arabian male. But lest you offend, stand your ground! If you do not, they may chase you all over the office in the attempt to have a polite conversation. Or worse, they may conclude that you dislike them or their culture.

The more formal Japanese might shake hands or bow at our customary three feet, then step back one more foot. Do not try to shorten the distance when that happens. You could spend your day in frustration, chasing these people all over town trying to violate their more distant personal space. This will not win high marks in the rapport-building Olympics.

India has some very complex rules on how closely members of one caste may approach members of another. Here, the best thing to do is to wait a moment and let the client take the lead. Be polite and patient until you see what distance an Indian client prefers.

Although some cultures seem similar to the American, their customs of personal space may differ radically from ours. Scots, Swedes, and many others of Northern European heritage require additional distance, for example. In Germany, private space is practically sacred and not to be violated, not ever. Severe consequences could ensue.

As always, avoid "natural" assumptions, however reasonable they may seem. Wait, see what your client does, and take your cues from that.

Physical Contact

Many cultures are not as tactile, or "touchy-feely," as the American. A male agent should never touch a traditional Japanese woman, as this would be the near equivalent of sexual assault. Similarly, a male agent should not put his hand on a Chinese woman's forearm or shoulders, however friendly he might mean the gesture. The German culture is also very formal and considers any greeting other than a firm handshake highly offensive.

In contrast, Puerto Ricans have a friendly, tactile culture. A recent study observed people from this island country in social settings with other cultures. Puerto Ricans touched each other an average of 180 times an hour while people in Florida made physical contact only twice per hour. Among the British, no intentional contact was observed at all.

Studies show that African American males touch each other while conversing more often then European American males. African American women tend to make physical contact about twice as often as Caucasian females.

Gift Giving

You may want to bring a small but thoughtful gift to a meeting with new clients. While Americans may think that gift giving in a business relationship smacks of bribery, other cultures use presents to break the ice. Therefore, you should know which cultures regularly exchange gifts in a business setting and have some idea of what is fitting. Business gift giving is common, or expected, in South Korea, India, and Japan.

The Japanese are the most enthusiastic gift givers in the business world. They celebrate most American holidays and have even added opportunities for gift giving by inventing a few of their own. They exchange presents as a matter of course, especially at midyear (July 15) and year's end (January 1). It is also considered good manners to bring flowers, cake, or candy when invited to a Japanese person's home.

One caveat about exchanging gifts with the Japanese: outspend your clients and you cause them to lose face. Having lost face, they may never be comfortable in your presence again. Give to them eagerly, but with careful attention to the future of the relationship.

The trick, then, is to select a gift that is neither more expensive nor more generous than your clients' before you know what they are giving you. My solution has been to ask permission to open their gift in their presence. While this is not done in Japan, they readily accept it as an American custom. I then excuse myself, apologizing for forgetting to bring their gift in from my car, where I have three items of different values ($25, $50, and $100) waiting in the trunk. I do my best to pick the most appropriate one. When in doubt, I always err toward a slightly less valuable present than they have given me. If my gift still seems more costly than theirs, I simply explain that I am friends with the distributor and imply that I got it for next to nothing.

The surest way to choose an appropriate present for any client is to probe gently for their interests when you first speak on the telephone. For those with an avid interest in sports a set of golf balls of a respected brand usually sets well. For people who drink alcohol a bottle of good liquor—many Japanese are partial to good Scotch—makes an excellent gift, while a high quality crystal piece is a most impressive offering.

While the eagle is the national symbol of the United States, be aware that it is a symbol of bad luck in China and Saudi Arabia. The wisest practice, therefore, is to avoid giving gifts bearing the American eagle to clients from these countries.

Learn all you can about how the culture of your clients may affect gift giving. This will help you avoid some potentially embarrassing and deal-killing situations. For example, most people know that the Islamic religion prohibits its believers from drinking alcohol. Giving an Asian a knife or a pair of scissors carries an inherent risk. In a number of Asian cultures, anything that cuts symbolizes the severing of a relationship, the polar opposite of what you meant to create. It is also a good idea to avoid giving clocks to Asians, as they symbolize death, or the winding down of life.

Avoid giving an Asian a present consisting of a set of four since they may consider the number unlucky. As proof, you may have noticed that Japanese and Chinese tea sets usually come with either five or six, never four, cups.

Do not give handkerchiefs to Middle Eastern clients. They suggest sadness, tears, or pity.

Exercise caution when giving flowers to people because they can carry all sorts of unexpected symbolism. For instance, in Mexico and Brazil purple flowers are associated with death. White flowers, such a carnations, have a similar connotation in Japan and many European countries.

How you wrap your gift is also important. The Japanese prefer rice paper and soft pastel colors to the bright hues often displayed on Americans' gifts. Both Chinese and Japanese shy away from using white wrappings, since the color is identified with death in both cultures.

Fortunately for the average agent's budget, most other Asian cultures are less disposed to gift giving than the Japanese. Indeed, many Europeans consider it an insult to give a gift before business is completed. Or they take it as an overt attempt at bribery. Check before you choose a gift with agents familiar with clients from the culture you are meeting.

Getting Acquainted

After the greeting comes the critical stage of rapport-building, where agent and client get acquainted. Depending on how that goes, they then decide whether they wish to proceed with the relationship. This step is crucial for cultures who are more concerned with personal qualities than they are with degrees, awards, or even experience, the agent might possess.

As with any potential client, talk about any subject that seems natural—anything but real estate. Take an interest— ask about family, work, or leisure activities. Almost any subject is acceptable in search of common interests other than the usual taboos: sex, politics, and religion. The agent should not discuss business until the client brings it up. It will rarely come up before the client feels there is sufficient rapport. Take care not to carelessly lump cultural groups together. While Pakistan is literally next door to India on the map, it is not a good idea to discuss your Indian clients with Pakistanis. The two countries have a long history of animosity and conflict. Puerto Ricans consider themselves distinct from longtime Puerto Rican residents of New York. Remember that China, Korea, and Japan have had their differences over the years. You must keep them as separate in your mind as in your conversations.

If stuck for appropriate questions, remember the reporter's five "W's": Who, What, When, Where, and How. "Who are you?" "What country did you or your ancestors come from?" "What size is your family?" Other questions might be, "What languages do you speak?" "What schools did you attend?" If you have clients from Mexico you might ask, "What state do you come from?" Again, that country is divided into states much like the United States.

The "When" question might lead you to ask, "When did you arrive in America?" or "What time do you usually take your evening meal?" Some good "Where's" are, "Where are you living now?" or "Where have you traveled over the years?" A "Why" question could address issues such as "Why did you choose to live in this area?" or "Why have you come at this time?"

Finally, your "How" questions could include, "How did you travel to America?" "How long do you plan to live here?" "How do you like to spend your free time?" If conversation is not natural and free-flowing by now, you may never develop rapport with this client. Frankly, you may want to consider referring the client to another agent and expect a referral in exchange.

Filipinos do not particularly like to ask questions. They are proud that, at 85 percent, their country possesses one of the highest literacy rates in the world. Consequently, asking too many questions could make them feel you think they are not very smart. Therefore, the agent should check their understanding of real estate by beginning with open-ended questions about matters of opinion, instead of fact or knowledge.

Hispanics have a strong sense of pride in their ethnic roots. With this in mind, find out their country of origin and learn as much as you can about it. With any multicultural client, see if you can establish a mutual education agreement wherein you promise to teach them all they need to know about real estate. In exchange, they will give you information about their language and culture.

Different and distinct groups live side by side in the Saudi Arabian peninsula. Three in number, they are, nomadic and seminomadic pastoral peoples, farmers, and urban dwellers. Each group has its own special traits and interests. You are most likely to find property buyers among urban dwellers, since they are the group most likely to have the means to purchase American real estate. Again, you will probably be expected to brag openly about your accomplishments with this group.

Saudis, most of whom subscribe to the Islamic religion, place great value on the family. As with most cultures, discussions of family history are always a good place to begin building rapport. It is vital in relationships with believers to understand that Islam affects all facets of life and behavior. Especially significant: it teaches its faithful that only Allah decides the future.

Koreans use a specialized vocabulary for different degrees of social status, depth of intimacy, and in formal and informal occasions. When meeting a fellow Korean they begin tentatively with small talk to determine which kind of language is appropriate. American agents working with Koreans should also begin with topics other than real estate.

Americans are emphatic in communications, as evidenced by the common use of such words as "absolutely" or "positively." We tend to be indirect only on sensitive subjects like politics or sex. Other cultures like the Japanese are more ambiguous and speak in terms of "maybe" and "perhaps." This leads some to believe, erroneously, that the Japanese are indecisive or evasive. Clearly they are not, but they are cautious about giving premature agreement.

Many Asian cultures don't like to be disagreeable. The Japanese have perfected this to a high art and in doing so have developed some seventeen different ways to say "no" without having to actually utter the word. If you hear a client from this culture say, "This is very difficult," take that as a "no." Further, if your client inhales between his teeth very loudly take that sign as a very emphatic "no."

Some cultural groups are very open in conversation and ask searching personal questions of the agent. It is common for the family-oriented Chinese to inquire about your marital status and children. You will find that most immigrants are quite family-oriented. Questions you ask on this subject usually elicit lengthy and intense responses. Keep in mind that some queries that are considered intrusive in our culture are expressions of good will in theirs.

People from collectivist countries may ask seemingly intrusive personal questions of those from individualist areas. Such inquiries as, "How old are you?" "Are you married?" and "How much do you earn?" are common. This line of questioning helps them know what socioeconomic group you belong to. While seemingly inappropriate to us, they help them deal more comfortably with strangers.

Like the Japanese, Puerto Ricans try not to be confrontational. People from this island seem to distrust purely verbal communication and rely more on actions than on words. For them, what is not spoken is more important than what is.

Hispanics are generally diplomatic and make efforts to show respect for the feelings of others. They are indirect in order to preserve others' dignity. In return, they expect to be treated with the same sensitivity.

African Americans can be very assertive in their communication style. Sometimes stating their opinions in loud voices can be a common way to express disagreement.

Most cultures outside America are less verbal than ours. Asians expect the listener to read between the lines. When a conversation with a Japanese lags, most Americans feel they must step in and get it going again. We feel constrained to fill a conversational void with almost anything, even pointless chitchat. To a Japanese, that suggests that you are not a very deep thinker or, worse, that you hope to conceal something with your chatter.

Silence plays an important part in communication with Eastern Indians as well. Hindus believe that wisdom and peace come from communion with yourself in such silence as that found in meditation. Success with clients from these cultures requires that you to learn to be comfortable with silence—a condition most of us Americans find unsettling at best.

In Japan, it is believed that truth emerges from silence, not from words. Likewise, Native Americans prefer more silence than Europeans. It protects them from people they don't know because through years of betrayals, many of these once trusting and open people have become defensive, cynical, and aloof. Talk is now reserved for more established, intimate relationships.

This is the opposite of Europeans and Americans, who encourage talk in their attempts to ascertain the truth. We are more likely to be silent in our most intimate relationships, and for relatively short periods.

Arabic cultures use exaggeration to strengthen and emphasize the point. Instead of stating a simple "no," an Arab may declare, "I swear it by God. No!" Far from blasphemous in context with the speaker's religion, this combines a strong statement of position with a declaration of faith.

Culture dictates how we display emotions more than any other factor. The various cultures express themselves in gradations. European Americans are relatively detached in communication; many find the emotional and animated style of African Americans threatening, perhaps intimidating.

Nevertheless, Americans in general are more likely to show emotion than Asians, who believe that, especially in public, control over the body is control over the mind.

Also, the magnitude of people's self-expressions is culturally diverse. The French are quite animated with their friends. A spirited but amicable debate may appear to be a heated argument. Arabs speak loudly as a sign of sincerity, believing those who talk softly are devious. Some less vocal groups think that the loud talk of cultures such as the French, Koreans, Arabs, and African Americans is rude. Obviously, loud talk is not rude per se, it is just a different style of communicating.

Americans should not be offended that a multicultural client asks about things that we think of as personal, like "How much do you make?" Some cultural groups may ask these questions to get a sense of what social position you are in so they know how to relate to you. People in almost all other countries think every American is fabulously rich. Television shows like "Lifestyles of the Rich and Famous" lead all but the best informed immigrant to believe that everyone in this country has solid gold toilet seats and dog bowls.

However you decide to answer, your reply will nearly always be less than expected. Inform them about how little you really do make and how hard you work compared to the real estate myths and there will be fewer demands for part of your commission. Even if you are a top agent in your company or service area, it is probably best not to mention it. Many such clients find these facts unimportant. They might even see them as negative indications.

Many groups value cooperation over competition; pointing out your own accomplishments could be understood as proof of a flawed character. The Japanese say, "The nail that sticks up gets hammered down." Among cultures that are more cooperative than competitive are African Americans, Asian and Pacific Islanders, and Hispanics.

A Japanese conversational peculiarity that bothers American agents is the habit of speaking at the same time as others. This trait exasperates Americans, who perceive it as rude and inconsiderate behavior. We take turns in conversation. "You speak, I answer. Perhaps I add a thought of my own." But the Japanese believe that speaking simultaneously is harmonious and pleasing, like singing in unison or karaoke.

A good illustration of contrasting conversational styles in America occurs when people from the southern states are upset by Northeasterners—those from New York in particular, who habitually complete one other's sentences. While this seems rude to others, New Yorkers say that it shows that they are participating fully and paying attention.

Some cultures take longer to acquire rapport than others. Chinese and Japanese clients may need many seemingly pointless meetings during which the conversation covers just about anything but real estate. The agent who patiently endures such sessions will find the clients will get down to serious business the moment they conclude they are dealing with someone who is trustworthy and honest.

For similar reasons, Jamaicans want their relationship with a real estate agent to develop slowly and without pressure. They want time to decide that you are more interested in their needs than in your commission. Because there is a shortage of available homes on their island, agents usually meet clients at the property. Let Jamaicans know what services you perform and what you expect in return. Include punctuality on the latter list—Jamaica is a tourist spot with a very relaxed pace.

Jamaican men take an overtly macho attitude and portray themselves as uninterested in everyday details, while the women are notably strong-willed. Between the two, the woman usually makes the home buying decision. Since the culture calls for stating one's thoughts bluntly, Jamaicans' conversation may startle some Americans. Although their passion and directness may lead some to think they are perpetually angry, the people of that island are the friendliest in the hemisphere.

Children are treasured regardless of culture. Rapport builds quickly for the agent who expresses sincere kindness and concern for the client's children. Be aware, though, that clients will see your behavior toward family members in the light of their own culture. However friendly it is meant, an improper gesture can upset the whole relationship. Touching the head of anyone from Vietnam, Laos, or Cambodia offends the belief that the head is sacrosanct because it houses the spirit. This is particularly true for children from Southeast Asia because the body could become ill if the child's spirit is not yet strong enough to be touched. This is similar to the American belief that the soul lives in the chest area near the heart. Who's to say who's right and who's wrong?

The same prohibition against touching the head holds true for African American children, for different reasons. Slave owners used to rub the heads of slave children "for good luck." Understandably, this remains a sensitive issue of respect to people from this culture.

Inexperienced agents may be pleased to know that other cultures are most concerned with the quality of the person they are contemplating doing business with. They are not easily impressed by long years of experience or a long history in the business. They recognize that while experience can be gained, the quality of being trustworthy cannot. If they find you to be a good, honest person they will probably be glad to work with you regardless of your experience.

You can talk about almost anything with multicultural clients, but some subjects are best avoided. Many of these are political: nearly anything about the People's Republic of China is a sore subject with Taiwanese. Most Koreans prefer not to discuss the perpetually burning issue of North and South reunification.

Personal matters can be equally sensitive. The Chinese are generally very reserved on the subject of sex. African Americans prize their families but more than half of their households are headed by women. Single parenthood has been a sensitive subject since male African American slaves were often removed from their families and required to work apart while the women headed the household.

But initiate a conversation about children and you will rarely go wrong in any cultural environment. Children are a universal subject. Americans, especially salespeople, love to talk. It is a good idea, though, to keep the conversation specific to the people you are speaking with and out of general areas that might be culturally sensitive.

French and German people are inclined to be formal in conversation and may prefer to stick with the sorts of impersonal subjects which their cultures enjoy. The French are so serious about appreciating their food and wine that it is probably better to postpone any business discussions until after the meal.

Arabs habitually boast among themselves about their own culture's superiority; but never discuss personal shortcomings. Anyone doing business with them is expected to show this social trait. While they rarely talk about their own, they are not shy about pointing out others' shortcomings, real or perceived. Pity the poor real estate agent who fails to serve them well. That unfortunate person will become the subject of after-dinner conversation for a long time to come!

Make educating your potential clients about the real estate business a normal part of the rapport-building process. Your explanation of the process will engage them, not just how you make your living and how much you earn but also about the mysterious way they can go from looking at a house to actually owning a home. Their professional respect for you will grow with every opportunity you take to inject business talk gently into matters that do not directly relate to the business at hand.

Multicultural Women

Most of the world is simply not as sexually liberated as the United States. In many places, every aspect of intimate relationships is considered an entirely private matter. The American assumption of spiritual and mental equality of the genders is just plain incomprehensible to many people from unfamiliar cultures.

A case in point: In the Middle East, Saudi women are sometimes assumed to be less capable than men. Their life roles are strictly prescribed by the Holy Koran. Women are expected to yield subserviently to men in all matters. Women are not permitted to attend the same university classes as men. By traditional teaching, Saudi women are not to drive cars or even ride bicycles. They cannot leave the house alone or speak to any man other than their husband or a blood relative. An understanding of these facts is indispensable in any relationship with Saudis.

Unless he brings it up, you should not mention the subject of his wife to a male client from the Middle East. Don't suggest that he bring her along to tour likely properties because she may not accompany him to look at property or sign papers. In these countries, everything—including the wife herself—is the property of the man. If she must sign to make the transaction legal, you must spell it out, then be emphatic and firm. You will probably have to show them that some governmental authority requires the wife's signature.

Japan is another country where women have traditionally been homemakers. This is now beginning to change.

Both the Hispanic and Filipino cultures are very male-dominated and do not always afford women the rights they have here. American women may become uncomfortable and perhaps irate when confronted with unequal treatment. Whether you are a male or a female agent, be aware that this can and will occur. Determine in advance how you will respond.

Women Agents

Women agents need to prepare themselves for different attitudes they are likely to encounter. It is a good idea to dress conservatively when working with clients from other cultures. Many of them view short skirts as not just unfashionable, but downright offensive. Asians, for instance, are most comfortable if a woman's skirt covers the knees when she stands.

Saudi Arabian men are more comfortable when working with women agents who cover their arms and legs. In some Middle Eastern countries, a woman who shows any skin but the hands and that part of the face around the eyes commits a crime punishable under Islamic law. Bare shoulders could be quite distracting to Arab men who are not used to this sight outside the home. Under strict interpretation, a man may touch the skin of no woman but his wife's, even accidentally.

Latin American men, especially Brazilians, may stare and openly make comments about women. You need to be polite but firm when dealing with men from this culture and you hear such remarks.

When working with Japanese clients, you should be aware that this culture has considered the nape of the neck an erogenous zone for many centuries. Women may want to avoid becoming a distraction and keep the client's mind on business by covering the neck with a scarf or high collar. At the same time, they should understand that, however senseless this may seem to them, it is equally futile to try to resist the product of centuries of tradition.

American women learn to "stand up straight" to project confidence and business ability. Unfortunately, Asians consider this too masculine a stance; a more humble, slightly hunched pose is preferable. It is especially important for taller women to adopt such a position. A woman who towers over a shorter Asian male client might make it impossible for him to be comfortable in negotiations.

Women agents must learn to be businesslike but still retain their femininity when working with people from other countries. Most multicultural men would prefer to deal with women who are unassertive.

Perhaps unexpectedly, men from the Philippine culture may actually prefer female agents, thinking them more forthcoming and trustworthy than men. Paradoxically, the practice of *la gai* is not expected to be adhered to by women.

For the same reason, Middle Eastern men may prefer working with female agents. While their culture does not encourage them to give American women the level of respect they are accustomed to, they may be more trusting because the usual fierce male-to-male competition is absent. Thus, they may actually find that they are assumed to be more honest and credible in a business situation than their male counterparts.

Women agents should not invite male clients to their home alone. It might be interpreted by certain cultures as improper. It is better to build rapport with male clients at your office or entertain them in a restaurant.

Some cultures have deeply ingrained restrictions against women holding jobs outside the home. For instance, more Latino men than European Americans feel that women should not hold jobs other than as homemakers. Female agents should be aware of these issues and deal with them accordingly.

Dining with Multicultural Clients

Much of your rapport-building with people from other cultures will likely take place over lunch or dinner. Americans may be confused by the many cultural variations in manners, food, and eating. What is polite and proper varies somewhat even within our own culture, so it is only logical to expect to see differences between ours and other lands. Tradition requires that a Chinese offered more food at lunch or dinner refuse two or three times before reluctantly accepting. Be ready to ask at least three times or your guest might go hungry! The Taiwanese who learns that you haven't had lunch feels obliged to drop everything and take you somewhere to eat.

Any time you take prospective clients out to eat during the rapport-building phase, be sure you know what kinds of food they like as well as what they might find repulsive. The Chinese do not eat raw meat, so do not take them out for a meal of steak tartare (raw ground beef mixed with onions).

Hindus will not eat beef because it violates the religious belief that cattle house the souls of the departed. As a tenet of their faith, Pakistanis, being Muslims, will not eat pork or any scavenger animal like pigs or goats. Although Westerners sometimes confuse their religion with that of India, the two faiths are separate and dissimilar. People from India, Pakistan, and Bangladesh are often vegetarians.

During each day of the month of Ramadan, Muslims do not eat or drink from sunrise to sunset. It is considered extremely poor manners for non-Muslims to eat or drink in the presence of those observing Ramadan, the holy month.

On the other hand, many traditional dishes from other countries may disgust Americans. Common foods are octopus in South America, sheep's brains in Jordan, raw monkey's brains or sea slugs in China, raw fish in Japan, sheep's eyeballs in Saudi Arabia, reindeer meat in Norway, dog meat in South Korea, or toasted grasshopper in Mexico.

You also need to be aware of eating practices of the country from which your clients immigrated. Chinese and Japanese eat with chopsticks, while traditional Arabs eat with the fingers of the right hand while scrupulously holding the left, the unclean hand, in the lap. Even today, Middle Eastern women usually eat separated from the men.

The Chinese will engage in boisterous discussions over a meal, but many Japanese prefer silence with their food. If conversation lags during a meal with a Japanese, remember to fight off the temptation to fill the void with idle banter. But feel free to pick up the slack when the talk slows during a business lunch with Chinese clients. Saudi Arabians prefer to talk after the meal. Chileans talk freely over a meal. Indonesians also prize silence as evidenced by their proverb, "Empty cans clatter the loudest." The only way to know what the rules of eating etiquette are for your clients is to watch carefully and do as they do.

Time for eating can also vary in different parts of the world, which may continue when those residents live in the United States. In America, three meals a day are common, with breakfast usually eaten before 9:00 A.M.; lunch around noon; and dinner, the "big meal," somewhere between 6:00 P.M. and 8:00 P.M.

In Iran and many other Middle Eastern countries the midday meal after 2:00 P.M. is the most important and a light dinner is served after 8:00 P.M. Mexicans also consider lunch as the primary meal of the day. Maybe because it is a U.S. commonwealth, Puerto Rico recognizes the main meal as dinner. Europeans generally consider dinner at around 8:00 P.M. to be the main meal.

In some Mayan, mestizo, and Middle Eastern families women eat separately from the men or after they have eaten.

Americans commonly eat out at restaurants while other peoples may be more comfortable cooking at home for friends and family. Cuban families rarely eat in a restaurant in that country because they are all state-owned and expensive.

There are also many ways that the end of a meal is signaled around the world. In the United States and Europe diners simply place their silverware on the main plate to indicate completion. In Indonesia, burping at the end of a meal is not considered in bad taste—it is a compliment. In India, the *namaste* gesture is often used to decline more food. In most of Asia, leaving even a single grain of rice on your plate implies the meal was not satisfactory. However, in other countries like Egypt it is polite to leave a few morsels to symbolize abundance and to compliment the host. Again, it is best to ask or watch what others in your party do and to do likewise.

During the meal many cultures serve different beverages. In America, water is generally served before and during the meal with coffee or tea served after. In Asia, tea is usually the drink of choice, served hot throughout the meal. It is common practice to signal the waiter or waitress for more tea by leaving the lid of the teapot open.

Again, there is no uniformity of custom when it comes to tea, even in Asia. In Thailand people drink water at the end of the meal but not during. This habit is also true in some South American countries.

Americans may order beer or wine with dinner, which is also true for many European countries. Other cultures may drink different alcoholic beverages during lunch or dinner. In Italy and France wine is freely consumed during meals. In Argentina, wine is also served with meals—but never pour it with your left hand or hold the bottle by the neck as it is considered in bad taste.

Holidays

Nothing shows how different people around the world are than in how we celebrate seemingly similar holidays. Many agents send Christmas cards but not all cultures believe in this holiday, which can make this a dangerous practice if you have a multicultural client base.

Jews celebrate Hanukkah, which is an eight-day celebration starting on December 13. It is a historical holiday, not a religious one, and has nothing to do with Christ's birth. Instead, Hanukkah celebrates the rededication of the Temple of Jerusalem after ancient Jews were victorious over a Greco-Syrian king who attempted to wipe out the Jewish faith. Jewish folklore says that a miracle occurred at the rededication of the Temple when the victorious Judah Maccabee and his followers prepared to light the menorah (candelabra) at the Temple. They only had enough oil to last for one day. Miraculously, the oil lasted for eight days. Hanukkah is celebrated by eating potato pancakes, telling stories, and lighting the menorah. Many Jews do not believe in giving gifts although some do. Be sure to ask your Jewish clients for permission before giving presents. Rosh Hashanah is the Jewish New Year.

Ramadan is a month-long period during which Muslims abstain from food and drink from the time the sun rises until it sets. Fasting symbolizes self-control and patience for this group. Obviously, it would be in very poor taste to invite a client of the Muslim faith to a noontime Christmas party where food and drink will be served. At the end of Ramadan is "Eid al Fitr", which is a three-day feast. While Ramadan usually occurs around our Christmas celebration, it follows the lunar calendar so it does not occur on the same date every year. It traditionally begins and ends on the sighting of the first crescent new moon in the month of Ramadan.

Traditional Buddhists may celebrate Bodhi Day. This celebrates the day when Prince Siddhartha on December 8 in the year 448 B.C. sat down under the Bodhi tree and realized enlightenment. As a result, he was given the title of Buddha, "The Enlightened One." A special service is held in Buddhist temples on the Sunday closest to December 8. During this service Buddhists express gratitude to Buddha and reflect on his teachings. The Buddhist New Year is a three-day celebration scheduled according to the Chinese lunar calendar so it occurs in April.

In Mexico and Latin America the Christmas (*la novena*) season begins on December 12. This is the feast day of the Virgin of Guadalupe, patroness of Latin America. The Virgin is an important figure because she represents the marriage of indigenous and Spanish cultures. Las Posadas begins on December 16. This reenacts the journey of Mary and Joseph to Bethlehem and their nightly search for a place to stay. Music is an important part of Las Posadas. Friends and family go on a procession each night for eight nights, going from one house to the next singing a song that asks for a place to stay. Various foods, breads, and hot chocolate are an integral part of the festivities. Piñatas are broken on December 25, the ninth night of Las Posadas.

Kwanzaa is a seven-day African American celebration which honors their cultural heritage and begins on December 26. It was begun in 1966 by Maulana Karenga, a black studies professor, at California State University at Long Beach. Kwanzaa is based on seven important African principles: unity, self-determination, collective work and responsibility, cooperative economics, creativity, purpose, and faith. It is a joyous event that also stresses the importance of family.

While the Japanese don't celebrate Christmas they have another celebration around the same time of the year. It is the tea ceremony to mark the end of the year, which is a time to reflect on the events of the past year. It is a very quiet, introspective ceremony where the host serves tea while guests appreciate the changing of the seasons and the new life that spring brings.

Chinese New Year is celebrated for a week during January or February according to the Chinese lunar calendar. Iranians celebrate their New Year around the end of March to mark the spring equinox.

It's interesting to note that most South Koreans celebrate Christmas while the majority of North Koreans do not. Russians mark their most popular holiday of Christmas on January 7 in accordance with the Greek Orthodox Church calendar.

In Cuba religious holidays, like Christmas, are not officially recognized but may still be celebrated with feasts and religious services. The Greeks hold the Blessing of the Waters on the first Sunday after January 6. It begins with the Divine Liturgy followed by a procession and Blessing of the Waters ceremony.

Finances

With any client, it is good practice to get loan preapproval before you show property. Knowing the financing they can obtain saves a great deal of fruitless work, as does knowing when they are not credit-worthy. Use care and sensitivity in approaching the subject of loans with people who are unfamiliar with the requirements.

Almost all new immigrants are at least somewhat private about their financial affairs. Put yourself in the buyer's position: You have recently arrived in a strange country after much planning and hard work. Perhaps your home country is rife with poverty and suspicion. It may be one in which owing money is considered disgraceful. You decide to buy a home in this new land, and a person you hardly know is in a position to sell you one. But first, he wants you to reveal the most intimate details of your personal life and finances. Would you freely and easily reveal your assets and debts?

Borrowing must be defined as a normal business practice. Few new immigrants are familiar with American lending practices. In fact, many Asian cultures consider it shameful to owe money to anyone. Tell them that here it is customary for a bank to lend money to a borrower, who pays it back with interest to compensate the bank for the use of its cash. Again, it is a standard business arrangement.

At another point on this subject are the Germans, who hate to owe money for reasons of financial security. They are always concerned that an economic downturn or rampant inflation could devastate someone who owes a great deal of money, as happened to Germany in the early twentieth century. As a result, relatively few Germans use credit cards compared to Americans. Home buyers from this country usually put 50 percent down and finance the balance.

How much of a down payment the client will make is another delicate subject. Asians in particular are reluctant to give out this kind of information. As mentioned earlier, just asking about the down payment could quite literally endanger the client's life. Sound odd? Many Asians do not believe in banks due to historic instability in the home country. Instead, they may keep huge sums of cash savings in the family home. This is why there are so many home robberies of Asian families. It isn't that they have more expensive stereos and televisions than everyone else. It's because home is often where they keep their cash.

Distrust of banks is equally common within the Hispanic community. Home robberies are nearly as familiar within that culture as in some Asian communities. The author personally knows of one Hispanic investor who lost over $75,000 cash in such a crime.

The reason most people do not know the real motive for home invasion robberies is a general rule in law enforcement which dictates that the amount of cash taken in a home robbery is not disclosed. Police believe that there might be a virtual torrent of home invasions committed by people from outside such communities if the general public were aware of the amounts some groups keep outside banks.

Many Hispanics deal strictly in cash, at least for the down payment. They may not have any money in the bank and virtually no credit cards. People who know Mexico understand why Hispanics don't trust their money to banks. In the past, savings have lost value drastically while they sat around producing bank profits at little or no interest to the depositor. Worse yet, the rampant corruption they have seen as common banking practice could cause the loss of their entire life savings.

In order to obtain a loan for Hispanics without verifiable credit history you must seek out a loan officer who understands the issue. Those who are willing to use alternative credit checking measures will verify that the client makes prompt payments for gas and electricity, and pays other bills on time such as telephone, cable television, and medical bills.

So, if you can't ask about the down payment, how can you know which homes to show Asian or Hispanic buyers? The simplest method is by use of the "menu." Show the buyers what would be required for 10 percent down and the monthly payments if the bank finances the remaining 90 percent. Show the figures for 20 percent, 30 percent, and so on until you see interest indicated. Of course, inform them that paying all-cash is a possible alternative.

Remember to add the required private mortgage insurance (PMI) to any loan granted under 20 percent down if required by the lender. Neglecting this additional monthly amount may lead your clients to assume you lied to make the deal look better than it was. In that case, they might expect the agent to pay for it. Lawsuits have resulted from failure to disclose smaller issues.

Two important facts are that Asians are good savers and that they may not believe in banks. It is possible that they sold their property in the home country and have a large amount of cash on hand when they get here. So the option that interests your clients most may call for telling you how much they have for the down payment. It's possible, too, that they will want to make an all-cash purchase.

For most Asians, buying a house is not the emotional purchase it is for most Americans. They tend to think of property as an investment, so rarely will you see them "fall in love" with it. They will usually have done their homework and know how much they have for a down payment and what the payments will be. Thus, when they choose from your financing menu they usually can be expected to have the down payment and monthly income to support the option they select, as would any investor.

Building trust is the crucial step to building rapport around financial issues. With any real estate client, establishing your honesty is going to be critical. Telling them how much you earn is seen as an act of honesty—they know they will have to give you their personal financial information and so expect you to be just as candid. From their viewpoint, if you won't trust them with yours, then why should they tell you theirs?

On any level, discussing money with clients from other cultures calls for a cautious, sensitive approach. Some Asians believe that owing money to another person is shameful and that all purchases, including homes, should therefore be paid for in cash. Thus, the first discussion of money is always a delicate moment.

Despite its prevalence here, buying on credit is not an accepted practice worldwide. A case in point: Major credit card companies have offered MasterCard and Visa for a relatively short time in Korea. As a result, many Koreans do not understand that a payment due on a certain date is not acceptable a week or a month later. Because the principles of credit are poorly understood there, some buyers from this culture have a history of making late payments. It does not necessarily mean that they are poor credit risks, but you must find someone who knows about this and is willing to handle the loan in spite of this cultural propensity. Failing that, check with your lender about the requirements for obtaining a "quick qualifier" or "no-document" loan. Often it requires 20 to 25 percent down and if this is the case the client may have the incentive to come up with this amount.

In Jamaica, conversely, credit is easy to obtain with little paperwork. For these clients, you must assert the importance of a proper credit procedure, loan applications, verification of credit, employment, deposit funds, and so on. Being direct in such matters is by far the best way to deal with Jamaicans. Since American lending practices are not within their experience, they need to understand that these things are required to obtain a real estate loan. Let them realize that shopping around for other lenders will only waste time and demonstrate that standard procedures are not optional.

Finally, remind them that these requirements are not yours, but every bank's. Failure to comply with all the qualifying factors and answer every question will result in getting application after application rejected. Expect to apply all your professional knowledge, making sure all the i's are dotted and all the t's are crossed.

Most of your multicultural clients will be first-time home buyers who are unfamiliar with American customs and our legal system. True, the ground rules may be unfamiliar, but be assured that they will learn at lightning speed. They got here, after all, and are sharp enough to be able to buy property. You will find that a lifelong clientele may emerge from slowly and carefully going through the process and the required paperwork.

A 1998 study by the Federal National Mortgage Association (FNMA) showed that while nearly 70 percent of white households in the United State reside in homes that they own, only about 45 percent of African American families and 44 percent of Hispanics are home owners. Although they have a greater desire to own homes than the dominant white culture, around half of all African Americans and a third of Hispanics expect special obstacles to home ownership, as contrasted with Caucasians. Many seem discouraged about home buying because they expect discrimination in housing and lending to hinder their efforts. Old beliefs die hard, even with multiple state and federal laws that make discrimination on racial and ethnic grounds a very risky business.

Survey after survey shows that this impression cannot be dismissed as mere paranoia. It is indisputable that some mortgage loan officers still require more documentation and paperwork from African American and Hispanic loan applicants than from Caucasians.

Hence, many who believe they will suffer these kinds of discrimination are turning to the Internet for loans. They find that they can apply, verify all needed information, and receive approval for a loan on-line without face-to-face contact at the bank. They believe there is less likelihood of prejudice as a factor in this process.

Mortgage lending on Native American tribal lands has always been a major problem. One of the biggest obstacles is that the title on the land can't be transferred. Also, there is a general lack of knowledge about mortgage lending on reservations. Borrowers must go through the tribal council and the Bureau of Indian Affairs. It's also difficult to get a HUD loan because it requires a construction warranty. Many Native Americans build their own homes rather than working through a builder.

Even today, there is discrimination in the mortgage lending industry. The Federal Financial Institution Examinations Council, which oversees bank regulators, reported in 1996 that lenders rejected mortgage applications from nearly 49 percent of those received from African Americans, 24 percent from whites. The study further showed that 34 percent of Hispanics', 50 percent of Native Americans', and 14 percent of Asian Americans' loan requests were disapproved in the same period.

Also in 1996, the Southern Suburban Housing Center sent out thirty pairs of testers to document contrasts in the treatment of whites and minorities in the mortgage market. Although the minority and nonminority testers had virtually identical income, credit statistics and other loan qualifications, the Housing Center found that African Americans were twice as likely as whites to be steered toward mortgages from the Federal Housing Administration (FHA). FHA loans are insured by the federal government, reducing risks to the lenders.

A study by the National Community Reinvestment Coalition based in Washington, D.C., showed that subprime lenders received 29 percent of mortgage applications from African Americans in 1997 compared to 14 percent from European Americans. These loans have higher fees and interest rates than those offered by prime lenders.

Inexperience and lack of information are other roadblocks to home ownership for African Americans and Hispanics. The same FNMA study showed that around one-third of both of these groups did not believe that a history of late payment would adversely affect their ability to obtain a home loan. Yet a credit history showing such things as timely car and credit card payments is crucial to getting a mortgage.

Some minorities hesitate to even apply for a mortgage. They may not be aware of the options available in home loans. Some may believe that you must have perfect credit and a 20 percent down payment to get a mortgage.

Be considerate of all your multicultural clients. If possible, provide information and loan applications in their own languages. Many lenders, as well as agents and title companies, keep translated materials on hand for the use of such clients.

As you work with people from other cultures, make an effort to educate them about requirements home buyers must satisfy. Lay out at the outset the importance of having at least one year of on-time payments for all bills before applying for a mortgage. Detail for them the other information that the lender will expect, such as employment and down payment verification, copies of past tax returns, and all else that applies.

Unless they know well in advance that they will have to satisfy such requirements, the clients may consider them unwarranted intrusions or, worse, they might believe you created them yourself. Spell out early and clearly that all this information is required of every borrower. If they don't know, it is quite possible that they will indignantly seek out an agent who they think won't make them jump through hoops.

Why People Buy Homes

Different groups buy homes for different reasons and this, too, can affect real estate transactions. A FNMA study shows that African Americans tend to buy for reasons of financial security while Hispanics look at a home as the chance to do what they want with their own space. This is one reason why many Hispanics have little interest in condominiums or townhouses because of the various restrictions that their controlling associations impose. Asians usually buy real estate for investment or to be near good schools for their children.

Therefore, smart agents customize their buyer presentations by stressing financial security more with African Americans and the freedom of owning over the restrictions of renting with Hispanics. Never assume that Chinese buyers will become emotionally attached to a house because chances are they won't. These Asian investors are usually more interested in the economic aspects and appreciation potential of the property.

Koreans coming to America show an avid desire to own real estate. For many centuries, only a tiny handful of powerful families have held almost all of the land. Taking advantage of the opportunity to own real estate in this country is also a major goal for Koreans. Again, because of their unfamiliarity with the home buying process you must go very slowly as you project the details for them. Your patience will reward you with loyalty for a lifetime.

Setting Limits

Hard-working Filipinos expect their agent to work just as hard as they do. They may call you at home in the evening or on the weekends, expecting you to be awake, alert, and working diligently on their behalf. Other new immigrants may behave in the same way. You would be wise to set boundaries in this area by telling them that the hours after 10:00 P.M. and before 8:00 A.M. are "family time" at your house. Off-hours stated in these terms will usually be understood and respected by people from all cultures.

Setting limits can also refer to behavior as well. Some agents comment that Vietnamese parents tend to be slower in monitoring and redirecting their children's behaviors that are unacceptable in this culture. This may be due to the fact that they have lived through some horrible conditions and pamper their children so they don't "flash back" to the difficult times.

There is nothing wrong, however, about setting limits in your listings, your car or properties you are showing as long as you enforce them equally with everyone.

Decision Making

Treat the family members of your multicultural clients with respect. Your buyer or seller may seek their approval before committing to a certain house. Relatives may also be providing part or all of the down payment as either a gift or a loan. In addition to that kind of help, family members often have further vested interests in the transaction.

While seniors in America are often the butt of jokes and criticized by some as worthless, other cultures revere their elders because of the wisdom and knowledge they believe they have accumulated over the years. At the other extreme of life, children are greatly valued in a majority of cultures. Compliments and thoughtfully chosen presents to these family members can bring big rewards.

The opinions of family and elders will often be sought before the final decision to buy or sell a house is made, even after a written agreement has been signed. Therefore, be sure to seek the input of all those present before having a contract signed. Whether they are parties to the purchase or not, a courteous and thoughtful attitude can only bring you benefits.

Many agents have expressed confusion when confronted with extended families. If you want to know who makes the decisions in a large family, watch who they generally look to for guidance on the "big" decisions.

Older relatives and other family members may also accompany your purchaser on the final inspection before close of escrow. In such cases, be sure beforehand that everything—from the light in the refrigerator to the float in the toilet—is in perfect working order. All experienced agents remember stories of times when a grouchy uncle or in-law squelched a good sale. These recollections seldom have to do with ethnicity; there are few families without at least one compulsively negative member. Be prepared.

Explaining the Process

Be prepared to carefully and patiently explain the home buying process to first-time buyers from any culture. It is complicated and unfamiliar, even to most Americans. Add a new language and complex legal system, and the explanation becomes even more complicated.

Purchasing a home can create overwhelming anxiety in the buyers. Some cultures have a harder time dealing with uncertainty than others. Asians in particular appreciate being educated about the process because it helps reduce the fear associated with buying property. All buyers like to know what is going to happen and what is expected of them.

Questioning the agent on details helps European Americans reduce uncertainty, but other cultures may not be comfortable with this technique. Many African Americans and Asians are reluctant to ask questions because they do not like to seem as if they don't know the answers. It's important for real estate agents to keep in mind that stupidity should not be inferred from simple lack of knowledge.

For these groups, agents must take care not to educate condescendingly. Be respectful and do not talk down to the clients. At least as important, we must also listen actively to make sure they understand the complex material we are presenting. Constantly asking if your understanding is correct is the only way to know if you are on the right track.

Self-disclosure is another technique that helps reduce anxiety around the home buying process. This involves disclosing information about yourself of a non-real estate nature—facts like marital status, children, hobbies, schooling, and the like. Openly telling this sort of thing makes the agent appear more accessible and further reduces fear of asking questions.

As with any group, African Americans in particular want

to be respected and appreciate others being real and authentic with them. Self-disclosure increases the feeling that the agent is genuine, trustworthy, and trusting.

> *"Let your clients get to know you first before ever talking about real estate."*

7

Showing Property to People from Other Cultures

Once you have prepared the clients and have built the necessary rapport, the time comes to take the buyers out to look at property for the first time. Here again, cultural issues can have a profound impact. Before you put clients in the car to show them homes, let's look at some of the potential differences.

You will find that most people from other cultures prefer single-family homes. Condominiums, townhouses, and cooperatives tend to have less appeal to those who want to own a piece of American soil. Hispanics, in particular, want the flexibility that owning a home brings. They like to be able to renovate and make changes without the rules and regulations imposed by homeowners' associations.

Unwitting agents may experience being "blindsided" on the issue of time. They are dumbfounded to discover that other cultures do not always place the same value, stress, and importance we do on the "fourth dimension."

According to the National Association of Realtors®, the average resale home buyer in a typical real estate market spends fifteen weeks looking and will physically view about eighteen homes before purchasing one. New-home buyers will take more time looking because it is often a long-term home purchase.

People who are moving a long distance tend to look at more homes before they buy. On the other hand, they normally work faster, spending about twelve weeks looking. It appears that they need to get a better sense of the market since they are unfamiliar with the area, but are usually under some time pressure to get settled.

Differences in Time Perception

We Americans are fond of saying "time is money." We place great value on promptness and like to get down to business without delay. A delay of five minutes, though, is not considered unusual or disrespectful here or in England. Others often view time in a different light. People from Germany, Austria, and Switzerland tend to be sticklers for promptness; in these countries, being one minute tardy is considered rude.

On the other hand, fifteen to thirty minutes is quite acceptable in the Middle East. Japanese may be consistently thirty minutes late but will expect you to be prompt—without exception. Your waiting for them is how you show respect.

In contrast, Latin Americans often expect you to arrive late. This is a sign of respect for your hosts. Latinos believe in *mañana*, meaning literally "tomorrow." This does not imply laziness but rather a concept that the future is not definite. Therefore, one should take time to enjoy the here and now. This is also true of people from Italy and Spain.

Americans have a very rigid view of time, in which it's almost tangible. We see time as a linear progression of seconds, minutes, and hours with appointments set along this line. In other countries time can be much more flexible, even changeable. For them, time is a series of events and is a general guideline that outside circumstances can change.

America is a task-oriented culture in which getting the job done is crucial. Here we can do business without first establishing personal relationships because it is efficient. Many other cultures are more relationship-oriented—people are most important. Therefore, it is crucial to take the time to develop relationships because you do business with people you know and trust. In flexible cultures, the needs of people are placed above such things as contracts.

Many Europeans think that American real estate salespeople are pushy and just want a quick sale. Europeans want to feel confidence in the company and agent they are dealing with before consummating a deal. The relationship is crucial but because Europe is so densely populated and congested they tend to build relationships slowly.

Even walking pace is significant within many cultures. English and Americans walk much faster and more purposefully than Taiwanese and Mexicans. Some cultures view a person in a hurry as undisciplined, others as inconsiderate. Still others may consider someone who does not hurry in the same way. Be aware of your clients' conduct in this respect while you lead them through properties.

Again, there are big differences in the use of time from culture to culture. In a great number of places, time is treated in a relaxed and flexible manner. In Italy, it is perfectly acceptable to be two hours late while an Ethiopian may be even later. In fact, it's not unusual for someone from the island of Java to miss an appointment altogether.

This sometimes frustrating cultural characteristic makes it important for agents to set the parameters in the rapport-building stages of a relationship. Explain why it is important to be on time. Agents need to tell clients that because their days are busy, one task or appointment scheduled after the other, someone else may not be willing to work with someone who isn't available as expected.

With some, you might even make light of this bad habit we have in America of "rushing around twenty-four hours a day." But make it clear that it is vital to conform to it. A good way to present the concept of timeliness to people from some cultures is to explain that if your other clients have to wait, you lose face.

People from the Caribbean resort island of Jamaica probably differ the most from Americans' attitude toward time. Their relaxed attitude often results in showing up two or more hours late. The agent must educate them from the start about the importance of punctuality for appointments and close of escrow. If you must, pick them up at home or at the office, on the way to their appointment. But don't be surprised if they are not ready when you arrive to get them.

The Jamaican home market is so competitive because of the scant number of available properties that agents simply get up and leave when a buyer does not arrive on time. In fact, it is such a seller's market that agents who represent buyers do not drive clients to the property but expect instead to have the anxious buyers meet them there.

People from Jamaica's nearby Caribbean island of Haiti have a similar perception of time. They have the same relaxed attitude and will often be two or more hours late for appointments. Education as to the value of your time is most effective, if done at the outset.

As mentioned earlier, Japanese buyers often arrive a half-hour late but nonetheless expect the agent to be waiting on the premises. Fortunately, it is not too difficult to satisfy this mind-set and avoid wasting your time. The author always arrives on time for the first meeting, assuming that Japanese clients will be punctual. If they get there thirty minutes after I do, I adjust my schedule to arrive ten minutes late next time. Now I am only twenty minutes early. This goes on until I learn their usual appointment timing. Then I adopt the practice of showing up just a few minutes before the clients.

Like the Japanese, Filipino clients regularly arrive a half-hour to an hour late. However, like the others, they expect the agent to arrive on the dot. Making you wait reflects positively on their importance in the context of the business being done, which is considered significant in that culture. In ours, we call it "pecking order."

Clients from other countries, except those from Germany, England, and a few small nations, seem to adopt a more relaxed attitude toward time than most Americans are used to. You will find it necessary to educate all of your clients from the start about the value of your time and the fact that other clients are on time for most meetings. Otherwise, they may be perpetually late, yet expect you to spend the entire day with them.

Be aware that the word "midday" does not necessarily mean "noon" in all cultures. In Mexico, a midday meal will be served at 1:30 P.M. or later and can last to 3:30 P.M. or later. Be sure to ask what time they want to meet you.

Workdays differ around the world. Americans follow a Monday through Friday, 9:00 A.M. to 5:00 P.M. work week. However, in Islamic countries, Friday is the day of rest while Saturday and Sunday are workdays. While many Hispanics and Latinos may take long lunch hours, they begin work at around 9:00 A.M. and end at 7:00 or 8:00 P.M.

Smoking

While the habit of smoking among Americans is declining it tends to be much more prevalent and accepted in other countries. If you prefer that clients not smoke in your car or in sellers' houses, you should explain your preference.

Outside the United States, smoking is done without even thinking, especially in Cuba, Poland, Japan, Canada, China,

Greece, and Hungary. If you smoke, be aware that people from many cultures will not verbally object while they might actually prefer you didn't smoke in their presence. To be safe, it's probably best not to smoke.

Selecting the Right House

It goes without saying that you must treat each client individually, but there are some general tendencies you can reasonably expect.

The Japanese prefer newer homes since those in Japan are often torn down after only thirty or thirty-five years. Asians tend to like bright, spacious kitchens for cooking and formal dining rooms for family dinners. The Chinese generally want natural gas stoves because they are more preferable for wok-style cooking than electric stoves.

Some Hispanics like the stucco exteriors and tile roofs that are reminiscent of architecture in their home countries. They may also prefer arched doorways and tile in the kitchen.

Filipinos like homes that look expensive and opulent like palaces. Friends and family members get tremendous enjoyment from trying to outdo each other. They are greatly competitive in the matter of residential purchases. A Filipino client who hears that a friend paid $200,000 for a house might insist that you find them one costing $250,000.

They also have an affinity for high ceilings and formal dining rooms as well as spacious family rooms for entertaining. They will ask for homes with three or more bedrooms and two or more full baths so guests can be proudly invited to stay. Some of this cultural group look forward to having guests, with an eye toward showing them how successful they have become. In the Philippines, evidence of success is believed to attract more of the same.

Around the home, successful Filipinos look for large lawn areas for entertaining, gardens for growing vegetables and flowers, and a fish pond filled with carp for good luck. Multicar garages are often a high priority, since they and their driving-age children are all likely to have expensive cars to house out of the weather and sun. Two or more garages imply that they have achieved a certain level of status as well.

Many African Americans like formal dining rooms for traditional family Sunday dinners. Like many other Americans, they appreciate large yards for entertaining friends on holidays and weekends. The living and family rooms are also important areas for entertaining. They may also want a home that looks unique or distinctive. Uniqueness is often taught from childhood. African American children are encouraged to do their best and not compare themselves to other children who may have more advantages.

Jamaicans appreciate homes with a certain sense of "class" and appeal. They care greatly about the impression the home gives to friends and family. Obviously, the definition of desirable characteristics depends on the client, but the house ought to look good from the outside and testify to high status. Pay close attention to what your Jamaican prospects do and don't find pleasing as you take them through various properties.

Jamaicans work hard to attain success. Most of the island's people live in grinding poverty. Those who have done well strive for perfection and want their homes to reflect their prosperity. If the home they select needs some initial work, these hard-working clients will turn it into a palace with paint, furnishings, and decorations.

A word of explanation: From shortly after discovery by Christopher Columbus until 1961, Jamaica was under the rule of the British Empire. The island's culture still reflects British manners and mores strongly. The inhabitants still retain the typically British facade of dignity and propriety. Thus, the impression their homes make from the outside is very important.

Jamaicans enjoy homes with airy, expansive rooms. They like to surround themselves with grounds with enough room for extensive plantings of lush flowers and vegetables. The yards of Jamaican-owned houses sometimes enhance the neighborhood as showcases of tropical beauty. You can often guess that a home owner comes from the Caribbean by the banana or papaya tree in the front yard.

A typical home on the Jamaican island is prohibitively expensive, so properties in the United States appear to be bargain-priced in comparison. A property that sells for $150,000 in California could easily cost $2 or $3 million there.

Haitians, by contrast, are not native English speakers. Their French-based heritage tends not to associate with African Americans to any great degree. Yet Haitian social and family groups are more similar to African Americans' than Jamaicans'. Tending to be close-knit, they prefer one-story homes with multiple bedrooms for housing their entire family and possibly extended family members. Many especially like trim and paneling in dark wood finishes. They often prefer to buy homes in neighborhoods populated by other Haitians.

Puerto Ricans make up 10.5 percent of the Hispanic population in the United States. Two distinct groups of Puerto Ricans live in America. The first are those who moved to New York in the 1950s to work in the factories. Now in the second and third generations, these English-speaking blue-collar workers are moving to Orlando, Florida, and other places that enable them to get away from some of the problems of the big city such as crowded schools and gangs. They are selling their homes and moving south with the cash proceeds.

Unfortunately for their hopes and dreams, there are few blue-collar jobs in tourist locations like Orlando. Unable to find comparable work, many have had to sell their Florida homes at a loss after only a few years or less and move back to New York. It might be wise to counsel your Puerto Rican American clients gently about job prospects before they buy a house in a new area.

Puerto Ricans from the island, whose members may be very recent arrivals, frankly consider themselves separate and a class above earlier immigrants. It is probably best not to discuss your other Puerto Rican American clients with them, as they may perceive that you lump them together. They are often here to buy second or vacation homes in the United States and have very different housing needs from Americans of Puerto Rican descent who are buying primary residences.

Cubans make up 4.7 percent of the Latino population in America, most of whom live in Florida. Most live in and around the Miami area.

Brazilians often prefer homes in gated communities for safety. Security is one of their major concerns in their home country. They may ask you to show them homes with direct entry from the garage for the same reason. They also seem to prefer windows and high ceilings. The land surrounding the house is generally not as important as the layout.

Venezuelans have housing needs similar to Brazilians'. They particularly want as many bedrooms and full baths as they can afford so that friends and extended family can be invited to stay over. The author has a Venezuelan friend who grew up in a house in that country with seven bathrooms.

Argentines have housing needs similar to Brazilians'. They especially like fashionable designer touches and enjoy customizing their homes to their own taste.

Latins in general prefer decoratively tiled floors. Owing to the destructive effects of high humidity, carpeting is not common in their country. Tile roofs and Spanish-style homes are more familiar to them as well. When they buy homes, they plan to pass them down to future generations as part of the family heritage. Therefore, they may be interested in the property's potential for expansion.

Homes in India are quite inexpensive compared to those in the United States. A Mediterranean style house that costs $50,000 there could go as high as $400,000 here, depending on location. Both construction materials and labor are much cheaper in India than here.

Pakistanis favor big houses of 3,000 to 3,500 square feet and more, selling here in the general range of $400,000. Although there are real estate agents in that country who provide services similar to those in this country, you should define what you do for a living and how you get paid. In every case, potential misunderstandings are avoided in proportion to the amount of clarity you inject into the relationship.

Colombians tend to look for modern-style homes that are relatively affordable. In that country, a three-bedroom, two-bath house costs about $50,000 while a classic Spanish- style house could cost as much as the equivalent of $1 or $2 million. Colombia's real estate practices differ significantly from ours. In that country the seller customarily pays the agent 10 percent commission for bringing in a buyer. Using an agent to list the property is unusual in this country.

Many new immigrants look for houses similar to the ones in their home country. In Panama the average price is around $50,000 for a three-bedroom, two-bath home. Most houses are one-story since it is a very hot and humid country. Many look for these types of homes in the United States although they are generally more expensive here.

Costa Rican homes also average $50,000, but beach properties can go as high as $400,000 or more. An interesting feature of better homes is that many are raised well off the ground to keep snakes out.

Schools with good records and high reputations especially appeal to people from other cultures. Despite what we may hear about the declining quality of American education, immigrants usually view it as the main prerequisite for their children to get ahead in this society. Therefore, if there are good schools in the area, you should emphasize that fact in your presentation. If possible, have supporting test scores from the schools available for clients to review.

Some cultures prefer homes within walking distance to good schools. Close proximity saves on commuting expenses, but that may not be the only factor. In some cultures, the traditional Japanese and Middle Eastern in particular, women do not drive the family car. Nearness to schools makes it easy for parents or servants to escort the children there.

Showing Property

I cannot stress too much that you are likely to be showing homes to first-time buyers who are unfamiliar with American real estate practices, law, and customs. As protection for both yourself and the client, move slowly and explain every aspect in detail.

The order in which you show properties requires forethought, unless you and your clients find endless touring through a random collection of houses pleasurable. Assume for a moment that you have selected four properties to show. You have decided that house A has the best possibilities, while B is similar but doesn't fit the clients' wishes quite as well. C is the fixer-upper of the lot; it might do very well but only after substantial repair and rehabilitation. Finally, home D barely fits their needs and will require considerable work before it can be truly habitable.

Many agents make the error of showing in order of increasing desirability, D-C-B-A. While this may seem to make sense at first, consider what goes on in the clients' minds as they view these properties in this order. As they view D they think, "What a dump! Does this agent know what we want?" At C they say, "Now this is better." Viewing B they may respond, "Now this is good. We're finally on the right track!"

Then comes the problem. Once they have a look at A they will likely say, "This is even better." So far, so good, but then comes, "We can't wait to see the next one!"—and your whole day is wasted. Showing properties in this order causes prospects always to expect more from the next one. The D-C-B-A order is going to build unrealistic expectations that put both client and agent on an endless, frustrating, and probably fruitless course.

Arranging these properties in this order is proven and effective practice: First D, then C, followed by A, with B the final selection. Instead of the former mental process, consider what goes through buyers' minds as they view the properties. At D, they think, "Well, I suppose it's something like what we had in mind, but it's in terrible shape. I hope the others are better!" Now they look at C and think, "Now this is an improvement!" After going through A they may think, "Say, this is really good. I can't wait to see the next one!" At B they will likely say something like, "You know, that last house was much better. Let's go back to A for a closer look and talk about it."

This technique is effective with any culture because it makes the best choice obvious. If you are still showing properties in order of improving condition, you may now understand why your clients always want to see more houses, even after you have carefully saved the best for last. Switch to D-C-A-B and you will likely find you are showing fewer properties before you write an offer. Your time will be more efficiently used, and you just might find that your list of satisfied clients who clamor to bring you referrals is growing.

Once you meet with your clients at your office, their home, or the first scheduled property, you must handle getting everyone on the road. It is not uncommon for multicultural clients to bring along extended family members, some or all of whom may have brought their own transportation. If you possibly can, get agreement on travel arrangements ahead of time. The fewer cars that wander around between properties, getting lost on the way and blocking driveways, the better.

On a related subject, Filipino clients often expect their agent to drive them around in a prestigious car since they themselves will often work at two or three jobs to afford the best vehicle possible. Germans also consider a late-model, spotless car with no dents important.

Some Filipinos may look down upon an agent who personally drives them around to look at properties. In their home islands, assistants known as "leg men" do the job until the clients find something they like. Only then are they taken to the agent, who writes an offer and compensates the leg man with a small part of the commission. Some of the more successful agents who work with Filipino clients have an assistant show property. This leaves the agent free to do more productive work and is a more familiar practice to their clients. You may want to consider instituting this practice with your clients depending on your office policy. In most parts of the country an unlicensed agent can take clients through open houses but is forbidden by real estate licensing law and some multiple listing rules to use the employing agent's lock box key. Check your real estate state law and local rules before you have an assistant show property to clients.

Check your map carefully before driving a Chinese person or family to look at property. Take care to avoid passing cemeteries or funeral homes on the way because they are perceived as bad luck. A California real estate agent relates an experience when he lost what seemed to be the solid sale of a $2 million property. Unaware of Chinese cultural beliefs, he happened to drive past a cemetery. The prospect recoiled, stated that property would be plagued by bad luck, jumped out of the agent's car, and took a taxi home. Every subsequent attempt to resurrect the deal was indignantly refused.

It is essential to treat the Hispanic woman of the house with respect. Unlike some other cultures, chivalry is not dead in this one; it is usually appropriate to open doors for a Hispanic woman (unless the husband has already done so), solicit her opinion, and be sincerely attentive to her comments throughout the showing. The female spouse is the one most likely to kill the sale if she doesn't like something. And since their house buying discussions will likely take place in their present home, you probably have the opportunity to be there to offer your counterarguments.

Most people from other cultures will not make the decision to buy at the prospective property. They generally resist high-pressure tactics and quickly leave an agent who employs them. They customarily go home and talk things over in detail before making a final decision. A home purchase is a big investment and they are unfamiliar with our property values, the legal system, and almost everything else about American real estate. The systematic efforts you make to provide good and reliable information early in the relationship can become fruitful at this stage.

Differences in Measurement

It is surprising to Americans that most people around the world do not measure homes or land in square feet and acres. A majority use square meters for interior measurements and hectares, or "apples," for outside dimensions. One hectare is 2.2 acres; an apple equals 1.8 acres. These units are much more familiar to clients from Europe, South America, and most other countries.

Koreans call their unit of interior measurement the *pyung*; it equals one square meter. Japanese measure the inside of their homes using units called the *tatami* because it is the size of the traditional sleeping mat of the same name, or approximately 3 feet by 6 feet or 18 square feet. Thus, an 1800 square foot home would be 100 *tatami*, quite large by Japanese standards where 50 *tatami* homes and apartments are the norm. Japanese land is measured by placing two mats together to equal an area 6 feet by 6 feet or 36 square feet called a *tsubo*. 36,000 square feet of land would be 1,000 *tsubo*—a huge parcel to a Japanese in whose country the average person is unable to afford even the smallest lot.

Given unfamiliarity with our system of weights and measures, it would be a thoughtful gesture to convert measurements into the units your clients find most familiar. Obviously, ask them first if they would like you to do the conversion.

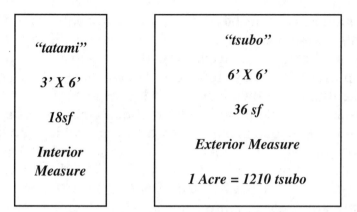

Length of Ownership

A study by the U.S. Census Bureau shows that while Caucasian home owners keep their houses for an average of 8.4 years, Asian/Pacific Islander home owners only hold their homes an average of 5.2 years. They then upgrade. African Americans keep their homes for slightly less than the average at 8.1 years, Hispanics move after only 6.6 years.

This is another good reason to take the time and trouble to become familiar with the special needs of other cultures—the turnover rate is higher. Higher turnover rates mean more transactions over the same amount of time.

Buying Signs

Most real estate salespeople rely on reading the body language of their clients to know whether they like a home being shown or not. Although this is an effective technique with most multicultural buyers as well, it just doesn't seem to work, particularly with Asians. They often express no body language—none at all. When that happens, you have encountered the common Asian belief that control over the body is control over the mind. While they may be absolutely enamored with the property, there may be no outward evidence of their feelings.

The most obvious buying sign likely to come from Asian clients whose body language is nonexistent is the very thing American real estate agents usually fear most: The whole group moves en masse to a corner of the house to converse spiritedly in their own language. Most of us find this behavior rude and some may secretly fear that when others speak in a foreign tongue in our presence they are talking about us.

Consider: Does any buyer, regardless of culture, talk about a house they have no interest in buying? No, they leave the property as fast as they can and go on to the next one. So what exactly are clients from other countries talking about when they begin speaking their native tongue in a property? "Do we like this home?" "Would we enjoy living in this neighborhood?" "Will our children be comfortable in this schools in the area?" Abstract concepts such as these must be discussed in your primary language. Factual issues like the number of bedrooms and baths or size of the lot can easily be handled in a second language, but it's hard to conceptualize abstract ideas in a language you have learned from a book. Very often, people who primarily speak a language other than English slip into their native tongue automatically without thinking. They truly do not intend to leave you out of the conversation.

So if potential buyers go off and speak in another language, encourage them. Quietly exit from the room and let them talk—the longer the better. Real estate agents should watch for and welcome these interludes because they might be the only obvious buying signs they see.

The only other clear buying sign you may get from cultures that exhibit little body language presents a very thorny problem. Minorities who are seriously considering a property may ask, "Are there other people from our culture living in the neighborhood?" While you can understand that people from a physically distinct ethnic group may not want to be the only one of their background in an area to be targeted for discrimination, a whole plethora of local, state, federal, and real estate laws prohibit agents from even discussing the issue.

When asked about the ethnic background of a neighborhood, about the only thing you can legally do is to refer them to sources where they can satisfy their curiosity. Such resources as the local Chamber of Commerce, police department, school district, or newspaper may be able to provide the information they seek. Some buyers are so concerned about this issue that they will sit for hours in their cars watching neighbors come and go from a neighborhood. Obviously, this is their right but you must be extremely careful how you handle the issue. Professionals in real estate and related fields are prohibited by fair housing laws from discussing anything regarding ethnic, racial, religious, age, familial status, or disabilities of any of the home owners in an area.

Recognize that few cultures in the world have come to the point the United States has in equality for women. In many places, the man does all the talking for a married couple. Some Asian and Middle Eastern males simply expect the woman to like whatever the man selects. Filipino men make the ultimate decision to buy the house while the wife will have decided on its style and location. This may understandably irritate some American women agents; in such circumstances it is probably best to refer these clients to another agent. Rest assured that you will not dispel thousands of years of cultural imprinting with a passionate lecture on women's rights and will surely lose the client in the bargain.

Not long ago, Brazil was a very male-dominated society, but its women have made great strides toward equality in recent years. Nowadays, Brazilian women usually make the decision on which house the family will buy. That done, the husband then negotiates the actual details of the purchase.

Careful listening is the key to finding the right home for any client. Pay attention to every comment made during the showing process. If buying signals are going to appear, that's where they will first surface. Once again, no client is going to spend much time talking about a property that is not under serious consideration.

Be warned that people from cultures outside the United States are often quite sophisticated at negotiating strategies and closing techniques. To ask a Hispanic client, "Do you want to make an offer now or tonight?" is instantly recognizable as the classic "alternative of choice close" and could be taken as a demonstration of lack of respect for their business acumen. Instead, a proven and effective practice is to encourage them to tell you when they are ready to make an offer. It can cause you some anxiety, but is the only sure way to proceed.

Steering

It is especially important—ethically and legally—not to assume that people from a particular culture want to live in an area occupied by people from the same culture. While most people of color do not want to be the only ones of their group to live in a neighborhood, they do want to be free to choose where they live, as is their right in this country.

Apart from all else, assuming a preference constitutes illegally "steering" the client. The best practice is to disclose full information on all areas where the clients are qualified to buy and let them make the decisions. You should tour all areas with them first so that their decisions are well informed. It is good business practice to keep accurate records of properties you show every client in case you are later called upon to refute charges of steering or other illegal discriminatory practices in our increasingly lawsuit-prone society.

> *"Differences can impact the home showing process—be aware of and plan for them."*

8

How Beliefs Affect Home Purchases

It is good to find out early what beliefs any client, regardless of culture, might hold that could affect their purchase of real estate. Do not hesitate to ask them as you would any potential home buyer about colors, floor plans, or how many bedrooms and bathrooms they require. It is as important, or even more so, to know if they require special features of any kind.

You may want to show your buyers this book to demonstrate that you have more than a passing interest in meeting the needs of other cultures. You might tell them, "This book discusses cultural beliefs and practices that may influence the purchase of a home. Is it possible that any of yours might affect which house you choose?" Most multicultural clients truly appreciate this question and will go out of their way to educate you about their cultural beliefs.

It is certainly true that some cultures have virtually no convictions that influence the purchase of real estate. Others have whole systems of applicable rituals. For instance, Middle Easterners, Pakistanis, and Haitians tend to prefer single-story homes, but cultural impact may end for some at that point. On the other hand, some Asian groups hold profound religious beliefs that dictate the direction an acceptable house faces, where it is located on a street, its address, how it is designed, and more.

Feng Shui

Some Chinese believe in *Feng Shui* (pronounced *fung showway*), literally, "wind and water," an entire system of beliefs concerning the role of natural harmony. It prescribes, among other things, that the stove and sink must not sit opposite each other because fire and water do not mix, and that doors should open inward instead of outward so that good luck does not leave the home. A stairway should not lead directly to the front door because it tempts bad luck to enter and good luck to leave.

Feng Shui also teaches that bad luck travels in straight lines. It says that these lines create "secret arrows" along which negative energy or *chi* luck travels. On the other hand, good luck moves along curved paths. Thus, for those who believe *Feng Shui* strongly, curved or spiral staircases are preferred over straight and round windows over rectangular. In addition, some followers of *Feng Shui* prefer windows that open completely as opposed to sliding up and down. This can create bad energy or luck. The author has consulted with home builders who were trying to appeal to Asian home buyers and demonstrated how they could make a straight walkway curved with just a few extra pounds of cement.

One of the most often-asked questions from agents who are dealing with clients who are followers of *Feng Shui* is, "Why don't they want a house on a T-intersection or on a cul-de-sac."

From the following diagram you can see why believers in *Feng Shui* do not like homes situated at an intersection or on a cul-de-sac. Look how bad luck traveling down a street creates secret arrows which can enter the home without impediment. This could also be true to a lesser degree for the homes on the sides or the end of a cul-de-sac.

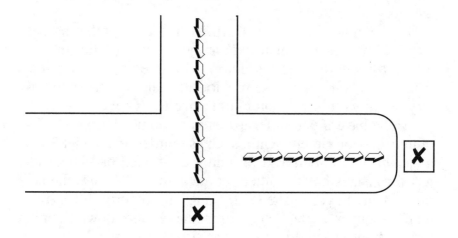

One possible "cure" for this bad *Feng Shui* would be to put a plant to block the negative energy or a water fountain to absorb it. However, the potential home buyer must want this house badly enough to go to the trouble of implementing a cure.

Colors can have special meanings to followers of *Feng Shui*. For instance, yellow connotes good health, red brings fame and fortune, white increases the chances of having children, black improves a career, blue is for knowledge, green is for family happiness, and purple brings wealth.

The beliefs of *Feng Shui* are too numerous and wide-ranging to put in this book in fullest detail. Ultimately, the way you will know what your particular clients believe is by asking them. This book is meant to give you a head start at knowing what to ask, why, and how those beliefs will impact a real estate transaction.

Death in the Home

Death in the home is another significant issue for many people, especially Asian home buyers. Some Asians, in particular, believe that a former owner's good or bad fortune foretells the kind of luck subsequent owners will experience. For this reason, many prefer new homes since they cannot have a history of bad luck.

On the other hand, most Americans also prefer homes without any negative history. Ask the agent who tries to rent or sell a property where a notorious crime has taken place. Conversely, a home whose previous owner won the state lottery might well bring a premium price from buyers.

Asians have a particular aversion to homes with histories of untimely or violent death, such as murder or suicide. Such a background is believed to induce continued bad luck, not just for Asians but for other people as well. Witness the actions of the buyer of the O. J. Simpson property in California. The buyer, a non-Asian, immediately tore down the notorious house to build a new one with no negative history.

Even if they plan to rent the property out, some shrink at the thought that bad fortune may follow the rental money back to the owner. In China, those who believe the tenets of "predecessor death" will often burn a house with bad history to the ground to free the evil spirits within.

For the average American buyer, having a cemetery in plain sight of the home is not overly objectionable. In fact, many real estate agents are fond of joking, "At least you won't have noisy neighbors." However, in the minds of Chinese who believe in *Feng Shui,* the negative energy will travel directly from the gravesites to the house and render the property unlucky.

Be aware that for almost every bad luck secret arrow there is a countermeasure to nullify it if your client is willing to go to the trouble. The careful placement of a mirror, rock, tree, or fountain can absorb, deflect, or reflect the bad luck. However, a believer in *Feng Shui* may be willing to go to the trouble of taking countermeasures only if the deal is perceived good enough to warrant the effort. You will likely have more success in pointing out the benefits of the purchase than in trying to overcome the secret arrows with these buyers.

Like the Chinese, Japanese followers of traditional culture will avoid buying a home where a murder, suicide, foreclosure, or some other catastrophic event has caused the sale of the house. They believe that it is wrong to gain advantage from others' misfortunes.

Vastu Shastra

Feng Shui is but one of many belief systems that can affect home choice. In India, an ancient principle called *Vastu Shastra* is believed to promote happiness and prosperity. According to *Vastu*, the home should be surrounded by a wall at a greater distance from the house on the east and north sides. This philosophy also dictates that the building should be at least three feet above road level and oriented toward the cardinal points of the compass, such as directly north, south, east, or west. Part of the explanation for this belief could be the Indian subcontinent's history of annual monsoons.

In a complex and detailed set of rules, *Vastu* prescribes that the main entrance (front door) be the largest, and the exit door (back door) the smallest to keep good luck from easily leaving the home. The center of the building is supposed to be free of beams, pillars, or columns. Ideally, the north and east sides open onto verandas.

Valuables such as important documents, money, and jewelry should be placed in the corner of the southwest portion of the home and face toward the north. The southeast is for the kitchen, to position the cook toward the sacred East while meals are being prepared. The sink should stand in the east or northeast side of the room.

The master bedroom should be located in the southwest or

niruthi of the home. The occupants are advised to sleep in the southwest corner with their heads facing south. The beds must not touch the walls of this room. The west side of the house is for the children's rooms, with the beds positioned on the southwest side so their heads face toward the west.

The room in the northeast corner is called the *puja*. *Vastu* teaches that medicines stored here will develop enhanced healing properties. The northwest part of the house is for incidental use, like garages, guest rooms, toilets, and storage. Also, the garage should not be in front of the house or good luck will be blocked from entering the home.

On the south and west sides of the property, deciduous trees like guava or coconut are recommended. Windows that let in plenty of light are encouraged, but the total area of openings on the north and east sides must exceed that of the south and west. Finally, staircases can be in the west, south, southwest, or southeast sides. The top step of each should angle toward the south or the west. Obviously, the complexity of this belief is further evidence that the only real way to know what your clients believe is to ask them directly.

House Orientation

You can see how Asian Indians are quite concerned about the direction the home faces. So, too, are other groups. Some Chinese believe, like the Indians, that a home should face to the east. Other groups, Koreans, for example, are used to southward-facing homes like those in their cold native land, which take advantage of maximum sunlight throughout the day. They prefer that the head of their beds not face north since this is the direction in which the dead are buried, toward the mountains which lie in that direction.

Many Chinese do not want the front door to face north because ancient folklore says this is where the devil lives— with his home on a direct line of sight, he might see yours and send bad luck your way. In the same way, the some Japanese like eastern or southern exposure to fit the weather patterns of their home country. They prefer that the headboard in the master bedroom not be on the north wall. They, like the Koreans, bury their dead facing in that direction.

Some people from India prefer to live on pie-shaped lots that are narrow in front and wide in the back, which they call *gaumukhi,* or cow. Many will avoid the opposite orientation, a wide front and narrow rear, called *shermukhi*, or lion.

Again, ask your clients if orientation of the home is a concern. You might also want to add a compass to your business tools if you work with many multicultural buyers.

Hispanic Preferences

Most Hispanics do not harbor complex systems of beliefs that relate to the home but some features are more attractive to members of this culture. A large, well-equipped kitchen is a major selling point for Hispanic women. When showing a home with an outstanding kitchen to a woman from this culture, let her view that room first. They also like well-appointed and clean-looking bathrooms.

A few culturally unique appointments for Hispanics might include tile roofs, earthen-colored tile on the kitchen floor, and arched doorways. Natural wood is often preferred over stained or painted. Many Hispanic home buyers prefer green or red counter tiles.

Attractive grounds, prized in this culture, are usually small or nonexistent in multiple family buildings. As a result, Hispanic families may even prefer a smaller single-family home over a larger condo or townhouse in an otherwise more attractive neighborhood.

Like their Latino brethren, Hispanics may look for homes with a greater number of bedrooms and bathrooms because of the common practice of inviting extended family and valued friends to stay with them. Therefore, given the ability to qualify, four or five bedrooms and three to four baths would be preferred over smaller homes.

The oldest son or daughter in a Hispanic family may be present to speak for the interests of the younger children in real estate transactions. Give this family member respect and let them handle the papers like any other person involved in the transaction.

Hispanics are inclined to be more fatalistic, some say from the influence of the Catholic Church. Americans, a majority of whom are Protestant, tend to believe they have a partnership with God and therefore have control over their own success. Many Hispanics subscribe to the belief that their destiny is entirely in God's hands and that there is little the individual can do but make the most of it. A wise agent will avoid such philosophical differences during negotiations.

For generations, 80 percent of the land in Mexico has been owned by only 2 percent of the people, the upper and ruling class whose ancestral home lies in Spain. The average Mexicans, the mestizos and Indios (native Indian ancestry), are not accustomed to owning land in their home country, but it is certainly a major goal for those coming here. It may be the chief reason for many.

Numerology

Americans may find it surprising that the belief in numerology can affect the choice of a home for people from other cultures. A superstitious reliance on numbers is certainly not limited to new immigrants. Many Americans would not want to be treated on the thirteenth floor of a hospital. In fact, the author was riding in an elevator with several Japanese businessmen and as we watched the floor numbers go from 12 to 14 they wanted to know why 13 had been skipped. To my amusement, they thought it was some sort of special "club level" to which they wanted to belong. After I explained that it is an American belief that the number 13 is unlucky they exclaimed, "Americans are so superstitious!"

There is probably no culture on earth lacking in curious beliefs about numbers. In many Asian countries the number eight is considered lucky and four unlucky. In Chinese dialects, these numbers are "homophones": The word for eight (*baat*) sounds like the word for rich or luck, which is also pronounced *baat* but with a different emphasis. Four (*sei*) sounds very much like the word for death (*sei*). Likewise, the Japanese word for "four" sounds exactly like their word for death and the word for "nine" sounds like the Japanese word for suffering. As a result, there are few hotels or hospitals in that country with the number four or nine for floors or rooms.

Not every Asian group believes the number four unlucky. Many Filipinos believe that three is equally ominous. In fact, some are convinced that three steps leading to a front door signify inescapable misfortune. Others believe that any multiple of three is a bad sign. This stems from the Filipino adage "oro, plata, mata," meaning that the first step represents gold or *oro*, the second silver or *plata* and the third step death or *mata*. If the top step is the third or any multiple of three they may not want to buy it. It is not unusual to see real estate agents and their Filipino clients meticulously counting steps and subsequently making the decision to buy or not to buy a property based on this belief.

Koreans' lucky numbers are three and seven while the number four is unlucky for a similar reason as it is in China. In Korean the number four is pronounced *sa* while death is also *sa*.

In contrast to many other Asian groups, many Filipinos believe seven to mean luck or *suerte*. Former President Ferdinand Marcos carefully followed the dictates of the number seven while he ruled the country for over twenty years. One who asked him the simplest question could almost count on Marcos taking seven days, minutes, or hours to respond. He also usually wrote laws consisting of seven parts.

Those who believe in numerological precepts follow them religiously. For example, a wealthy gentleman in Hong Kong paid over $1.5 million for the personalized license plate 88888, which he took to mean "rich-rich-rich-rich-rich." Think a moment before you laugh about this "frivolous" purchase. Where did he get so much money? Could it have been the result of his belief in numerology? Further, imagine for how much more he might later sell the plate to another believer! It might be hasty to make light of this common belief in the power of numbers. How many who scoff at numerology would have the money to buy such a plate?

Numerology affects the purchase of real estate in many ways. Homes with addresses like 444 or 4444 will probably not sell to Asians, who believe that these numbers signify triple or quadruple death. Building departments in cities where significant numbers of people believe in numerology have been besieged by requests for address changes. Some authorities have turned this belief to their profit by agreeing to an address change for a substantial fee, as long as it does not disrupt the logical sequence of houses. As a practical solution, adding an eight or other lucky number can remedy the reputed bad luck brought by a given address.

One possible solution to property with a bad luck address is to explain to the clients that the house address is merely so the post office can deliver the mail to the right house. Tell the buyers that the official address really consists of the lot and block numbers that (hopefully) has no bad numbers and a plethora of good ones. Despite your best efforts, however, you may be left with no alternative other than finding another house.

Some real estate agents attempt to attract believers in numerology by prominently featuring the number eight in the listing price. A price like $108,888 may indicate that this tactic has been employed.

Other cultures may place a great deal of importance on different phases of the moon. Some Filipinos believe closing escrow during a full moon is lucky. This can cause difficulties if the lucky day falls on a Saturday, Sunday, or holiday, since most county recorders are not open on these days. About the only solution to this dilemma is to explain that once all of the parties have signed papers, they basically own the property. Recording those documents is only a formality. The earlier you can ascertain this issue, the more options you will have to resolve it.

People from India may consult astrological calendars for good and bad auspices. This practice is recommended by *Rahu Kalam*, a belief system based on the negative influence of the planet *Rahu*. Inauspicious days and hours are: Mondays from 7:30 to 9:00 A.M.; Saturdays from 9:00 to 10:30 A.M.; Fridays from 10:30 to noon; Wednesdays from noon to 1:30 P.M.; Thursdays from 1:30 to 3:00 P.M.; Tuesdays from 3:00 to 4:30 P.M. and Sundays from 4:30 to 6:00 P.M. These ninety-minute increments are recalled by the mnemonic device, *M*other *S*aw *F*ather *W*earing *T*he *T*urban on *S*unday.

Again, many people who profess strong beliefs in numerology may modify their faith if they like the home enough or think it enough of a bargain. The author remembers the firm followers of numerology who purchased a home with the address 1142. Despite the fact that there was an unlucky four in it, they reasoned that the numbers added together to make eight and thus bought the house.

Pets

Pets can present unique difficulties for some multicultural buyers. Dogs and cats are domesticated in the American culture, but in other parts of the world some cultures consider them to be food. Pay attention to your clients as you tour homes with them. Notice if they object to animal smells in the house. When they have them, Asians generally prefer pets like fish or birds, which emit little or no odor.

Filipinos and other Asian cultures like the Southeast Asians dislike the smells of domestic animals in the house just as most Americans would dislike the odor of chickens or pigs. If you are showing a property that you think is perfect in every respect except for the presence of sellers' pets, ask them to put their animals in the garage or back yard and give the house a good airing out before you arrive.

In the Middle East, dogs are used for hunting and guard duty but are not kept inside the home. While dogs are often treated with affection and respect for the function they serve, they are not considered worthy to share the living space of their human masters. In fact, to call someone in that country a "dog" is to imply that they are a dirty, low form of life.

Pets in a home being shown may present further problems. Dogs are not domesticated in every other country and are not regarded with the same affection everywhere. Certainly few Americans have been attacked by packs of vicious wild dogs, which is a common experience in some places. If you sense fear or hesitancy, take this to mean your clients do not like pets. It is best to ask the sellers to take them to a neighbor's house for the duration of any showing.

Colors

Color takes on different meanings in different cultures. Asians tend to avoid white houses as that color is associated with death. For the same reason, snow-white chrysanthemums are given to the mourners at Asian funerals. For people from Peru, Mexico, or Iran, yellow flowers have a similar meaning.

Red means good luck for the Chinese but has a different meaning in other cultures. People think the Hindus and Moslems are similar, yet those who follow the Hindu religion tend to consider green lucky, while many Moslems favor blue.

Red ink is used to sign the names of the dead at funerals in Korea, hence one should never write a Korean's name in red or hand them a red pen to sign their own name. Red is also the color of mourning in Ghana. In Western societies, black signifies mourning while white is worn to weddings. In many Asian countries it is just the opposite. In China, white clothing is worn to funerals and black to weddings.

Although purple is favored in most societies, Japan is the exception. There the color purple is thought to fade faster than all other colors. So it should never be worn at a happy event like a wedding or birthday party. It would imply that you expect the happiness of the event to be short-lived. Purple is the color of death in Brazil and Mexico, brown is the color for funerals in Persia, and blue symbolizes death in Syria.

The Philippine Islands are another exception to the Asian aversion to the color white. With centuries of history with Spanish culture, they believe like Westerners that the symbol of death is black.

Green is the national color of Egypt and therefore wrapping presents to clients from this country in green is as offensive as wrapping gifts to people in the United States in an American flag.

Other peoples' beliefs really aren't so hard to understand—no more difficult, in fact, than some of our own are to them, or to each other. In fact, most of the divergent beliefs found among Americans came across the seas with our ancestors. Recognize that every group, including Americans, have beliefs that other cultures could find difficult to understand. The first step to breaking down barriers to rapport and a lifetime relationship with clients, their friends, and their family is realizing this obvious fact. Everyone has beliefs—some are just different from ours.

> *"Every culture has beliefs—we need to learn about any beliefs our clients hold that will affect the real estate transaction."*

9

Writing the Offer

Contracts are one of the most frustrating parts of the real estate transaction. Dealing with people from other cultures merely accentuates the problems. The author has personally witnessed and had countless agents expound on the "unethical" behavior of certain groups. The most common complaint seems to be that they have a tendency to continue to negotiate after a purchase agreement has been signed.

Are people from other cultures really unethical, or do they just have different ideas about contracts? To answer this question, one must understand several points about writing a purchase offer for a client from another country. Remember that the United States is a "low context" country, meaning we use words to express our thoughts, instead of gestures, posture, and other conventions that mean as much in other cultures as verbal communication does here.

This cultural trait leads us to place everything we intend into wordy and lengthy contracts. That is the reason behind their often mind-boggling complexity. Everything from purchase price to closing date to inspections is placed into the contract in voluminous detail so that there can be no confusion over what was agreed on.

In "high context" countries like Mexico, China, and Japan, much more is implied and less is spelled out. In areas like the Middle East, having too many details in a contract implies the parties do not trust one another. In most of Asia, it is understood that the contract is the starting point of a relationship. It is an agreement that will necessarily change over time to suit the needs of all the parties. It is expected that when one party needs to adjust the terms, the other will actively help change the contract.

In the United States, signing a contract means that all negotiation and bargaining has ended. In countries like China, a contract could be taken as the first step in a period during which terms, conditions, and price are open to further discussion and change. Notice how easily confusion and charges of unethical behavior develop from differing views of the nature and purpose of contracts.

The author has heard dozens of real estate agents across the country who lament that they cannot understand why some Chinese clients try to stretch out the negotiations after the contract is signed, even after close of escrow and the final passing of title. These agents never knew that these clients' culture taught them to view signing a contract as the opening, not the end, of negotiations.

Another confusing area for American real estate agents involves the "ridiculously low" offers that many people from other cultures make. All too often, such practices insult sellers and make listing agents furious, resulting in a total rejection of the offer or, at best, full-price or higher counteroffers.

While the United States is not a country where protracted negotiating is common, it is a practical and essential art in most other countries. Through a long and drawn-out process, the participants get to know one another and build long-term relationships that make future relations more efficient. In these places, it is not unusual to start the haggling at what

American agents consider an absurdly low price. But others see a relationship-building process with negotiations the first, not final, step.

Agents must understand that multicultural clients are usually quite willing to pay a realistic price, but actually may feel cheated when there has been no opportunity to negotiate. You cannot have much of a chance at the serious fun of negotiation if you start near the asking price.

As negotiators, people from other countries make offers that American agents consider insulting. They are astonished to find that some are actually accepted. Unfortunately, starting low to leave room for negotiation presents a real problem in a seller's market. Such a tactic can deny the buyer desirable properties when they are selling at or above asking prices. Once you tell your clients that there are many good and serious offers coming in, they may be more willing to make a good initial offer. People from other cultures are just as likely as Americans to bid the price up if there are multiple offers. They, like anyone else, think it must be a good deal if so many people are interested!

You can remind clients that a signed and accepted offer ends the negotiations in America. You want to be blunt with people like your preapproved Jamaican clients and let them know that "Unless you drop dead you must complete the transaction as you have agreed." Chinese may understand that the seller who allows the buyer to renegotiate a signed contract "loses face." Otherwise, they may follow tradition and think that negotiations have barely begun. That tradition is thousands of years old and very hard to break.

Sellers may believe that anyone, regardless of culture, who tries to renegotiate the contract after signing should be taken to court to enforce the terms of the agreement. Unfortunately for them, buyers from other countries may not take threats of legal action seriously. The legal system in their home country may be even slower and less effective than ours. If so, that may lead them to believe that such threats are without force.

It is usually better for all involved to compromise or mediate disputes than to go to court.

Provide copies of the purchase agreement as far in advance of the signing as possible. Remember that the ancestors of people from some other countries were not always treated kindly by the American government. They may feel reluctant and fearful of signing official-looking documents if not given the opportunity to review them before being required to sign them.

The author gives every buyer a forty-page written guide that makes clear the entire home buying process and includes a sample purchase agreement. I provide this at the very first meeting in an effort to build credibility and provide value to the client. It gives clients an opportunity to review the contract at their leisure and know what questions to ask throughout the home buying process. Thus, since they are familiar with it, it is not as imposing as seeing it for the first time at the moment they are expected to sign on the dotted line.

Being provided a sample purchase agreement in advance also enables the buyer who needs it to obtain a translation and have it explained by someone in their culture who is familiar with real estate. The English language can be difficult and confusing for people from other countries to understand. Add the complexities of American real estate, which few Americans truly understand, and you have a very frightening document.

Spend some time with your buyers and go over each line of the contract, telling them what it means. Again, this gives them the opportunity to ask questions or obtain clarification. You may want to keep a bilingual dictionary handy, preferably one containing the definitions of real estate terms. These are available through most major bookstores.

Before you write the offer, show your clients what other buyers are paying for comparable properties by completing a competitive market analysis (CMA) just as you would use it to set a listing price. This helps your buyers better understand the value of the property they are offering to buy. Remember that they may come from a country where prices are a bargain compared to what they are being asked to offer here. Is it any wonder they want to start low?

Another fact that good negotiators appreciate: The asking price sets the absolute upper limit of the price the seller thinks the property will sell for. Whatever initial offer the buyer makes, it will rarely go down from there. As a practical fact, it can only go up. The wisdom of starting at a low—but not an unreasonably—low point, and letting the seller work up from there ought to be clear.

The way to handle the touchy issue of renegotiation of the contract is to be prepared in advance. Recognize that the buyers will probably try to change the contract after it has been ratified. Suggest to the sellers that they would not be smart to give everything to your buyers up front, but to save something for possible last-minute changes. As good negotiators, multicultural clients know they have the strongest bargaining position just before close of escrow. Therefore, always save your best bargaining chip for then.

Granted, that may seem like an odd tactic for one who legally represents the buyer. But if they should lose a house they genuinely wanted because their agent didn't effectively anticipate a renegotiation that clearly was coming, how well were they truly served?

The first step to successful negotiations with people from other cultures is always to ensure that the seller makes a counteroffer. Insist on one, even if the seller might accept the low offer as written because of an impending divorce, bankruptcy, or other factor. Have them take out the refrigerator, clothes washer or dryer, lawn mower, or anything else that could be a negotiable item. Otherwise, you run the risk that the buyers will eventually decide that they paid too much.

Despite all the above, you will find that some home preferences of new immigrants are not specifically culture-related. Many prefer to buy in gated communities because of the security and sense of community that these developments provide. From our earliest history, immigrants have taken the blame for problems ranging from unemployment to depression. Today's new arrivals are no different. The news carries stories of violence against Hispanics, Asians, Middle Easterners, and others. Gated communities offer a haven from fears of such violence. Do not be surprised if your clients express a preference for that kind of neighborhood.

Once an oral agreement is reached, the time has come to put it in writing. Here again, cultural differences make themselves felt.

In Asia and Latin America, personal relationships are considered more important than words on a piece of paper. Written obligations are unlimited and unspecified, leaving plenty of room for later amendments.

The detailed real state contracts required in the United States can be immensely confusing to people whose primary language is not English. Take whatever time is necessary to justify every line and paragraph. Better yet, provide contracts or contract explanations in the client's primary language. This shows sensitivity and reduces the chances of liability that may result from having a client sign a contract in a language that can later be claimed to have been misunderstood.

Also, people from high context countries expect others to know what is bothering them without having to have it specified in detail. We Americans are more direct—people from individualist countries prefer that style. We sometimes feel that an indirect and more ambiguous mode of communication is evasive and frustrating.

If you sense hesitancy to sign the contract, back up immediately. Try to determine where the source of the uneasiness lies. You may have to say something like, "I must have misunderstood when you said you wanted this house. Where did I go wrong?"

All else aside, don't allow your clients to become so dependent upon you that they fail to read the contract. You have no interest in their willingness to sign anything you tell them to. Have a relative or friend who is fluent in both the client's

language and English translate everything before they oblig-
ate themselves to the biggest purchase of their lives. You do
not want to end up in front of a judge and jury explaining
why you did not bring in a translator to render a complicated
legal document intelligible to the clients.

Treat your clients as you want to be treated. In their place,
you would want to be sure you understood every finest detail
before committing yourself to a real estate purchase. It's
called the Golden Rule, and it is a good policy to apply to
every client.

> *"Different cultures view contracts differently.*
> *In America we put everything in writing.*
> *In other countries being too specific implies mistrust."*

10

Negotiating

Just mention the word *negotiate* and the most experienced real estate agents will break out in a cold sweat. Say multicultural negotiations, and they may run screaming from the room.

On the subject of negotiation, there are two types of cultures: those that do and those that don't. Excepting two "big-ticket" purchases, cars and homes, the United States is a classic non-negotiating country. (We would prefer not to bargain over those, but the amount of money involved seems to overcome our usual reluctance.)

We are so uncomfortable with negotiating that the Saturn car company catapulted into popularity by providing a reliable car at a fixed price. This no-haggle method of purchasing a car became so attractive that even a mega carmaker like General Motors has selectively instituted its very similar Value Pricing policy. Others carmakers have followed suit.

This leaves real estate as the final bastion of negotiating in America. A home is also usually the largest purchase most families ever make, increasing the level of tension and discomfort dramatically.

Most other countries are negotiating countries where, outside major metropolitan areas, people bargain as a matter of course for everything from groceries to laundry services to rent. They have become masters of dickering simply by living through life's daily challenges. Don't forget that life is tenuous in most places, so every dollar, peso, dinar, yen, pound, franc, or rial that can be saved through sharp negotiating is crucial to survival.

In America, providers of goods and services have tacitly agreed with consumers to set prices with no negotiating in mind so that time spent in this activity is minimized. In the United States we say, "Time is money." But in other countries time is the currency of relationships and negotiating is a way that two parties can get to know one another. It is as much a part of the socialization process as the cocktail party is here.

Much of the confusion and frustration that real estate agents feel with people from other cultures centers around this issue of negotiation. Let's look at some of the differences.

The first and most obvious difference is the pace at which things move. Here we like to get down to business and get it over with right away. In Asia and Latin America, negotiations move at what seems to us an excruciatingly slow pace. The author did some negotiations in Japan in which he attended five consecutive client meetings during which business never came up. Not until we had built a relationship over lunches of sushi and saki did negotiations finally begin.

In Argentina, it may take a number of trips to reach agreement simply because several people who will not attend most of the meetings must approve every decision. This is a standard negotiating tactic that we call "The Higher Authority Ploy." Just as at American new car dealerships, no one Argentine negotiator seems to have the sole power to ratify the contract.

Second, negotiations might move at a slower pace than we are used to because other cultures count on the early stages to develop the relationship between the parties. The purpose is not the same as using it to determine bargaining positions, as is common here. Other cultures look forward with delight to negotiations and genuinely enjoy them. They feel it is important that, every bit as much as closing a deal, they are getting acquainted with the other party.

Each culture has its own unique negotiating style. In South Korea, you may have to ask a question over and over. Koreans are by no means dumb but rather are trying to explore all options to assure themselves that they are making the right choice. In Japan, saying "I'm sorry" repeatedly during negotiations is a sign of politeness. In contrast, veteran bargainers expect Germans to be direct and businesslike, perhaps even abrupt, in negotiations. People from Israel are very confrontational and emotional in their negotiating style, which can really intimidate Americans. Saudi Arabians and Egyptians will come very close physically when negotiating and often touch the other party, which we think of as being very aggressive.

A third difference in negotiation styles is in the weight and importance that attach to issues. Americans habitually concentrate on immediate substantive matters like price, quality, or availability while the Japanese are more concerned with the quality of the people with whom they do business. In other words, their interest is on building lifetime relationships.

Trust between the parties is crucial to successful negotiations. But different cultural groups establish trust in different ways. Some look to past experience, others rely on intuition and emotion, and still others count on ready acceptance rules that assure performance. Whatever criteria a given culture may use, the transaction will never get past square one until they are satisfied.

While Americans rely on the past history and reputation of those with whom they negotiate, the Japanese are more attentive to the nature of the relationship they are building with the other party. Especially in Asian societies, solid personal relationships are believed to help minimize potential social conflicts.

When presenting offers on behalf of multicultural home buyers, encourage the sellers to make a counteroffer, even when they want to accept the offer exactly as written. Even if the offer is perfectly acceptable to the seller, it is essential to write a counteroffer to make sure the deal survives to close of escrow intact. Otherwise the buyers might feel that they paid too much and try to kill the deal.

Why would a buyer want to cancel a contract that has been accepted with no counteroffer? Consider: The buyers make what they believe is a low starting offer. The sellers, perhaps because of an impending divorce or threat of foreclosure, accept that offer. The buyers rethink and wonder why the seller accepted so quickly. It is possible that they will forever regret the terms of the deal, believing that they must have offered too much or perhaps there is something wrong with the home.

Yet another point: People from negotiating countries take great pride in the bargaining skills they have spent a lifetime developing. If they think they are overpaying, they will likely begin bargaining all over again in order to kill the deal with the same enthusiasm that they used to put it together, regardless of how beneficial to them you honestly believe it is.

No matter how much the seller is tempted to accept the offer without any kind of counter, then, it is imperative that in most cases you convince them to make some small changes. If the deal is going to disintegrate, better to have it happen early than at close of escrow when all parties have invested tremendous amounts of time, energy, and money.

Suggest making some minor changes in provisions relating to personal property, perhaps a refrigerator or a washer and dryer. If they were excluded in the first place, you can always throw them back into the deal. The chief point is to inject something that reflects the buyers' viewpoint into the contract.

People from negotiating countries must believe they got a good deal or all too often they simply will not go through with it. The buyers may want to renegotiate after signing and prior to close of escrow.

Sharp negotiators know that they have the most leverage just before close of escrow. Around that time the sellers may have moved out of the home and told all of their friends that the home is sold. Also, any interest in the property prior to the pending sale has dissipated.

Negotiators may ask for items like new copper pipes, new paint, personal property, or other amenities. Many do this so they can feel proud that they put together a good deal for themselves. Rarely is the item they ask for of great significance, but most do want to be able to feel that they have crafted a good deal by their own efforts and skill.

This the standard negotiating tactic of "covering the bottom line," building in something to compensate the buyer just in case the price later proves too high for the property. After all, your clients are probably somewhat new to the country and may not be completely familiar with home values in the area. In all likelihood, they are paying a great deal more for a home in the United States than they would in their home country. A competent real estate agent looks for ways to structure the transaction in favor of all the parties' interests.

"Nibbling," asking for previously unmentioned small items as if they have just come to mind, is another technique of master negotiators. Because of the relief and the almost euphoric atmosphere that follows successful negotiations, this technique is especially effective immediately after the parties have come to an agreement. Nibbling could take the form of asking to store personal property in the garage before close of escrow, extending the closing date by a few days or weeks, or any of an infinite number of other concessions. Nibbling always wears a reasonable face, but, as with big requests dealt with earlier, it must be stopped in its tracks or there will be no end to it.

To put a stop to incessant requests for more and more, ask the buyers for a concession before ever granting one. If a client would like to extend escrow by two weeks, respond with, "What will you do in return for extending escrow? Would you pay the sellers' property taxes for that period? It would be an expense that they haven't anticipated, you know." Once the buyers know that every demand will bring a similar one from the seller, there is a good chance they will stop asking.

Some groups are less flexible than others. Filipinos and some other Asians may adopt a take-it-or-leave-it stance. You may be able to forestall this prospect by broaching the subject in the rapport-building stages. Inject into the conversation, simply and innocently, without direct reference to the client, that this ploy kills a lot of deals in this country.

If you have failed to clarify early everything you do for clients and how little you actually make, count on that commission quickly becoming the subject of negotiation. It's certainly worth a few minutes to detail these facts early on. Failure to discuss it early may cause you to invest many hours defending your commission to someone who is committed to getting a piece of it into her or his own pocket. If negotiations begin with a multicultural buyer believing that the agent does nothing to earn an exorbitant amount of money, be assured that the commission will become fair game for negotiation.

It cannot be overstressed: People from other cultures are often effective negotiators. They almost always start with a rock-bottom offer. This is particularly true of Chinese and Jamaican buyers. However, build good rapport and they will look to you as a friend, not just a salesperson. Point out the benefits of the home, then present a menu of offering prices.

Tell them, "Make a low offer and you will quite probably not even get a counteroffer. The sellers may feel that you have insulted them and decide not to do business with you. Medium—close to but below the listing price—and you will probably get a significant counteroffer. A high offer will likely be accepted with little or no counteroffer." Find out how badly they want the property and structure the offer accordingly.

If the buyer persists in making low starting offers even when several offers are being submitted in a seller's market, you may wish to refer them to another agent. Until they see the market change, many people from negotiating countries will not understand why they should make offers at or above asking price. You may waste a great deal of time working with buyers who refuse to adjust to current conditions.

When you make a low offer on behalf of any buyer, do everything you can to convince the sellers to make a reasonable counteroffer. Explain that your clients like to bargain and a counteroffer would help both you and the seller. This helps you to determine the seller's actual bottom line. It's probably not a good idea to tell the seller the cultural background of the buyer because it might give them an opportunity to discriminate, something the agent could be held responsible for. Again, just tell them that your buyers like to bargain, and after all, who doesn't?

It can be frustrating to present offers for multicultural buyers in a seller's market, especially when there are multiple offers, some even above the asking price. However, when your buyers see comparables showing the value of the property and understand that others are offering more than they are, they might become more reasonable. If not competently and completely explained, the vital process of educating people from negotiating cultures is a source of frustration for many real estate agents.

A counteroffer should be made to any home buyer regardless of cultural background and despite how low the initial offer may be. The key point, again, is that an offer that is accepted as presented may lead them to believe they are paying too much and cause them to try to back out.

If possible, present all offers in person. This gives you the opportunity to meet the sellers directly and try to ascertain the real reason they are selling. If you can, find out the absolute minimum terms and price they will accept. As best you can, exert some control over the terms of counteroffers, such as omitting personal property until close of escrow. It is essential to handle this openly with the seller if you suspect your clients are likely to utilize to the tactic.

The author usually tries to gain input into a counteroffer by saying something like, "I'd like to save a few trees, so please don't bother writing a counteroffer that my buyers can't accept." I pause, then say, "Take all the time you need to discuss our offer in private and let me know what you're thinking before you write a counteroffer." I have been very successful in getting the listing agent to restructure the counteroffer to meet the needs of both parties and handle the buyer's need to renegotiate before close of escrow.

If, for some reason, the seller insists on accepting your buyer's offer as written (usually for fear of losing it), please don't rush back to your clients with the good news. Take your time and carefully spell out how hard you worked to get them to accept the offer without changes, in spite of the fact that they did not want to. Few sellers don't want a higher sales price or to keep most of their personal property.

If you happen to be presenting an offer to a seller from a negotiating country, be prepared for the education of a lifetime! They will probably take their time with the offer, show little or no emotion when you present it, and play hardball on every issue. No matter how many professional negotiating courses you may have taken, you are up against people for whom hard bargaining is a way of life. Remember, they have negotiated all of their lives on everything.

Some cultural groups are quite fatalistic about negotiations. When the seller rejects their offer, a Hispanic may say, "God preordained the result." With the same meaning, a Pakistani might say, "Life goes on." This unemotional attitude makes some multicultural prospects tough on agents who are not accustomed to playing the game this way.

In fact, some Chinese will steadfastly not allow themselves to become emotionally involved in the purchase of a family home. It is only an investment; if they don't buy the property they are currently offering on, another will surely come along. One way to convince this type of negotiator to accept a counteroffer at higher than the offering price is to point out what an outstanding deal the purchase is. Show them comparable house sales and describe the unique benefits.

Japanese buyers and sellers often close their eyes during negotiations as a way to concentrate on what the other side is saying or has proposed. The ensuing long periods of silence will often drive Americans crazy, but it should not be broken until the client breaks it. You can take comfort in the knowledge that they are not withdrawing from the conversation. Despite appearances, they are listening intently and considering every word.

Japanese sellers and buyers will rarely say "no" and just because they don't does not necessarily mean "yes." People from this culture do not like to be disagreeable. However, there are definite signs that the Japanese do not agree with what is said, such as stating something like, "This is very difficult," or impatiently sucking air through their teeth. The Japanese dislike saying a direct no so much that they have at least sixteen ways to avoid uttering the word. Indonesians are similarly disposed and have twelve different ways to not state a negative answer.

Similarly, the aboriginal people of central Australia are another rather unassertive people who prefer strongly to avoid direct confrontation. They avoid having to say no by putting off discussions with which they might disagree.

Arabs rarely say "no" because their culture considers the word impolite. There is a saying that when an Arab says "yes," he means "maybe." When he says "maybe," he means "no." For the sake of good manners, Arabs may substitute the phrase "if God is willing" for a direct "no."

The Chinese can drive people who don't understand their methods of negotiation nearly to distraction. This group takes its time trying to wear down the other side. Or, they may delay responding interminably as a way to kill the deal without losing face.

Koreans customarily try to delay with a complicated panoply of contrived excuses. They often make the opposing side wait until the last minute for an answer. On the other hand, Koreans are the most likely of all the Asian groups to give a solid, clear "no." Contrived delays notwithstanding, they are more likely to be direct than most other people from the Far East.

By practicing the art of bargaining every day, people from negotiating countries have become masters. It is as natural to them as breathing. Their apparent effortlessness is one factor that can drive American real estate agents crazy. However, if Americans could observe how multicultural people negotiate with an open mind, we just might learn a few tricks that could save us and our clients a great deal of money.

> *"Most cultures negotiate everything every day—America is one of the few countries that does not regularly negotiate. We must learn to do it better."*

11

Working with Affiliated Professions

People in related professions—loan officers, title and escrow persons, various inspectors, attorneys, and contractors—can be a help or a hindrance to you when dealing with people from other cultures. The bank loan officer or mortgage broker is one of the first people your buyers will meet (unless they are paying all-cash). This makes it essential to send them to a competent and understanding bank, mortgage company, or loan broker.

Give the lender your résumé and encourage him or her to tell the clients something specific about you from it in the first few minutes after they meet. People from other countries rely heavily on such word-of-mouth.

Coach the banker to begin with a few brief words like, "Oh, you are Michael Lee's clients. Do you know that he's been in real estate over twenty years?" or "Did you know that Michael Lee is a pilot?" These few practiced words can buy you years of trust and loyalty—and a gold mine of referrals—from multicultural clients.

Have your co-professionals make you a real person to your clients by saying something about you that is not related to real estate. Have them learn things such as the number of children you have, any hobbies you engage in, languages you speak other than English. It is as important to your banker as it is to you to make you human, instead of "just a salesperson."

Make it a rule that every real estate-related company mentions some detail from your biography. It's clear that people from any culture connect better to a person with a pulse than they ever would to an impersonal corporation. The reference should include both professional and personal information.

Lenders should be sure to let new immigrants know that the process of buying a home in the United States isn't as complex and complicated as it probably was in their home country. They may also mistakenly believe that American lenders consider foreign home buyers a higher risk than domestic borrowers.

If there are any restrictions on lending to non-U.S. residents or citizens, let them know as early as possible. Don't forget to check FNMA and other sources for funds that can help lenders handle some of the nontraditional saving methods of foreigners.

Vietnamese and Hispanics in particular may join together to help one another buy homes. You must build a list of lenders who understand and will work with this kind of pooling of funds. They should be aware that multicultural groups, Hispanics and others, are first-time home buyers as a rule, so every step of the transaction must be explained thoroughly and carefully.

For other reasons, Middle Eastern people may not want to

obtain financing from a Middle Eastern bank or have someone of similar descent represent the lender. Again, the level
of mistrust they might hold for others of their culture makes
this necessary.

Many people are aware of long-standing discriminatory
practices that have occurred in the past in the lending industry. One-third of Hispanics still feel that there is prejudice
when applying for a home loan and half of African Americans believe they are subject to discrimination in lending. Do
whatever you can to demonstrate fairness in your application
and underwriting process because studies still show that minority mortgage applicants are rejected more frequently than
Caucasian buyers.

There is probably no procedure equivalent to the title
search in your buyers' home country. In some parts of the
United States, a title company does the job, while in others it
falls to an attorney. No matter who performs this important
task, it is critical for you to impress upon the buyers the importance of guaranteeing them a clear title to the property.

Once you elect to use an attorney's services, justify this
function in the real estate transaction to the client in detail. In
some countries—Great Britain is a good example—attorneys
earn their respect with hard and diligent work, while in others
(more than a few) anyone can call himself a lawyer by simply
hanging out an impressive sign. If your buyers come from one
of the latter countries, it is up to you to ensure that they have
confidence in the real estate attorney in this transaction.

In many states, it is customary for agents to use a neutral
escrow company to hold funds for the seller and to transfer
title to the buyer. The United States is fairly unique in this
practice, so every buyer should receive a clear explanation of
the escrow function. Most title and escrow companies have
brochures available explaining their duties and the steps required to accomplish a successful transfer of title. It would
be appropriate to have such materials translated into the language of the immigrant groups you most commonly serve.

Escrow officers should be sure to explain that you can only act with authority from both the buyer and seller. Otherwise, you may find yourself in the middle of a rather nasty battle.

Those concerned with title and escrow should be sure to get the names of buyers and sellers correct—failure to do so could have serious legal consequences. Remember to ask, "Which is your family name?" and not assume that just because a name looks like a surname that it necessarily is one.

Title officers or attorneys should be sure to ask every client, regardless of ethnicity or cultural background, if they have any beliefs that will affect the title or escrow process. For instance, the author wanted to close the purchase of his first home on his birthday, which was December 30. While not culturally driven, closing on one's birthday can be a rather universal goal.

Ask clients if there are any significant days on which they want to close escrow. Some Koreans and Indians may want to close during a full moon and other groups may have certain dates that are more desirable than others. Many Asians believe the date of August 8 to be lucky because it is "double eight"—the eighth day of the eighth month. Many Americans who claim not to be superstitious still would be reluctant to take possession of a house on a Friday the thirteenth.

The only way to know what closing dates are lucky or unlucky for a client is to ask. A fairly serious issue can arise if the date they want to close on falls on a weekend or holiday when the county recorder's office is closed. One way around this is to explain that when both the buyer and seller have signed closing papers the deal is done; the actual recording of the documents is merely a formality.

Title officers or attorneys should try to provide closing documents as early as possible before they will need to be actually signed. Recall that most minority groups in the United States have had its laws used against them in the past so there is a deep-rooted fear of government-looking documents. Giving closing papers in advance of closing provides clients the opportunity to look them over and ask questions of their friends and advisors before going through the rather hurried closing process.

Remember that for someone buying a home the paperwork, including loan documents, can easily exceed seventy-five pages or more of rather legalistic terminology. For anyone familiar with English language and basic American contract law this can be quite imposing. Just imaging how confusing and frightening it looks to someone from another country whose primary language is not English!

Above all, provide privacy when people from other cultures sign closing documents. Again, financial affairs are an extremely personal issue and they don't want others to know their business. Many escrow offices ask clients to sign papers sitting in front of a desk in the middle of an office floor when almost anyone can overhear the detail of the transaction. This is very insensitive to clients of any culture. A separate "closing room" with curtains that can be drawn for privacy is much more comfortable for the discussion of a home purchase or sale.

Nearly every bank requires some minimum amount of fire insurance; some also mandate liability insurance before they will provide a loan. In a number of cultures, mere discussion of potential catastrophes is tantamount to issuing an invitation for fires, floods, tornadoes, and earthquakes to descend upon the home and destroy it. Middle Easterners would call this *haboosh,* or an unpredictable desert dust storm. Carefully inform your clients of the importance of insurance before they run into the issue unprepared.

Several kinds of inspection are available—or required—in different parts of the country. The necessity for such inspections as roof, pest control, well water, structural, septic tank, geologic, toxic waste, soils, and others appropriate in your area should be defined for the buyers. This may or may not be their first purchase of property, but they are probably unfamiliar with our language, customs, and laws. Real estate agents are even more responsible for detailing any material facts affecting the transaction to new immigrants than to people who are more familiar with American customs.

As with any first-time home buyer, you should inform people from other countries that they should expect to hear some bad news from any inspector. It is their job to find flaws and point out potential problems. Let your clients know that flaws discovered in inspections do not necessarily mean that the house is about to fall down, but you will discuss the implications of the reports as they come in.

To avoid problems, introduce first-time home buyers to your real estate "team" and tell how each will help them to own the home of their dreams. Stress that real estate is a difficult profession requiring the services of many specialists to assure a sound purchase. Let the buyer know that your job is to coordinate all of these people's efforts and to make sure all documents are provided as required.

Do not give your buyers, especially new arrivals, unrealistic expectations about costs or deadlines. Otherwise, they may assume you have lied if things cost more than you estimated or take longer than expected. This can ruin an entire relationship for a few dollars or a few days. Always give yourself a cushion so that things cost less and are completed more quickly than the original estimate. Do this, and you will look like a genius.

> *"The job of a real estate agent is to coordinate all of the people needed to put together a transaction."*

12

Working with Multicultural Home Sellers

As more and more newcomers to America buy homes here, they will eventually become sellers. Cultural impact continues when they take the opposite role. The familiarity with the process acquired when they bought the property is incomplete at best. It now must be complemented with knowledge of the part the "other side" plays.

As with buyers, the first place where culture affects real estate is in the choice of an agent. If chosen by a new client, you must assume that the agent who originally sold them the property did not detail everything professionals do on behalf of sellers; if he or she did, you are ahead of the game. Still, make it a point to tell them how little you really get paid from each sale. Fail to do this, and you may run into that all-too-common problem of sellers asking for part of your commission.

That is the first discussion you should have with a seller of any culture. As with buyers, deal with the myth of overpaid, do-nothing agents at the first opportunity. Show them a list of things that you do to help them sell their house, like the following:

Exclusive Marketing Services

I do over a hundred activities to get your house sold faster and at a higher price. To earn my commission, some of things I do on your behalf include:

1) Order a complete property profile of your house.
2) Review the property profile for accuracy.
3) Perform a complete competitive market analysis of your house.
4) Calculate how long it will take your property to sell.
5) Determine the effect of similar properties on the market.
6) Help develop a pricing strategy for your property.
7) Compute an estimation of your proceeds from the sale.
8) Provide you with information on how to prepare your property for sale.
9) Tour your property from the "buyer's standpoint."
10) Conduct a complete "staging" analysis of your house.
11) Provide written instructions on how to stage your house for maximum effect.
12) Review the interior of the house to maximize attractiveness.
13) Assist you in locating suitable storage for large pieces of furniture.
14) Review the exterior of the house to maximize "curb appeal."
15) Assist you in making the exterior as attractive as possible.

16) Take photographs of your property for use in marketing materials.
17) Develop "just listed" postcards.
18) Place your property for sale on the Internet.
19) Explain the advantages of seller carryback financing.
20) Explain the disadvantages of seller carryback financing.
21) Review the status of any encumbrances against the property.
22) Review the significance of any easements affecting the property.
23) Conduct a thorough and diligent visual inspection of the property.
24) Review the state of any property tax liens against the property.
25) Obtain architectural drawings and permits relative to the property.
26) Assist in determining the square footage of the house.
27) Develop an attractive description of the house for marketing.
28) Place the house description into the multiple listing service.
29) Explain real estate agency duties and liabilities.
30) Review required flood disclosures, as required.
31) Review required seismic disclosures, as required.
32) Review required Mello Roos disclosures, as required.
33) Review the environmental hazards disclosures requirement.
34) Review the federal Foreign Investment in Real Property Tax Act.
35) Review the state Foreign Investment in Real Property Tax Act.
36) Review the smoke detector compliance requirement.
37) Review any swimming pool safety ordinances and laws, as appropriate.
38) Provide seller with "statement of identity" for completion.

39) Review competitive market analysis with seller.
40) Explain how commissions are split between listing and selling brokers.
41) Explain to seller how much the agent earns on the sale of the property.
42) Show seller how commission splits affect how often a house is shown.
43) Review the broker employment agreement with the seller.
44) Explain my "marketing guarantee" to the seller.
45) Sign "marketing guarantee" with the seller.
46) Review advantages of using a real estate lock box on the property.
47) Review disadvantages of using a real estate lock box on the property.
48) Review the benefits of placing a real estate sign on the property.
49) Arrange for pest control inspection of the property.
50) Arrange for contractor's inspection of the property.
51) Arrange for roof report on the property.
52) Arrange for septic tank inspection, as necessary.
53) Arrange for county inspection, as necessary.
54) Arrange for well water inspection, as necessary.
55) Arrange for asbestos analysis, as necessary.
56) Arrange for smoke detector inspection, as necessary.
57) Arrange for energy conservation inspection, as necessary.
58) Arrange for soil inspection, as necessary.
59) Assist seller in correcting anything significant revealed in inspections.
60) Provide transfer disclosure statement to the seller.
61) Complete listing agent's portion of disclosure statement.
62) Provide transfer disclosure statement to buyers.
63) Place a professional "For Sale" sign on the property, as authorized.

64) Place appropriate riders on "For Sale" sign.
65) Place brochure box on "For Sale" sign.
66) Keep brochure box filled with flyers.
67) Place lock box on property, as authorized.
68) Directly contact agents with qualified buyers about the property.
69) Respond to agent questions about the property.
70) Respond to buyer questions about the property.
71) Design attractive color flyers for the property.
72) Place flyers in flyer stand inside the property.
73) Order an academic report on local schools.
74) Prepare sheets for potential buyers showing financing options.
75) Prepare an open house guest register.
76) Develop an open house schedule with owner or tenants.
77) Assist home owner in preparation of the property for showing.
78) Conduct telephone calls to target market, as necessary.
79) Develop a profile of the most likely buyers for the property.
80) Update marketing program, as necessary.
81) Stay in close contact with the seller about the status of the marketing.
82) Write advertising copy for various media.
83) Place ads in various media.
84) Print color flyers.
85) Provide clear flyer display stand for inside the house.
86) For vacant properties suggest the use of appropriate rental furniture.
87) Show owner how to obtain copies of building permits.
88) Order copies of covenants, conditions, and restrictions, as appropriate.
89) Place appropriate information into multiple listing system.
90) Order professional photo of the property to be take for the MLS.

91) Conduct door-knocking campaign in neighborhood, as appropriate.
92) Send "just listed" postcards to neighbors.
93) Follow up with agents who show the property.
94) Meet potential buyers to show them the property.
95) Follow up with potential buyers from open house contacts.
96) Canvass centers of influence to locate potential buyers.
97) Arrange for a tour of the property by all agents in the area.
98) Develop a program to attract agents to brokers' open tour.
99) Obtain other real estate agent's opinions of the pricing of the property.
100) Obtain other real estate agent's opinions of the condition of the property.
101) Provide a weekly status report to seller by phone or fax.
102) Review local news sources for changes in the neighborhood.
103) Place "open house" advertisements, as appropriate.
104) Strategically place open house signs to attract buyers.
105) Hold property open house for potential buyers.
106) Provide refreshments for open house guests.
107) Make sure every visitor signs the open house guest list.
108) Review results of the open house with seller.
109) Prequalify all potential buyers before offers are made.
110) Periodically review progress of the marketing program with seller.
111) Send "thank you" notes to agents who show the property.
112) Periodically update MLS information.
113) Assist seller in complying with fair housing laws.
114) Assist seller in complying with fair lending laws.
115) View all competing houses for sale.
116) Coordinate presentation of offer to purchase the house.
117) Write counteroffers, as necessary.

118) Make sure escrow is properly opened.
119) Make sure purchase deposit is properly credited to seller.
120) Make sure that any encumbrances are paid off at close of escrow.
121) Make sure seller is provided with correct amount at close of escrow.

The next aspect of selling affected by culture is the important action of staging the property for maximum appeal. The owners may like colors and furniture that a majority of buyers are likely to find unattractive. Insist that they must prepare the property for sale at the best price. They need to know that most buyers find neutral colors and a minimum of traditional furniture more attractive. Tell them that buyers need to be able to visualize the changes they will make to fit the house to their taste and lifestyle, as they undoubtedly did after they bought it.

Another issue you will likely have to address is the offering price. Just as people from bargaining countries like to pay the least possible price when they buy, they want to get the most when they sell. So expect some multicultural sellers to ask you to list their property well over the real value of comparable properties. It is imperative that you inform them that a house that sits on the market for an inordinately long time will probably bring a lower price in the end because buyers and agents may begin to be afraid that something must be wrong with it.

If they still insist on an unrealistically high listing price, do not hesitate to suggest they seek the services of another agent. Let them understand that it simply is not worth your time and wastes your professional skills trying to sell an unrealistically priced property. Another factor: The real estate profession does not need more "OPTs" (overpriced turkeys) on the market to give agents an even worse image than we already undeservedly have.

Some multicultural groups are more concerned about the offering price than the terms and conditions. It is important to many Saudis, for instance, to sell the property as close as possible to their asking price. This is further evidence of the business acumen for which their culture is well known. But this fact makes it even more important to set a realistic listing price.

Still another sensitive issue is whether to leave things in the home that indicate that the owner came from another culture. Maximizing value for the seller should be a major concern of every listing agent. Should that mean removing some furniture or taking family photos off the wall, you must bring up the subject confidently. The *Wall Street Journal* has published several articles about how some listing agents suggest that African American and other minorities make their homes "culturally neutral" in order not to prejudice any home buyers. Personal considerations aside, every real estate professional must know the market and make appropriate judgments on this issue.

Because of a desire for privacy, people from other countries are often secretive about loan balances and other financial matters. You will need to tell your sellers that a smooth payoff of their existing loan requires you to know both the account number and present balance. Assure them that no one who does not need this information will be able to obtain it, and that their desire for confidentiality will be respected whenever possible.

As good negotiators, multicultural sellers who are going to list with you and are also considering buying a new house using your services may want a discount on your listing commission, and may even ask you for kickback on the purchase side. It's important to say that, as a professional, you will do just as much work on the two separate transactions as you would with two individual clients.

If you should decide to give your current seller/future buyer a discount because of the increased efficiency of working with one party for two transactions, the author suggests that you do not discount the listing commission. Any concession should be offered on the purchase of their next house, provided they buy it through you. Without this incentive, you will probably discount your fee to a bare breakeven point, hoping to make it up on their next purchase. Yet it is not unusual for buyers, especially skilled negotiators, to walk into a new home development or for-sale-by-owner that does not cooperate with agents. Or they might remember a friend or relative in real estate. Promise a concession on the purchase of the next house, and you will provide them with the incentive they may need to stick with you as their agent.

If multicultural buyers make an offer on your listing, suggest that the sellers exclude something, such as personal property, that they are willing to give at the first sight of an offer. Sellers from most other cultures will have little difficulty understanding and agreeing in order to prevent reopened contract negotiations before close of escrow. Have them decide in advance which negotiable items the seller will hold back until just before close of escrow.

Remember to explain to every seller about the requirements of the Internal Revenue Service Foreign Interest in Real Property Tax Act (FIRPTA). Tell them that since January 1, 1985, the act has required that a buyer withhold 10 percent of the gross sales price from the seller's proceeds and send it to the Internal Revenue Service if the seller is a "foreign person."

A foreign person is defined as a nonresident alien individual, or a foreign corporation that has not properly made an election to be treated as a domestic corporation, or a foreign partnership, trust, estate, or other entity. A rough rule-of-thumb is that an individual is not a foreign person if he or she is a United States citizen, or is a resident alien (holds a valid "green card"), or meets the "substantial presence" test (contact the IRS for details).

All sales, including installment sales, exchanges, foreclosures, deeds in lieu of foreclosure and other transactions by a "foreign person" of a U.S. real property interest, are subject to FIRPTA unless an exemption applies. If the seller is a "nonforeign" person, he or she can be exempted from the requirements of FIRPTA by providing a "nonforeign affidavit" stating under penalty of perjury that the seller is not a foreign person and including the seller's taxpayer identification number.

The buyer can obtain a "withholding certificate" (also called a "qualifying statement") from the IRS, stating that no withholding is required. The certificate may also be issued to reduce the required amount of withholding.

The transaction can likewise be exempt from FIRPTA if it is a "nonrecognition transaction" for the seller and the seller furnishes a notice of nonrecognition transaction. This is a notice given by a seller to inform the buyer that no withholding is necessary because of a "nonrecognition" provision in the tax law. Examples of nonrecognition transactions include like-kind exchanges under Internal Revenue Code §1031 or a seller who is covered by a U.S. tax treaty that results in nonrecognition of gain on the sale.

A buyer should not close a sale relying on a notice of nonrecognition transaction except on the advice of a certified public accountant, attorney, or other professional tax advisor. Personal liability to the buyer can result from reliance on an improper notice of nonrecognition transaction. In addition, a buyer who relies on a notice of nonrecognition transaction must send a copy of the notice to the IRS by the twentieth day after the transfer of the property.

Remember that it is the buyer's responsibility to make sure the funds are withheld from the seller. If the buyer wants protection from potential personal liability for tax that should be withheld, he or she should have the seller complete and sign an affidavit of nonforeign status. This insulates the buyer from liability to the IRS if the seller is an individual (or multiple sellers are all individuals), unless the buyer has knowledge that the affidavit is false.

The buyer generally has no way of actually knowing whether the seller is a foreign person. Therefore, it is suggested that the seller's affidavit of nonforeign status, or buyer's affidavit that the property will be used by the buyer as the buyer's residence for the required amount of time, or other appropriate documentation that no withholding is required be obtained in every transaction.

The agent should also be sure to comply with FIRPTA for protection from potential personal liability. The penalty is potential liability to the IRS for the 10 percent of the sales price that should have been withheld, or for the seller's actual tax liability in the sale, or for the amount of commission or other compensation received by the agent, whichever is less, plus interest and penalties.

If the buyer fails to withhold the seller's funds when required the IRS can assess the full 10 percent of the sales price that should have been withheld, or the seller's actual tax liability in the sale, whichever is less, plus interest and penalties, against the buyer. This can occur if the buyer does not obtain the seller's affidavit of nonforeign status and the seller fails to pay taxes due on the sale. Even if the seller eventually pays taxes on the sale, the buyer can be liable for interest and penalties if the seller is a foreign person and no nonforeign affidavit was furnished.

There is also an exemption for sales of residential property selling for no more than $300,000 if the total sales price does not exceed $300,000, and on the date of transfer the buyer "has definite plans to reside in the property for at least 50 percent of the number of days that the property is used by any person during each of the first two 12-month periods following the date of transfer." Days that the property will be vacant are not taken into account for this purpose. The buyer is considered to reside in the property on any day the buyer or his or her brothers, sisters, ancestors, dependents, or spouse reside in it.

Withholding is normally done by having the escrow agent (title company, escrow corporation, attorney, financial institution, etc.) withhold the funds required. The funds collected will usually be sent to the IRS at close of escrow. While the law does not specifically state that the withholding must be done through escrow, doing so eliminates the possibility that a buyer might withhold funds at close of escrow and then not send them to the IRS as required. Withholding and transmittal of funds will, of course, require agreement between the buyer and seller in the deposit receipt or other sales agreement, or in the escrow instructions.

Withholding under FIRPTA must be reported and paid to the IRS by the twentieth day after the close of escrow. However, the transmittal of funds is normally made simultaneously with the close of escrow, as in the case of other disbursements of the seller's proceeds.

A withholding certificate is a form issued by the IRS specifying that no withholding, or a reduced amount of withholding, is necessary. A withholding certificate will normally be granted when, for example, taxes due on the seller's gain will be less than 10 percent of the sales price. A withholding certificate will also be granted when the seller has made other arrangements with the IRS to ensure payment of the taxes due. Either the buyer or the seller may apply for a withholding certificate. Usually though, it will be the seller's responsibility to obtain the withholding certificate and provide it to the buyer, to avoid withholding. The agreement between the buyer and seller should make it clear whose responsibility it is to obtain a withholding certificate, if applicable.

While all sellers should complete the FIRPTA statement, sellers who do not qualify for a FIRPTA exemption need to be informed of the requirements of this law so they do not think you are stealing their money or are engaged in some other illegal transaction. It will also help them with planning for the use of the sale proceeds.

Be aware that individual states may have their own FIRPTA-type regulations, which can differ substantially from the federal rules. For instance, California law defines a "foreign person" as anyone who does not live in the state or is going to move out of the state. Therefore, while sellers may be exempt from the requirements of federal FIRPTA they could be subject to state FIRPTA rules. Check with a real estate attorney or other knowledgeable professional such as a title or escrow officer about these complex rules.

> *"Multicultural sellers must be educated about what agents do for a living and how much they make."*

13

Marketing to Multicultural Clients

There are marketing issues to be aware of if you want to attract new immigrant clients to your real estate practice. First, people from other cultures do not customarily find real estate agents through newspaper and yellow pages advertising. As a rule, they prefer to receive a reference from trusted friends and relatives.

It is vital to ask your current multicultural clients for the names of people they know who might be thinking of buying or selling a home. It is equally important to get them to introduce you personally, since personal recommendations are crucial to trust building. Ideally, they should speak positively about you before they introduce you to their friends or relatives.

You may decide to advertise in newspapers and various other media that serve the interests of diverse cultures. However, realize that if a different language is spoken and your ad is written in that tongue, potential clients are probably going to expect you to speak it. Agents who don't know the language should not try this strategy.

The usual method of advertising in the United States is known as "low context," meaning that it relies on a lot of words to familiarize clients with the product and its features and to motivate buyers. Low context cultures include North America, England, Switzerland, and Germany, among others.

In contrast, high context cultures, like those found in most Asian and Latin American countries, as well as the Native American culture, rely more on pictures and nuances to convey meaning. These cultures consider low context ads and techniques pushy and aggressive. The saying, "One picture is worth a thousand words," epitomizes the preferred method of marketing to this group. This is also a good reason to do less talking when speaking to people from high context cultures. Recognize that you cannot market to all groups in the same way. You must find out how the groups you are trying to reach receive their information.

To people from other cultures, traditional ads that feature European Americans are virtually invisible. Use appropriate models and language for the group you are trying to reach.

Remember that the dominant religion of the Middle East is Islam. Do not use symbols or words in your advertising that imply Judeo-Christian values. Things such as stars, crosses, and even asterisks may be taken the wrong way by such readers.

Eighty percent of Hispanics listen to Spanish-speaking radio stations and 75 percent watch Spanish television. Members of this group are fiercely loyal to their language and culture and prefer that ads directed toward them be in the Spanish language. Hispanics tend to receive less direct mail advertisements and so are more likely to read it. Seventy-two percent say they always read direct mail and 33 percent say they would like to receive more.

Hispanics are very brand conscious and loyal to leading brands. If your real estate company is a member of a large, nationwide franchise, you may wish to stress this attribute. On the other hand, members of this culture are very family-oriented and if your company is family-owned and family-operated you may prefer to call their attention to this feature.

It is little known that 70 percent of Hispanics consider Christopher Columbus as beloved a figure as do the Italians. Making use of his image, where appropriate, would certainly not hurt any effort to attract this group.

Statistically, Hispanics have been slower than Caucasians to embrace technology for communication. They lag behind in the use of the Internet and e-mail so these media may not be as effective in reaching Hispanics.

Asians seem to prefer to read newspapers for information, as contrasted with radio and television. Do not make emotional appeals to this group, like "You'll love this home!" Never forget that Asians consider it poor taste to display emotions in public and they do not respond to emotional pitches. Any attempt to appeal to an Anglo-Saxon viewpoint about property is likely to fall upon deaf ears, and might well be counterproductive.

To appeal to Asians, accent the longevity, reputation, quality, and reliability of yourself and your company. Boldly stating that something is "new and improved" will not attract people from a five-thousand-year-old culture. Some may even find it humorous.

It is important not to knock your competition when marketing or working with Asians. They believe that doing so makes the one who speaks the negative comments lose face. Instead, stress the benefits and strengths your company offers them.

Avoid telling Japanese clients that your company is distinctive or unique. Remember that they value group harmony and "fitting in." The Japanese have a saying that exemplifies this philosophy: "The nail that sticks up gets hammered down." Asians want to promote accommodation and strongly prefer working with companies that show a cooperative attitude.

Stressing time-saving features of a home will win you the undying loyalty of most Koreans. Many regularly work fourteen to sixteen-hour days and six to seven-day weeks. Time is at a premium and they often feel guilty about not being able to spend more time with their families, especially the children. To save time, Koreans often seek out properties to buy that are close to their work, schools, churches, or shopping centers. Such features as microwave ovens, dishwashers, and trash compactors are also greatly appreciated.

Explain to Korean buyers that you can quickly narrow the search for the perfect house through your expertise and a computer. Telling sellers from this culture that you take on all of the work involved in marketing a house will have more impact than years of real estate experience.

Many Koreans work for high-technology companies in the United States. Thus, it may be possible to market to them through a Web site or e-mail. Many Indians are engineers and are also very "savvy" technologically. You may also be able to reach them through on-line marketing.

Asian Indians often have large families, and may prefer to do business with family-oriented companies. From centuries of British rule, they are usually very Westernized and speak excellent English. Consider using Indian models in ads showing families. Many Indian-English language newspapers are relatively inexpensive to advertise in, by the way.

It is important to recognize that African Americans are not just dark-skinned white people, but comprise a distinct culture. Most believe this to be the case, but within it are a number of subcultures, as from Haiti and other areas of the Caribbean. In addition, the South American heritage of many black-skinned people reflects even more varied points of view. This culture has developed many of its own newspapers, radio stations, and television stations to meet its unique needs.

Seventy percent of African Americans read community newspapers geared specifically toward their culture. Use models from this culture, but use caution when showing what you may believe to be traditional families. Remember that over 50 percent do not have a male head of household.

Marketing your real estate company to African Americans calls for deemphasizing size and longevity. Large, impersonal companies and governments have historically treated this group very badly. They prefer to work with small, personalized, entrepreneurial agents and companies with whom they can feel comfortable that phone calls will be returned by the person they want and that mail is answered personally.

Many African Americans dislike things that imply traditional American white, middle-class values. Many believe that these values have been used against them since they were brought over from Africa as slaves. African Americans like to express their own unique and individual styles when it comes to home ownership and design.

Like the Hispanics, African Americans have been slower than Caucasians to embrace technology for communication. For many reasons, they lag behind in the use of the Internet and e-mail so these media may not be as effective in reaching African Americans.

Certain words are particularly attractive to multicultural people, words like *family*, *security*, *prestige,* and others that describe features they esteem as desirable. But be careful: Stay out of trouble by verifying with your advertising outlet that seemingly innocent words do not inadvertently violate fair housing or antidiscrimination laws. A little personal research with members of the ethnic communities you hope to reach can go a long way toward achieving success with people from other cultures.

Many people come here from places where it was not unusual for a family business to operate in the same location for generations. If your business is long-established (at least ten years, preferably longer) you may wish to suggest trustworthiness by featuring this fact. The mind-set you want to create is the idea that it is unlikely that your business could have lasted so long while being dishonest. Also stress the family aspect of your company, if appropriate.

Be careful when offering coupons to new immigrants or even longtime residents like African and Native Americans. These are proud and self-sufficient cultures who, for the most part, don't favor things that look like preferential treatment, food stamps, or welfare.

Keep in mind the significance of colors to some cultural groups. Consider using red ink or red paper to advertise to Chinese; in their culture, that color represents good luck and prosperity. But again, use caution. Know whom you are dealing with. The same red that the Chinese celebrate as a harbinger of good fortune is the Korean's color of death.

Always have someone fluent in the language of the people you are trying to reach double-check your ad for any mistakes or cultural gaffes. Companies who ought to have known better have suffered great embarrassment that they could have avoided with better planning.

It is said that Pepsi Cola executives had a hard time understanding why sales were slow when the company first began distributing its product in Taiwan. In time, someone explained to them that their slogan "Pepsi brings good things to life" had been mistranslated to say "Pepsi brings your ancestors back from the dead." Those Chinese who weren't amused might have been offended, since ancestors are subjects of reverence in that culture. Pepsi Cola's gross miscalculation was more than embarrassing. It was a potential disaster for both sales and public relations.

A similar story about a translation error is told about the management at General Motors who were severely disappointment when its popular Chevrolet Nova line flopped miserably in Mexico and South America. They had believed their compact model, so popular here, couldn't miss in that new market. Sales projections were optimistic when the campaign kicked off but turned out to be nonexistent. Eventually, a kind soul made them aware that the name sounded like the Spanish phrase *no va*, meaning "It doesn't go." Millions of dollars in promotional costs were wasted because no one took the time to do their cultural homework.

Until you are confident in your ability to deal with ethnic differences, find your own expert to confirm that your approach is acceptable. It is not a good idea to try saving a few dollars with the rusty, formal high school Spanish you learned twenty years ago.

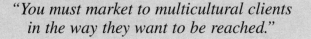

"You must market to multicultural clients in the way they want to be reached."

14

Using Interpreters and Translators

S poken as well as written real estate words and concepts may need a specialist to translate them into English. Few countries outside the United States utilize title and escrow systems and other real estate-specific services. Important as they are here, such functions must be explained using skill and patience. Be prepared to handle the ethnic and cultural diversities you encounter with three things: empathy, patience, and understanding.

One language cannot always be accurately translated into another. In fact, it can often become an impossible task because words can have more than one meaning. In addition, some words have no meaning outside their specific culture.

Modesty, which is highly valued in many other cultures, can justify the services of an interpreter. Add a compliment, and there should be no ensuing problems. "Mr. and Mrs.

Client, your knowledge of my language is so much better than mine is of yours that I believe I need an interpreter to be sure we understand each other."

Employing interpreters and translators is a common business practice in working with unfamiliar cultures. The two are not the same thing. An interpreter converts the spoken word to English, while a translator deals with the written word. If possible, find one with real estate experience. Whatever the case, a good one will be worth considerably more than you pay.

An extra benefit in using an interpreter during negotiations is that it gives you additional time to consider your response. So it is important for your interpreter to understand your goals in the transaction. The purpose is to meet those goals, so brief anyone you hire in advance to explain the nature of the deal and the part you expect them to play.

Locating a competent and experienced interpreter or translator can be crucial to your success. Colleagues or clients with whom you completed good property transactions should be your first source. You might also want to contact the nearest consular office for the appropriate country. Local colleges and universities might have foreign-born students or faculty who can fill the bill admirably.

It can be disastrous to accept the first person who applies; a poor interpreter can do irreparable damage. Most people have heard of the legendary story. When former President Jimmy Carter visited Poland in 1977, his interpreter butchered his official arrival message. When he said that he had left the United States early that day, the translator told those assembled that Carter had "abandoned his country." When the devoutly religious Carter talked about Polish "desires for the future," "desire" was mistranslated as "lust." If that wasn't bad enough, the interpreter ended the ill-starred address with, "The president says he is pleased to be here in Poland grasping your secret parts."

Interpretation of American-style English is difficult. Our language is filled with colloquialisms, acronyms, idioms, slang, and jargon. Add to these the special requirements of technical real estate terms, and the task can be just about impossible for an inexperienced interpreter. A bad job can easily lead to misunderstandings—even lawsuits. Once you select a candidate or two, hand them a few documents and ask them to tell you what they mean. Even though your knowledge of the language may be poor, your expertise in real estate can help avoid mistakes in this aspect.

Using an interpreter effectively requires the establishment of three-way rapport: between yourself and the interpreter; between yourself and your client; and between the interpreter and the client. This takes time and should be allowed for when planning a meeting using an interpreter.

Before the meeting starts, explain to your interpreter any technical terms that will be used. Ask him or her to explain any cultural differences in eye contact or other nonverbal nuances. Check on local customs such as the most appropriate time to hold the meeting, the client's concept of time, feelings about the consumption of alcohol, and any other issues that may affect your meeting.

Once the meeting begins, speak directly to your guests, not to your interpreter. Not doing so would be seen as rude to your clients. It is helpful to work out a few simple signals with your interpreter so that he or she can let you know when you are speaking too quickly or too slowly. It's easy to lose control of the conversation when using a surrogate so get your signs straight. You will probably not use them, but it's good to be prepared in advance. Before meeting with the clients, practice speaking in short phrases and pausing from time to time so your interpreter can catch up.

Never, *never* try to tell jokes through an interpreter. It rarely works and can be disastrous when not done just right. A story or subject that is perfectly acceptable in our culture could well offend people from another. Or, just as bad, it might not be funny in a different language.

There is the old story about how an American in Japan was telling a joke through an interpreter and the audience broke into uproarious laughter at the punch line. Beaming with confidence, the speaker remarked to one of his colleagues, who spoke Japanese, how well-received the joke was. His friend confided that the interpreter had actually said in Japanese, "The speaker has just told an American joke that does not make sense in our language. Please laugh."

Recognize that direct translation of English into other languages is often impossible. Too many words have more than one meaning and may have unexpected connotations in other tongues. Common real estate terms may have no direct equivalents. And, of course, cultural orientation itself can have an impact on the translation. Despite the help an interpreter can provide, it's still a good idea to draw diagrams and write figures down to improve communications.

Agents who use interpreters know from experience that it increases the time needed for communications. Plan for that when you allocate the time for a meeting with multicultural clients. Don't be shy about telling them why the meeting may be a long one. "I want to be sure to communicate everything so we all understand it, Señor Client, so I am allowing for the extra time we will need for three people to talk."

Interpreting is a difficult and taxing job, both mentally and physically. That's true even for the most experienced professional. Provide your interpreter with lots of water and snacks, as well as plenty of breaks. Treat the interpreter well because most clients look at how this member of your team is being treated and assume they will be treated the same.

Your first consideration after competence is to employ an interpreter with whom you are comfortable and who you think can work effectively with you as a member of your team. The person you choose should behave like you in terms of such personality characteristics as friendliness and communication style. For instance, if you are outgoing, try to find an interpreter who shares the same trait. In this way every word will be consistent with your own style.

Make certain that the dialect the interpreter speaks is the same as the people with whom you are going to communicate. Chinese, for example, is a language with hundreds of dialects, all classified in the West as Chinese but sometimes mutually incomprehensible.

Once more: Take the necessary time to hire someone with real estate experience, someone who knows the unique terminology of the profession. It may cost more, or it may not, but in any case the dividends of choosing someone who is as professional at his or her job as you are at yours will be great. Don't have a lifetime relationship ruined by a poor translator or interpreter.

> *"Try to find an interpreter who has real estate experience."*

15

Closing the Transaction

As an experienced real estate agent, you know it is good practice to keep your buyers and sellers constantly up-to-date on the progress of the transaction. The most common complaint heard about real estate agents across the nation is, "They don't stay in touch." That's especially true during the final stages when close of escrow is pending. Although there is not much to do except wait, remember that this is the time when buyers and sellers can become terribly nervous. A weekly phone call is probably about right, but it is helpful to determine in your first meeting how often they would like you to contact them regarding the status of their transaction.

The biggest fear of listing agents is having to call their sellers to tell them that nothing is happening with their property. Far worse, though, is for *them* to call you anxiously, only to learn that nothing is happening. Conventional wisdom says that this is a surefire recipe for a disgruntled seller. But a worse scenario is the one with a nervous seller sitting at home imagining all kinds of bad news. Even when you have little or nothing to report, make it a point to stay in regular contact.

Don't be lulled into a false sense of security from the relaxed atmosphere some cultures project. It practically never lasts. A typical Jamaican client may be weeks late in providing the documents needed to close. Later, that same apparently lackadaisical person may wear your ear to a nub with phone calls demanding to know why nothing is happening. If such is the case, remind them that nothing is ever going to happen until they provide the necessary papers. It is almost impossible to overcommunicate with any client.

Again, do not expect people from other cultures to blithely sign a stack of official-looking documents without some reluctance. Even someone from this country can find that mountain of papers quite imposing. The effect is doubly so for persons who are unfamiliar with the American language and culture. Remember, too, that certain peoples have not had good experiences with the U.S. government. Bad past experiences just increase their reluctance to sign official documents.

Be sensitive about presenting closing documents to people from the African American culture. Their long history of poor treatment by some, part of which can be attributed to the government, leads them to be careful about what they sign. For similar historical reasons, Asians are not always trusting of the paperwork necessary to transfer property. They also have their own history of maltreatment at the hands of earlier American government policymakers.

Given this bit of history, the best way to handing the huge pile of closing documents that both buyers and sellers of all cultures must sign is to obtain a pro forma set from the title company or attorney well in advance of closing. Give the clients at least a week to review all papers before expecting them to sign. Explain in detail anything that might be a concern. Also alert them to the fact that on the day of closing they will be expected to sign them rather quickly, so they should take time to look everything over and ask questions before that day.

It's interesting to note that Hispanics are more likely to be trusting of the U.S. government than any other group. In fact, they are twice as likely as European Americans to believe that the government can be trusted.

Don't forget that some Filipino buyers may want to close escrow and move during a full moon. This can be tricky when the full moon falls on a weekend. One way the author has handled this problem is to inform the clients that once everyone signs the papers the buyers own the house, for all intents and purposes. In that sense, recording the title on the following business day is only a legal formality.

Expect new Filipino home owners to bring a full sack of rice and some salt or garlic to their new home. Tradition dictates that they do so for luck before moving anything else in. So these will usually be the first items to be brought the door. That ritual accomplished, a priest will give his blessing upon the new family abode.

Other cultures frequently have special ways of christening a new home. Ask your clients if there will be a ceremony and whether it would be fitting for you to participate. You will probably find it interesting and enlightening, and the interest you show by simply asking will help to cement your relationship.

> *"Providing closing documents in advance and staying in touch with clients will win the undying gratitude of everyone you work with."*

16

New Homes

Immigrants are having a tremendous impact on American home construction. The million people coming into the country annually have helped assure the continued growth of this $800 billion industry. Without these people, experts estimate that the building industry's growth rate would stagnate or turn in a negative direction.

New arrivals often have great enthusiasm for owning property. In many cases it may be a case of centuries of pent-up demand. Historically, working or "lower-class" people have had little access to real estate in either Asia or Europe. Over the centuries, the term *real* has become associated with the word *royal*. In other words, if you weren't a member of royalty you could not own land.

This situation has taken centuries to remedy. After decades during which real estate ownership was illegal, even the People's Republic of China began allowing its citizens to buy and sell real estate again in 1998.

There are a number of reasons why new immigrants have become so important to the new home industry. New homes can be especially attractive to members of some cultures. Many Asians prefer brand-new property because there are no previous owners who have suffered ill fortune. Hispanics might favor new properties because the rooms may be larger than those in older homes. African Americans can customize homes so they reflect their own unique style. In fact, almost every culture would probably prefer a new home to a used one if price and location were no object.

Besides, what other accomplishment says so well that a new immigrant has achieved success in this new homeland? No picture could make the family back home prouder than one of a recently immigrated son or daughter standing in front of their brand-new American house.

However, buying a new home can be troublesome to people from countries where negotiating is common. Most developers will not negotiate the price because doing so could lower the value of other homes in the area where the owners previously paid a higher price. To overcome this obstacle, explain to your clients, especially Asians, that in order for the developer to "save face" with previous buyers, the purchase price must remain fixed. Nonetheless, upgrades or other amenities obtained as part of the deal may enable you to show the client how you helped reduce the net purchase price with each apparent upgrade.

Almost all developers allocate their salespeople a discretionary fund of from a few hundred to thousands of dollars, to provide some flexibility in making a sale. The amount varies with the price range of the home, how long the development has been marketing the properties, the builder's profit margin, and so on. Developers are reminded not to give them everything up front in case renegotiation becomes a factor and there is nothing left to give. When the author consults with home builders he shows them how to build a "renegotiation factor" into discretionary funds so salespeople cannot give it all away at the beginning.

Home builders should be aware of the influence immigrant groups can have on their business. The best sources of information regarding the wants and needs of people from other cultures are their own salespeople who interface with clients every day. If multicultural clients begin having a large impact on sales, developers may want to consider planning properties to satisfy these clients' needs.

Again, many Asians prefer that the walkway leading to the house be slightly curved rather than straight; straight walks are believed to create "secret arrows" that provide paths for bad luck. They may also favor round windows over the trendy triangular ones because the latter represent three straight lines. Practitioners of *Feng Shui* will prefer certain home orientation, room layouts, and appliance placement, as previously discussed. The rules of *Vastu Shastra*, described earlier, have substantial effects on Asian Indian clients who subscribe to this belief system.

One of the most requested options for people from other cultures seems to be vents that direct kitchen exhaust outside the home. Many of today's developers simply vent cooking odors back into the kitchen to save money. People who cook a lot of fish or use strong spices know the smell stays in the house for a long time, sometimes permanently. They often want assurance that it will be blown outside by a strong fan surrounded by a large hood over the range.

Another popular new home feature is the "granny unit" option, which substitutes a room designated as a library or study for a smaller bedroom and a bath. Many people from other countries expect to have friends and relatives stay over when they visit. An extra room where they can sleep and bathe is certainly more useful than a place where they can read. Also, quite a few immigrants plan to bring family members here to live with them.

The author has consulted with many home developers to show them how simple, inexpensive changes can make their properties more attractive to this unique clientele. It should go without saying, but the only way to know what your specific clients prefer is to ask them. Have your salespeople regularly survey the market as most home developers do, asking such questions as: "What color exterior do you prefer?" or "What changes in layout would you suggest?" or "How do the appliances suit your needs?" Finally, "Any other suggestions?" can reap a wealth of good advice.

One difficulty that home builders have is getting their salesforce to have visitors to model homes complete surveys. Well-thought-out survey forms provide valuable information as well as vital contact data for future follow-up. This problem is rather easy to understand because salespeople believe, correctly, that they get paid to sell, not to get questionnaires filled out. But this information is too valuable not to obtain, so new home sales agents need to be rewarded for obtaining it.

One developer brings balloons filled with various denominations of bills inside to the weekly sales meeting. Salespeople who have turned in more than a certain number of completed surveys get to pop them against a dart board. For each completed survey over the minimum, the person gets one dart. Balloons usually contain lots of $1 and $5 bills, some $20's, a few $50's, and one $100 bill. The balloon popping ceremony is usually the highlight of the meeting and encourages other salespeople to obtain completed survey cards. This game adds amusement to the meeting, and the developer gets valuable and needed information on prospects.

Salespeople should be asked if visitors regularly request custom features that the developer does not provide. If a sufficient number of requests come in, perhaps the developer should consider offering them.

In general, multicultural home buyers tend to prefer things they are familiar with. Many Jamaicans like the block and steel construction that is common in their homeland. They often ask builders to use concrete blocks between rooms instead of the sheetrock found in most construction here. This gives them a greater feeling of security against inclement weather like the hurricanes that are familiar to those who have lived in Jamaica.

Some new home buyers demonstrate unusual (to us) taste in color and style. Red is thought lucky for some Asians, so they might prefer crimson or plum-colored carpeting. However, as not all buyers would make this their first choice of colors, builders should be careful not to install such unique decor until the sale is well assured. Many developers have found themselves trying to resell new homes with custom features that made it difficult to find a new buyer.

If a new development is heavily impacted by multicultural home buyers, everyone on the selling team must understand the special needs of such clients. It would be wise to set aside specific training time for the sales force to learn about special needs, interests, and requests that might affect the selling and escrow processes.

Many immigrants who buy a new home like to visit the site and watch their home as it is being built. Loud arguments and other evidence of discord between the workers may be a sign that this will be a home filled with disharmony. An accident during construction might have a similar effect. How the developer handles these and other issues affecting multicultural buyers is crucial.

Be aware that the multicultural buyer may want to consecrate the ground before beginning construction. If this comes up, be careful to coordinate with their religious representative before any work like trenching or foundation pouring begins. If this opportunity is lost so might be the sale.

Everyone who works for a new home developer should be made aware that they can be affected by cultural differences. Not just the salespeople on the front line but decorators, carpenters, roofers, electricians, people in finance, and all others can help determine the success a project has with its potential multicultural market.

First, salespeople must understand the importance of getting the clients' names right. As noted earlier, they must be sure to get spelling and pronunciation correct, including first and family names (surnames). When sending this information on to other people within the company, give them a phonetic pronunciation and note which are the husband and wife. It is very embarrassing to call a client's workplace expecting to speak to a man, and having a woman answer. This small mistake makes the entire company seem callous and culturally insensitive, even when it may have only been the fault of one person.

New home salespeople, like other agents, should relate in detail what they do for a living and how much they make. This is as vital in new home sales as it is in resale because buyers, culture aside, seem to believe that new home salespeople are the same as resale agents. The same old myth holds true that new home salespeople do very little and earn a huge amount of money. You do not need to tell the buyer exactly how much you make but give them a percentage of the sales price if you are paid on commission. Deduct your income taxes and expenses so that they can compare your take-home pay with their own.

Next, spell out the new home model touring procedure. Many new home buyers, regardless of culture, do not know how to tour a new home nor are they always aware that the model furniture is not included in the purchase price. Once they know that, both you and they might avoid future disputes and embarrassment.

Point out any custom features that might be of interest and explain what can and cannot be done. Inexperienced new home buyers may think that all builders can totally customize a home or build it on the lot of their choice somewhere else in the area.

New homes can be a tremendous opportunity to help multicultural buyers own the ultimate American dream. However, as you can see, you might have to adjust your thinking and practices to do so. For more details about selling new homes to people from other cultures, see Michael Lee's book, *BUILDING BRIDGES: Selling to Multicultural New Home Customers*.

> *"Nothing says that people from other countries*
> *have achieved success in America more*
> *than a new home."*

17

Obtaining Referrals from Multicultural Clients

O nce you have a couple of multicultural clients who trust you, you will probably acquire more. As mentioned, the bulk of immigrants find service providers by word-of-mouth. A job well done can produce a steady current of clients for life. You will never have a more faithful relationship than one in which you have both served and educated a client. The Saudi Arabian reliance on the recommendations of friends, for instance, comes from centuries of trust in personal contacts to see them through periods of drought in their desert homeland.

It is always a good idea to give every client a gift at closing. The author has given every conceivable present over

twenty years in real estate. My list of gifts to new home owners ranges from door knockers and door mats to everything
in between. After spending thousands of dollars on small re-
membrances I have concluded that an effective closing gift
accomplishes one goal: It regularly reminds the client that I
am their real estate agent for life. A gift that does not satisfy
this paramount requirement is a waste of money.

The best closing gifts have personalized plaques and are
appropriate to the property involved in the transaction. A
business gift suits the sale of an office building, as a household item fits in the new home. Such things as pen and pencil desk sets and similar items are ideal. My most effective
closing gift is a glass and brass clock that spins every few
seconds. I put a matching brass plate at the base reading
"Congratulations on your home from your friend, Michael
Lee." Beneath that inscription I put the date of closing. The
wonderful thing about the clock is that the clients are reminded of me every time they glance at it, dust it off, or
change the battery.

For some cultures, however, clocks as closing gifts would
be quite inappropriate. They remind the Chinese of the winding down of life, or of funerals. Clearly, the Chinese consider
receiving a clock in itself an unlucky event. I give such
clients a pen and pencil set with the same brass plate as the
clock. It is also in poor taste to give knives to a Chinese or
Japanese because they stand for the severing of a relationship. Remember also that you should never give most Chinese or Japanese four of anything as those quantities remind
them of death. It would be the same for the quantities of three
for Filipinos or Southeast Asians.

Another good closing gift for many Asian cultures is a
green houseplant wrapped with a red ribbon. Green symbolizes growth and life while the red is for luck. Remember to
omit the red ribbon for Koreans.

I like to give my Japanese clients a small gift at the first meeting and another at close of escrow. These clients are likewise probably going want to give you presents on these occasions. To stress the point once more, it is my advice never to outspend a Japanese client. Your breach of etiquette will cause them to lose face and they will never be able to speak to you again.

Wrapping paper is another unexpected issue surrounding gifts. Never wrap a gift for a Chinese or Japanese in white paper. Again, white is the color of death in both lands. The Japanese culture passes out chrysanthemums at funerals, and everyone at the memorial wears white. Also, the Japanese consider brightly colored paper and fancy ribbons to be in bad taste. If you ever look for wrapping paper at a Japanese stationery store, you will find it very subdued. Chinese, on the other hand, frequently wrap their presents in red, their culture's color of good luck and happiness.

A strong small tree is a good closing gift for Koreans. This cultural group has a great affinity and affection for all growing things, especially trees. When Japan invaded the country it cut down all of the trees to provide a symbol of subjugation and to build ships for the Japanese Royal navy. Today, "Tree Day" is still a national holiday in Korea.

Food baskets, crystal glass items, and fine liquor are all excellent gifts for Chinese and Japanese clients. Unfortunately, I haven't found a good way to personalize any of these. The problem with gifts that do not have a plaque is that, if there is no reminder attached, the giver tends to pass from memory rather quickly, especially if not a family member. Most of us have received a gift that we have enjoyed while occasionally trying unsuccessfully to recall who gave it to us.

Whatever gift you give your multicultural clients, be certain it is of the highest quality and is not imported from their home country. Nothing but humiliation could result from a

Japanese client's turning over a fine piece of crystal only to read "Made in Japan." To give a Hispanic, an Arab, or anyone new to America a gift made in the place they just left would certainly not remind them of their new home in America.

Again, Japanese really appreciate high quality liquor. A word of warning on liquor is appropriate: Regardless of quality, nothing alcoholic must ever be given to anyone of a religion such as Islam, which frowns on all alcoholic beverages.

When you exchange gifts with Japanese, present yours with both hands like a business card, extend it forward with your left hand, and receive their gift to you with your right. It pays to give attention to the receiver as well as the gift.

You will discover that your Japanese, Chinese, and Mexican clients are extremely loyal and will almost automatically refer friends and family. These cultures place a high importance on loyalty. Gratitude also carries value as evidence of good quality and worthy purpose, so be sure to acknowledge the favor of a good referral in an appropriate manner.

The best time to ask for a referral is anytime a client expresses gratitude. If they say, "Thank you, I didn't know that," simply reply, "You're welcome. Is there anyone you know who might appreciate having the same information?" It is your duty to ask for a referral at the time they say thank you. Remember that the way they find trusted service providers in other countries is through referrals, so they want to refer you if you have done well by them. Give them the opportunity!

Providing you with a referral means several things to your client: (1) it's an ego boost for them to know more than their friends do about real estate; (2) they can help others with a referral; this is their chance to help them find a trustworthy agent; and (3) they pay you back for your service by referring a friend or family member.

The way you accept referrals is crucial to your success. When a client gives you a referral, say, "Thank you, John. I promise I will call them right after you tell them about me."

Then when you call the referred party say, "I promised John I would call you." This is considerably better than saying, "John gave me your name." You are keeping a sacred promise. This starts your relationship off in a very positive manner.

> *"People from other cultures want to make referrals—give them the opportunity to refer you."*

18

Conclusion

I wrote this book in the hope that you will take the information I have compiled for you over the past ten years and put it to work. I believe you will find working with people from unfamiliar cultures an enjoyable and beneficial experience. They can become your most loyal clients and best teachers.

Obviously, you cannot remember every detail about the various cultures that this book contains. The good news is that you don't have to. All you really need to learn is what is important to your clients, whatever country or culture they come from. Through this book you now have the tools to begin your studies. You are going to become the multicultural expert in your area by keeping an open mind and asking questions that come up because you are truly interested in learning about other people.

There are some basic rules that will help you be more sensitive to people from other cultures:

   1) Talk with other agents and people you know who are from other cultures about their language, beliefs, and

culture. You will find that they are usually happy to help you learn more.

2) Read as much as possible about the cultural background of people you most commonly encounter. There is usually plenty of information available at libraries or on the Internet.

3) Look at your own assumptions about people from other cultures. Stereotyping can easily lead to misunderstandings.

4) Take every opportunity to speak with individuals from cultural backgrounds that are different from your own. You will quickly discover that they aren't so different after all.

5) Take the time to learn a few words in the language of other people. They will really appreciate the effort spend in learning words like "hello," "good-bye," and perhaps your own name.

Never forget that these new immigrants all want what every American wants. They have dreamed of living in neighborhoods where they can raise their families in safety and harmony. They want their children to attend the best schools possible. They all want to have the greatest chance at success in the United States.

Every person you meet in the real estate profession is an individual with rights, interests, and visions of the future that are their own, yet much like everyone else's. Understanding their cultures and beliefs will help you to establish friendship, rapport, and sound business success.

If nothing else, don't assume a client wants to be treated in a certain way. Take the time to learn the culture your client came from. Then learn what changes have taken place in the client since coming here. You may be surprised. Be sensitive to cultural differences and it will pay you huge personal and professional dividends.

Once you have learned about their culture, take the time to get to know your clients personally—as husbands and wives, as fathers and mothers, as *people*. Don't be surprised that through this process your vocabulary changes from calling people from other cultures "those people" to "friends."

If you are ever in doubt about how to act or what to say around multicultural clients, follow the Golden Rule: treat them as you would like to be treated—with sensitivity, patience, and a desire to serve them with the best that is in you. You will never go wrong and you can expect to gain a lifetime of friendship and loyalty.

I wish you the very best of luck with opening the doors to real estate ownership for all your clients, regardless what culture, country or planet they may come from.

> *"The Golden Rule of Multicultural Relations:*
> *Treat clients as you would like to be treated."*

References

In addition to hundreds of interviews with multicultural real estate agents and clients, the following are some of the references used in the development of this book:

Abdrabbah, B. (1984). *Saudi Arabia: Forces of Modernism*. Brattleboro, VT: Amana Books.

Abrahams, R.D. (1976). *Talking Black*. Rowley, MA: Newbury House.

Ahmed, L. (1992). *Women and Gender in Islam*. New Haven, CT: Yale University Press.

Alier, A. (1990). *The Southern Sudan: Too Many Agreements Dishonored*. Exeter, England: Ithaca.

Allport, G.W. (1988). *The Nature of Prejudice*. Boston: Addison-Wesley.

Almaney, A.J. (1982). *Communicating with the Arabs*. Prospect Heights, IL: Waveland Press.

Altman, I. & Taylor, D.A. (1973). *Social Penetration: The Development of Interpersonal Relationships*. New York: Holt, Rinehart & Winston.

Amand, R.P. (Ed.)(1981). *Cultural Factors in International Relations*. New Delhi: Abinhav.

Argyle, M. (1975). *Bodily Communication*. London: Methuen.

Argyle, M. & Cook, M. (1976). *Gaze and Mutual Gaze*. Cambridge: Cambridge University Press.

Asante, M. & Newmark, E. (Eds.).(1989). *Handbook of Intercultural Communication*. Beverly Hills, CA: Sage.

Asante, M.K. (1987). *The Afrocentric Idea*. Philadelphia: Temple University Press.

Asante, M.K. (1988). *Afrocentricity*. Trenton, NJ: Africa World Press.

Asante, M.K. (Ed.). (1985). *African Culture*. Westport, CT: Greenwood Press.

Asian American Handbook (1991). Chicago: National Conference on Christians and Jews, Asian American Journalists Association.

Axtell, R.E. (1990). *Do's and Taboos of Hosting International Visitors*. New York: John Wiley.

Axtell, R.E. (1991). *Gestures: The Do's and Taboos of Body Language around the World*. New York: John Wiley.

Axtell, R.E. (1994). *The Do's and Taboos of International Trade.* New York: John Wiley.

Barth, F. (1969). *Ethnic Groups and Boundaries.* London: Allen & Unwin.

Beardsmore, H. (1992). *Bilingualism: Basic Principles.* London: Teitro, Ltd.

Bell, C. (1987). *The Unique Pacific.* London: The Centre for Security and Conflict Studies.

Benedict, R. (1934). *Patterns of Culture.* Boston: Houghton Mifflin.

Berger, C. & Chaffree, S. (Eds.). (1987). *Handbook of Communication Science.* Newbury Park, CA: Sage.

Bergman, P.M. (1969). *The Chronological History of the Negro in America.* New York: New American Library.

Berlin, B. & Kay, P. (1969). *Basic Color Terms.* Berkeley: University of California Press.

Berry, J., Dasen, P. & Saraswathi, T. (Eds.). (1997). *Handbook of Cross-Cultural Psychology.* Boston: Allyn & Bacon.

Beyer, S. (1974). *The Buddhist Experience.* Belmont, CA: Wadsworth.

Billingsley, A. (1974). *Black Families and the Struggle for Survival: Teaching Our Children to Walk Tall.* New York: Friendship Press.

Binh, D.T. (1975). *A Handbook for Teachers of Vietnamese Students: Hints for Dealing with Cultural Differences in Schools.* Arlington, VA: Center for Applied Linguistics.

Binnendijk, H. (Ed.). (1987). *National Negotiating Styles.* Washington, DC: Center for the Study of Foreign Affairs, U.S. Department of State.

Birke-Smith, K. (1959). *The Eskimos.* London: Methuen.

Blackbourn, D. & Evans, R.J. (Eds.). (1991). *The German Bourgeoisie.* London: Routledge.

Blaker, M.K. (1977). *Japanese International Negotiating Style.* New York: Columbia University Press.

Bloomfield, F. (1983). *The Book of Chinese Beliefs.* New York: Ballantine Books.

Blubaugh, J. & Pennington, D. (1976). *Crossing Differences: Interracial Communication.* Columbus, OH: Merrill.

Bochner, S. (Ed.). (1981). *The Mediating Person: Bridges Between Cultures.* Boston: Hall.

Bosmajian, H.A. (1983). *The Language of Oppression.* Lanham, MD: University Press of America.

Braganti, N.L. & Devine, E. (1984). *The Travelers' Guide to European Customs and Manners.* Deephaven, MN: Meadowbrook.

Briggs, V.N. (1977). *The Chicano Worker.* Austin: University of Texas Press.

Brigham Young University (1992). *Culturegrams.* Provo, UT: David M. Kennedy Center for International Studies.

Brislin, R. (1986). *Intercultural Interactions: A Practical Guide.* Beverly Hills, CA: Sage.

Buell, L.H. (1984). *Understanding the Immigrant Cambodian.* San Diego: Los Amigos Research Associates.

Buell, L.H. (1984). *Understanding the Refugee Laotian.* San Diego: Los Amigos Research Associates.

Buell, L.H. (1984). *Understanding the Immigrant Mexican.* San Diego: Los Amigos Research Associates.

Buell, L.H. (1984). *Understanding the Refugee Chinese.* San Diego: Los Amigos Research Associates.

Buell, L.H. (1984). *Understanding the Refugee Vietnamese.* San Diego: Los Amigos Research Associates.

Buell, L.H. (1984). *Understanding the Immigrant Iraqi.* San Diego: Los Amigos Research Associates.

Burbidge, L.C. (1993). *The State of Black America.* New York: National Urban League.

Burgoon, J.K., et al. (1988). *Non-verbal Communication: The Unspoken Dialog.* New York: Harper & Row.

Butturff, D. & Epstein, E. (Eds.). (1978). *Women's Language and Styles.* Akron, OH: L&S Books.

Campbell, C.P. (1995). *Race, Myth and the News.* Thousand Oaks, CA: Sage.

Campbell, I.C. (1989). *A History of the Pacific Islands.* Berkeley: University of California Press.

Campbell, L.R. (1994). *Learning about Culturally Diverse Populations.* Asha. 36 (6/7).

Canda, E.R. & Phaobtong, T. (1992). Buddhism as a Support System for Southeast Asian Refugees. *Social Work,* 37(1).

Caplan, N., Whitmore, J.K. & Choy, M.H. (1989). *The Boat People and Achievement in America.* Ann Arbor: University of Michigan Press.

Carbaugh, D. (Ed.). (1990). *Cultural Communication and Intercultural Contact.* Hillsdale, NJ: Lawrence Erlbaum.

Cardona, G. (1992). Indo-Iranian Languages. *International Encyclopedia of Linguistics,* 2. New York: Oxford University Press.

Carmichael, S. & Hamilton, C.V. (1967). *Black Power: The Politics of Liberation in America.* New York: Vintage.

Carrasquillo, A. (1991). *Hispanic Children and Youth in the United States.* New York: Garland Publishing.

Carroll, R. (1988). *Cultural Misunderstanding: The French-American Experience.* Chicago: University of Chicago Press.

Cashman, S.D. (1991). *African-Americans and the Quest for Civil Rights.* New York: New York University.

Casse, P. & Deol, S. (1985). *Managing Intercultural Negotiations.* Yarmouth, ME: Intercultural Press.

Chai, C. & Chai, W. (1965). *The Sacred Books of Confucius and Other Confucian Classics.* New York: Bantam Books.

Chambers, J.W., Jr. (1983). *Black English: Educational Equity and the Law.* Tucson: Karoma Publishers.

Chang, R. & Chang, M. (1992). *Speaking of Chinese.* New York: Oxford University Press.

Chang, S. (1991). *Asian Americans: An Interpretive History.* Boston: Twayne Publishers.

Cheek, J.M. (1976). *Assertive Black . . . Puzzled White.* San Luis Obispo, CA: Impact Publications.

Cheng, L.L. & Ima, K. (1989). *Understanding the Immigrant Pacific Islander.* San Diego: Los Amigos Research Associates.

Choy, B. (1979). *Koreans in America.* Chicago: Nelson-Hall.

Chu, C. (1991). *The Asian Mind Game.* New York: Rawson Associates.

Cima, R. (Ed.). (1989). *Vietnam: A Country Study.* Washington, DC: United States Government as represented by the Secretary of the Army.

Clark, S. & Kelley, S. (1992). Traditional Native-American Values. *Journal of Rehabilitation,* 58(2).

Cleveland, H. (1960). *The Overseas Americans.* New York: McGraw-Hill.

Clifford, J. (1989). *The Predicament of Culture.* Cambridge, MA: Harvard University Press.

Cogdell, R. & Wilson, S. (1980). *Black Communication in White Society.* Saratoga, CA: Century-Twenty-One Publishers.

Cohen, R. (1991). *Negotiating across Cultures: Communication Obstacles in International Diplomacy.* Washington, DC: U.S. Institute of Peace Press.

Condon, J. (1985). *Good Neighbors: Communicating with the Mexicans.* Yarmouth, ME: Intercultural Press.

Condon, J. & Yousef, F. (1975). *An Introduction to Intercultural Communication.* New York: Bobbs-Merrill.

Cordova, F. (1983). *Filipinos: Forgotten Asian Americans.* Dubuque, IA: Kendall/Hunt.

Costa, J.A. & Bomossy, G.J. (Eds.). (1995). *Marketing in a Multicultural World: Ethnicity, Nationalism and Cultural Identity.* Thousand Oaks, CA: Sage.

Cox, T. (1993). *Cultural Diversity in Organizations.* San Francisco: Berrrett-Koehler.

Dalton, B. (1992). *Indonesia.* Chicago: Passport Books.

Dance, F. (Ed.). (1982). *Human Communication Theory.* New York: Harper & Row.

Das, V. (Ed.). (1987). *Structure and Cognition: Aspects of Hindu Caste and Ritual.* Delhi: Oxford University Press.

De Bary, T. (1969). *The Buddhist Tradition in India, China, and Japan.* New York: Random House.

DeMente, B. (1989). *Korean Etiquette and Ethics in Business.* Lincolnwood, IL: NTC Publishing Group.

DeVito, J.A. (1986). *The Communication Handbook: A Dictionary.* New York: Harper & Row.

DeVos, G. & Romanucci-Ross, L. (Eds.). (1975). *Ethnic Identity: Cultural Continuities and Change.* Palo Alto, CA: Mayfield.

Dewart, J. (1989). *The State of Black America.* New York: National Urban League.

Dillard, J.L. (1972). *Black English: Its History and Usage in the United States.* New York: Random House.

Dodge, E.S. (1976). *Islands and Empires: Western Impact on the Pacific and East Asia.* Minneapolis: University of Minnesota Press.

Dovidio, J. & Gaertner, S. (Eds.). (1986). *Prejudice, Discrimination, and Racism.* New York: Academic Press.

Downs, J. (1971). *Cultures in Crisis.* Chicago: Glencoe.

Dresser, N. (1996). *Multicultural Manners.* New York: John Wiley.

DuBois, W.E.B. (1964). *The World and Africa.* New York: International

DuBois, W.E.B. (1969). *The Souls of Black Folks.* New York: New American Library.

Dudden, A.P. (1992). *The American Pacific: From the Old China Trade to Present.* New York: Oxford University Press.

Durkheim, E. (1965). *The Elementary Forms of the Religious Life.* Glencoe, IL: The Free Press.

Ebihara, M. (1966). Interrelations Between Buddhism and Social Systems in Cambodia Peasant Culture. *Anthropological Studies in Theravada Buddhism.* New Haven, CT: Yale University Press, Southeast Asian Studies.

Edwards, V. & Seinkewicz, T.J. (1990). *Oral Cultures Past and Present.* Cambridge: Basil Blackwell.

Eitel, E.J. (1970). *Handbook of Chinese Buddhism.* Amsterdam: Philo Press.

Elias, N. (1982). *The History of Manners.* New York: Pantheon.

Engineer, A.A. (1992). *The Rights of Women in Islam.* New York: St. Martin's Press.

Epstein, A.L. (1987). *Ethos and Identity.* Chicago: Aldine.

Erez, M. & Earley, P.C. (1993). *Culture, Self-identity, and Work.* New York: Oxford University Press.

Erickson, J. (1979). *Islands of the South Pacific.* Menlo Park, CA: Lane Publishing Co.

Ethridge, J.M. (1990). *China's Unfinished Revolution.* San Francisco: China Books and Periodicals.

Europa Publications Limited (1994). *The Middle East and North Africa* (40th ed.) Cambridge, England: Staples Printers Rochester Limited.

Famighetti, R. (Ed.).(1994). *The World Almanac and Book of Facts.* Mahwah, NJ: Funk & Wagnalls.

Farah, C.E. (1970). *Islam: Beliefs and Observances.* Barron's Educational Series. New York: Woodbury.

Farah, M. (1984). *Marriage and Sexuality in Islam.* Salt Lake City: University of Utah Press.

Featherstone, M. (1990). *Global Culture: Nationalism, Globalization and Modernity.* London: Sage.

Ferguson, H. (1987) *Manual for Multicultural Education.* Yarmouth, ME: Intercultural Press.

Fiatoa, L. & Palafox, N. (1980). *The Samoans.* Honolulu: University of Hawaii, School of Medicine.

Fisher, B.A. (1978). *Perspectives on Human Communication.* New York: Macmillan.

Fisher, G. (1980). *International Negotiation: A Cross-Cultural Perspective.* Chicago, IL: Intercultural Press.

Fixico, D.L. (1986). *Termination and Relocation: Federal Indian Policy, 1945 to 1960.* Albuquerque: University of New Mexico Press.

Forbes, J.D. (1977). *The Chicano Worker.* Austin: University of Texas Press.

Frazier, E.F. (1962). *Black Bourgeoisie.* New York: Crowell, Collier & Macmillan.

Frazier, E.F. (1963). *The Negro Church in America.* New York: Knopf.

Frederick, H.H. (1993). *Global Communication and International Relations.* Belmont, CA: Wadsworth.

Furlonge, G. (1971). *Traditional Islamic Society.* In M. Adams (Ed.), *The Middle East: A Handbook.* Cambridge, England: Anthony Blond Ltd.

Furnham, A. & Bochnew, S. (1986). *Culture Shock: Psychological Reactions to Unfamiliar Environments.* New York: Methuen.

Gall, S.B. & Gall, T.L. (1993). *Statistical Record of Asian Americans.* Detroit: Gale Research.

Gard, R.A. (1961). *Buddhism.* New York: George Braziller.

Gardwood, A.N. (Ed.). (1993). *Hispanic Americans: A Statistical Sourcebook.* Boulder, CO: Numbers & Concepts.

Garreau, J. (1981). *The Nine Nations of North America.* New York: Houghton Mifflin.

Geddes, R.W. (1976). *Migrants of the Mountains: The Cultural Ecology of the Blue Miau (Hmong) of Thailand.* Oxford: Clarendon.

Geertz, C. (1973). *The Interpretation of Cultures.* New York: Basic Books.

Giles, H. & St. Clair, R. (Eds.). (1992). *Language, Ethnicity and Intergroup Relations.* London: Academic Press.

Glazer, N. & Moynihan, D. (1963). *Beyond the Melting Pot.* Cambridge, MA: MIT Press & Harvard University Press.

Glazer, N. & Moynihan, D. (1975). *Ethnicity: Theory and Experience.* Cambridge, MA: Harvard University Press.

Glenn, E.S., Witmeyer, D. & Stevenson, K. (1977). Cultural Styles of Persuasion. *International Journal of Intercultural Relations,* I(3), 52–66.

Gochenour, T. (1990). *Considering Filipinos.* Yarmouth, ME: Intercultural Press.

Gorden, M. (1964). *Assimilation in American Life.* Oxford: Oxford University Press.

Gordon, M.M. (1978). *Human Nature, Class, and Ethnicity.* New York: Oxford University Press.

Gray, P. (1991). Whose America? *TIME Magazine,* 7/8 issue, 12–20.

Grebler, L., et al. (1970). *The Mexican American People.* New York: The Free Press.

Greene, M. (1993). *The Passions of Pluralism: Multiculturalism and the Expanding Community.* Educational Researcher, 22(1), 13–18.

Gronbeck, G., Farrell, T. & Soukup, P. (Eds.). (1991). *Media, Consciousness, and Culture.* Newbury Park, CA: Sage.

Grossier, P.L. (1982). *The United States and the Middle East.* Albany: State University of New York Press.

Gudykunst, W. (1984). *Communicating with Strangers: An Approach to Intercultural Communication.* Reading, MA: Addison-Wesley.

Gudykunst, W. (1989). *Theories in Intercultural Communication.* Newbury Park, CA: Sage.

Gudykunst, W. (1998). *Bridging Differences: Effective Intergroup Communication.* Thousand Oaks, CA: Sage.

Guernica, A. (1982). *Reaching the Hispanic Market Effectively.* New York: McGraw-Hill.

Gulliver, P.H. (1979). *Disputes and Negotiations: A Cross-cultural Perspective.* New York: Academic Press.

Gutman, H. (1976). *The Black Family in Slavery and Freedom: 1750–1925.* New York: Random House.

Gutmann, A. (Ed.). (1992). *Multiculturalism and the Politics of Recognition.* Princeton, NJ: Princeton University Press.

Hall, E.T. (1977). *Beyond Culture.* New York: Anchor Books.

Hall, E.T. (1981). *The Silent Language.* New York: Doubleday.

Hall, E.T. (1982). *The Hidden Dimension.* New York: Doubleday.

Hall, J. & Beadsley, R. (1965). *Twelve Doors to Japan.* New York: McGraw-Hill.

Hallowell, A.I. (1955). *Culture and Experience.* New York: Schocken Books.

Harris, P.R. & Morgan, R.T. (1991). *Managing Cultural Differences.* Houston, Gulf.

Hayakawa, S.I. (1978). *Through the Communication Barrier.* New York: Harper & Row.

Hayes-Bautista, D.E. (1992). *No Longer a Minority: Latinos and Social Policy in California.* Los Angeles: Chicano Studies Research Center, University of California.

Hecht, M.L. (1993). *African American Communication.* Thousand Oaks, CA: Sage.

Heider, F. (1958). *The Psychology of Interpersonal Relations.* New York: John Wiley.

Helms, J.E. (Ed.). (1977) *Black and White Racial Identity: Theory, Research, and Practice.* Westport, CT: Greenwood Press.

Henley, N.M. (1977). *Body Politics: Power, Sex and Nonverbal Communication.* Englewood Cliffs, NJ: Prentice-Hall.

Henry, W.A. (1990). *Beyond the Melting Pot.* Time Magazine, 135(15), 28–31.

Hinnells, J.R. (1997). *Dictionary of Religions.* London: Penguin Books.

Hobday, P. (1978). *Saudi Arabia Today.* New York: St. Martin's Press.

Hofstede, G. (1980). *Culture's Consequences.* Newbury Park, CA: Sage.

Hollinger, D.A. (1995). *Post-ethnic America: Beyond Multiculturalism.* New York: Basic Books.

Horowitz, D.L. (1985). *Ethnic Groups in Conflict.* Berkeley: University of California Press.

Horton, C.P. & Smith, J.C. (Eds.). (1993). *Statistical Record of Black America.* (2nd ed.). Detroit: Gale Research.

Hsu, F.L. (1963). *Caste, Clan and Club.* Princeton, NJ: Van Nostrand.

Hsu, F.L. (1981). *American and Chinese: Passage to Differences.* Honolulu: University of Hawaii Press.

Hurh, W.M. & Kwang, C.K. (1984). *Korean Immigrants in America.* Cranbury, NJ: Fairleigh Dickinson University Press.

Ikle, F.C. (1987). *How Nations Negotiate.* New York: Harper & Row.

Imai, M. (1981). *Sixteen Ways to Avoid Saying No.* Tokyo: Nihon Keizai Shimbun.

Ingraham, H. (1997). *People's Names.* Jefferson, NC: MacFarland.

Ingrams, D. (1971). *The Position of Women in Middle East Arab Society.* In M. Adams (Ed.), *The Middle East: A Handbook.* Cambridge, England: Anthony Blond Ltd.

Isaacs, J. (1980). *Australian Dreaming: 40,000 Years of Aboriginal History.* Sydney: Lansdowne.

Jandt, F.E. (1998). *Intercultural Communication: An Introduction.* Thousand Oaks, CA: Sage.

Jaynes, G.D., & Williams, R.M., Jr. (Eds.). (1989). *A Common Destiny: Blacks and American Society.* Washington, DC: National Academy Press.

Johnstone, P. (1993). *Operation World.* Harrisonburg, VA: R.R. Donnelly & Sons.

Jones, R.L. (Ed.). (1980). *Black Psychology.* New York: Harper & Row.

Jones, S. (1993). *The Right Touch: Understanding and Using the Language of Physical Contact.* Cresskill, NJ: Hampton Press.

Joy, A. (1989). *Ethnicity in Canada.* New York: AMS.

Karenga, M. (1982). *Introduction to Black Studies.* Englewood, CA: Dawaida.

Katriel, T. (1986). *Talking Straight: Dugri Speech in Israeli Sabra Culture.* Cambridge: Cambridge University Press.

Keesing, R.M. (1988). *Melanesian Pidgin and the Oceanic Substrate.* Stanford, CA: Stanford University Press.

Khuri, F. (1968, August). The Etiquette of Bargaining in the Middle East. *American Anthropologist, 4,* 698–706.

Kim, H. (1985). *Facts about Korea* (18th Ed.). Seoul, Korea: Samhwa Publishing Company.

Kim, Y.Y. (1986). *Interethnic Communication: Current Research.* Newbury Park, CA: Sage.

Kim, Y.Y. (1988). *Cross-cultural Adaptation: Current Approaches.* Newbury Park, CA: Sage.

Kincaid, D.L. (Ed.).(1987). *Communication Theory: Eastern and Western Perspectives.* New York: Academic Press.

Kitano, H. (1976) *Japanese Americans.* Englewood Cliffs, NJ: Prentice-Hall.

Kitayama, S. & Markus, H. (Eds.). (1994). *Culture, Self, and Emotions.* Washington, DC: American Psychological Association.

Kleg, M. (1993). *Hate, Prejudice, and Racism.* Albany: State University of New York Press.

Kluckhohn, F. & Strodtbeck, F. (1961). *Variations in Value Orientations.* New York: Row, Peterson.

Knapp, M.L. & Miller, G.R. (Eds.). (1985). *Handbook of Interpersonal Communication.* Beverly Hills, CA: Sage.

Kochman, T. (1981). *Black & White Styles in Conflict.* Chicago: University of Chicago Press.

Kohls, R.L. (1988). *The Values Americans Live By.* San Francisco: LinguaTec.

Koller, J.M. (1982). *The Indian Way.* New York: Macmillan.

Korean Overseas Information Service. (1986). *Focus on Korea.* Seoul, Korea: Samsung Moonwha Printing Company.

Korzenny, F. & Ting-Toomey, S. (Eds.). (1990). *Communicating for Peace: Diplomacy and Negotiation.* Newbury Park, CA: Sage.

Kozlowski, G.C. (1991). *The Concise History of Islam and the Origin of Its Empires.* Acton, MA: Copley Publishing Group.

Kremenyuk, V.A. (Ed.). (1991). *International Negotiation: Analysis, Approaches, Issues.* San Francisco: Jossey-Bass.

Kroeber, A. & Kluckhohn, C. (1963). *Culture: A Critical Review of Concepts and Definitions.* New York: Random House.

Labov, W. (1972). *Language in the Inner City: Studies in the Black English Vernacular.* Philadelphia: University of Philadelphia Press.

Landis, D. & Boucher, J. (1987). *Ethnic Conflict.* Newbury Park, CA: Sage.

Landis, D. & Brislin (Eds.). (1983). *Handbook of Intercultural Training*. Elmsford, NY: Pergamon.

Latino Legislative Caucus Hearings (1991). *Latinos at a Crossroads: Challenges and Opportunities into the 21st Century*. Los Angeles: Latino Legislative Caucus Hearings.

Lazarus, R. (1991). *Emotion and Adaptation*. New York: Oxford University Press.

Lebra, T.S. (1976). *Japanese Patterns of Behavior*. Honolulu: University Press of Hawaii.

Lemann, N. (1991). *The Promised Land: The Great Black Migration and How It Changed America*. New York: Knopf.

Leone, B. (1992). *Native Languages and Cultures*. Bilingual Basics, Summer/Fall 1992.

Levine, R.A. & Campbell, D.T.(1972). *Ethnocentrism: Theories of Conflict, Ethnic Attitudes and Group Behavior*. New York: John Wiley

Li, C.N. (1992). *International Encyclopedia of Linguistics*. New York: Oxford University Press.

Locke, D. (1992). *Increasing Multicultural Understanding*. Newbury Park, CA: Sage.

Long, S.O. (1992). *Japan: A Country Study*. Washington, DC: Department of the Army.

Lopreato, J. (1970). *Italian Americans*. New York: Random House.

Luce, D. & Sommer, J. (1969). *Viet Nam—The Unheard Voices*. Ithaca, NY: Cornell University Press.

Mackie, D. & Hamilton, D. (Eds.). (1993). *Affect, Cognition, and Stereotyping*. San Diego, CA: Academic Press.

Macrae, C., Stangor, C. & Hewstone, M. (Eds.). (1996). *Stereotypes and Stereotyping*. New York: Guilford.

Magnetti, D. & Sigler, M. (1973). *An Introduction to the Near East*. Huntington, IN: Our Sunday Visitor.

Major, J.S. (1989). *The Land and People of China*. New York: J.B. Lippincott.

Malson, M., Mudimbe-Boyi, E., O'Barr, J. & Wyer, M. (Eds.). (1990). *Black Women in America*. Chicago: University of Chicago Press.

Marin, G. & Marin, B. (1991). *Research with Hispanic Populations*. Beverly Hills, CA: Sage.

Matics, M.L. (1970). *Entering the Path of Enlightenment*. New York: Macmillan.

Mautner-Markhof, F. (Ed.). (1982). *Processes of International Negotiations*. Boulder, CO: Westview.

May, L. & Sharratt, S.C. (1994). *Applied Ethics: A Multicultural Approach*. Englewood Cliffs, NJ: Prentice-Hall.

McAdoo, H.P. (Ed.). (1988). *Black Families*. Newbury Park, CA: Sage.

McAdoo, H.P. & McAdoo, J.L. (Eds.). (1985). *Black Children.* Beverly Hills, CA: Sage.

McNaughton, W. (1974). *The Confucian Vision.* Ann Arbor: University of Michigan Press.

McWilliams, C. (1990). *North from Mexico.* New York: Greenwood Press.

Mehrrabian, A. (1981). *Silent Messages: Implicit Communication of Emotions and Attitudes.* Belmont, CA: Wadsworth.

Meier, F. (1971). *Islam and Its Cultural Divergence.* Urbana IL: University of Illinois Press.

Melendex, E. (1991). *Hispanics in the Labor Force: Issues and Policies.* New York: Plenum Press.

Menez, H.Q. (1980). *Folklore Communication among Filipinos in America.* New York: Arno Press.

Metz, H.C. (Ed.). (1990). *Iraq: A Country Study.* Washington, DC: Federal Research Division, Library of Congress. Headquarters, Department of the Army.

Miller, A.G. (Ed.). (1982). *In the Eye of the Beholder: Contemporary Issues in Stereotyping.* New York: Praeger.

Miller, G. & Steinberg, M. (1975). *Between People.* Chicago: Science Research Associates.

Min, P.G. (Ed.). (1995). *Asian Americans: Contemporary Trends and Issues.* Thousand Oaks, CA: Sage.

Moran, R. & Stripp, W. (1991). *Successful International Business Negotiations.* Houston: Gulf.

Morris, D. (1979). *Gestures: Their Origins and Distribution.* London: Cape.

Morris, D. (1995). *Bodytalk: The Meaning of Human Gestures.* New York: Crown Trade Paperbacks.

Mosher, S.W. (1983). *Broken Earth: The Rural Chinese.* New York: The Free Press.

Nakamura, H. (1964). *Ways of Thinking of Eastern Peoples.* Honolulu: East-West Center Press.

Nakane, C. (1970). *Japanese Society.* Berkeley: University of California Press.

Namamura, N. (1988). *Nippon: The Land and Its People.* Japan: Gakuseisha Publishing.

Nash, J.C. (1966). *Anthropological Studies in Theravada Buddhism.* New Haven, CT: Yale University Press of Southeast Asia Studies.

Nicolau, S. & S. Santiestevan, S. (Eds.). (1990). *The Hispanic Almanac.* New York: Hispanic Policy Development Project.

Nyrop, R.F. (Ed.). (1982). *Federal Republic of Germany, A Country Study.* Washington, DC: U.S. Government Printing Office.

Oey, T. (1993). *Everyday Indonesian.* Chicago: Passport Books.

Omi, M. & Winant, H. (1986). *Racial Group Formation in the United States.* New York: Routledge.

Padilla, A.M. (Ed.). (1980). *Acculturation: Theory, Models and Some New Findings.* Boulder, O: Westview.

Padilla, A.M. (Ed.). (1995). *Hispanic Psychology.* Thousand Oaks, CA: Sage.

Park, R. (Ed.). (1950). *Race and Culture.* New York: The Free Press.

Pedersen, P. (1988). *A Handbook to Develop Multicultural Awareness.* Washington, DC: AACD.

Penfield, J. (1990). *Understanding Asian Americans.* New York: Neal-Schuman Publishers.

Phillips, S. (1982). *The Invisible Culture.* New York: Longman.

Ponterotto, J.G. & Pedersen, P.B. (1993). *Preventing Prejudice.* Thousand Oaks, CA: Sage.

Portes, A. & Rumbaut, R. (1990). *Immigrant America: A Portrait.* Berkeley: University of California Press.

Posses, F. (1978). *The Art of International Negotiation.* London: Business Press.

Prosser, M.H. (1978). *The Cultural Dialogue: An Introduction to Intercultural Communication.* Boston: Houghton Mifflin.

Pye, L. (1982). *Chinese Commercial Negotiating Style.* Cambridge, MA: Oelgeschlager, Gunn & Hain.

Radhakrishnan, S. (1979). *Indian Religions.* New Delhi: Vision Books.

Reischauer, E. (1977). *The Japanese.* Cambridge, MA: Harvard University Press.

Robinson, P.W. (1978). *Black Quest for Identity.* Minneapolis, MN: Burgess Publishing.

Rodinson, M. (1981). *The Arabs.* London: Croom Helm.

Rokeach, M. (1972). *Beliefs, Attitudes, and Values.* San Francisco: Jossey-Bass.

Roosens, E. (1989). *Creating Ethnicity: The Process of Ethnogenesis.* Newbury Park, CA: Sage.

Root, M. (Ed.). (1995). *The Multiracial Experience.* Thousand Oaks, CA: Sage.

Rosaldo, M. (1974). *Women, Culture and Society.* Stanford, CA: Stanford University Press.

Rosaldo, R. (1989). *Culture and Truth: The Remaking of Social Analysis.* Boston: Beacon.

Roseberry-McKibbin, C. (1995). *Multicultural Students of Special Language Needs.* Oceanside, CA: Academic Communication Associates.

Rossman, M.L. (1994). *Multicultural Marketing: Selling to a Diverse America.* New York: AMACOM.

Rothenberg, P.S. (Ed.). (1992). *Race, Class and Gender in the United States.* New York: St. Martin's Press.

Rothman, J. (1992). *From Confrontation to Cooperation: Resolving Ethnic and Regional Conflict.* Newbury Park, CA: Sage.

Saitz, R.I. (1972). *Handbook of Gestures: Colombia and the United States.* The Hague: Mouton.

Salacuse, J. (1991). *Making Global Deals: Negotiating in the International Market Place.* Boston: Houghton Mifflin.

Samovar, L.A. (1981). *Understanding Intercultural Communication.* Belmont, CA: Wadsworth.

Samovar, L.A. & Porter, R.E. (Eds.). (1996). *Intercultural Communication: A Reader.* Belmont, CA: Wadsworth.

Sarbaugh, L.E. (1979). *Intercultural Communication.* Rochelle Park, NJ: Hayden Book Company.

Saville-Troike, M. (1982). *The Ethnography of Communication: An Introduction.* Oxford: Basil Blackwell.

Schultz, B. (1998). *Smart Selling Techniques.* Boca Raton, FL: New Home Specialist.

Schultz, B. (1997). *The Official Handbook for New Home Salespeople.* Boca Raton, FL: New Home Specialist.

Segall, M.H. (1966). *The Influence of Culture on Visual Perception.* Indianapolis: Bobbs-Merrill.

Shack, W. & Skinner, E. (1979). *Strangers in African Societies.* Berkeley: University of California Press.

Sharma, I.C. (1965). *Ethical Philosophies of India.* New York: Harper & Row.

Shelley, R. (1993). *Culture Shock: A Guide to Customs and Etiquette of Japan.* Portland, OR: Graphic Arts Center Publishing Company.

Shorris, E. (1992). *Latinos.* New York: W.W. Norton Company.

Singer, M. (1987). *Intercultural Communication: A Perceptual Approach.* Englewood Cliffs, NJ: Prentice-Hall.

Sitaram, K.S. & Cogdell, R.T. (1976). *Foundations of Intercultural Communication.* Columbus, OH: Merrill.

Smith, A. (1986). *The Ethnic Origins of Nations.* Oxford: Basil Blackwell.

Sreenivasa Murthy, H.V. (1973). *Studies in Indian Culture.* Bombay: Asia Publishing House.

Stern, J. (1989). *The Filipino Americans.* New York: Chelsea House Publishers.

Stewart, E. (1972). *American Cultural Patterns: A Cross-cultural Perspective.* Yarmouth, ME: Intercultural Press.

Stryk, L. (1968). *World of the Buddha: A Reader—from the Three Baskets to Modern Zen.* New York: Doubleday.

Tajfel, H. (Ed.).(1982). *Social Identity and Intergroup Relations.* Cambridge: Cambridge University Press.

Takaki, R. (1993). *A Different Mirror: A History of Multicultural America.* Boston: Little, Brown.

Terkel, S. (1992). *Race: How Blacks and Whites Think and Feel about the American Obsession.* New York: New Press.

Thomas, R. (1991). *Beyond Race & Gender.* New York: AMACOM.

Tidwell, B.J. (1993). *The State of Black America 1993.* New York: National Urban League.

Triandis, H.C. (1994). *Culture and Social Behavior.* New York: McGraw-Hill.

Trilling, L. (1968). *Beyond Culture.* New York: Viking.

Tsujimura, A. (1968). *Japanese Culture and Communication.* Tokyo: NHK Books.

Veltman, C. (1988). *The Future of the Spanish Language in the United States.* New York: Hispanic Policy Development Project.

Wadley, S. & Jacobson, D. (Eds.). (1977). *Women in India: Two Perspectives.* New Delhi: Manohar.

Watson, O.M. (1970). *Proxemic Behavior: A Cross-cultural Study.* The Hague: Mouton.

Weiss, S.E. & Stripp, W. (1985). *Negotiating with Foreign Persons.* New York: New York University Press.

West, C. (1993). *Race Matters.* Boston: Beacon Press.

White, J.L. & Parham, T.A. (1990). *The Psychology of Blacks: An African-American Perspective.* Englewood Cliffs, NJ: Prentice-Hall.

Williams, R. (1976). *Keywords: A Vocabulary of Culture and Society.* London: Fontana.

Williams, R. (1981). *Culture.* London: Fontana.

Wilson, C.C. & Gutierrez, F. (1995). *Race, Multiculturalism, and the Media.* Thousand Oaks, CA: Sage.

Wiseman, R. & Koester, J. (Eds.). (1993). *Intercultural Communication Competence.* Newbury Park, CA: Sage.

Wong, A.M. (1993). *Target: The U.S. Asian Market—A Practical Guide to Doing Business.* Palos Verdes, CA: Pacific Heritage Books.

Woodson, C.G. (1968). *The African Background Outlined.* New York: Negro Universities Press.

Wright, A.F. (1962). *Confucian Personalities.* Stanford, CA: Stanford University Press.

Wright, G. (1981). *Building the Dream: A Social History of Housing in America.* New York: Pantheon.

Yee, A. H. (1984). *A Search for Meaning: Essays of a Chinese American.* San Francisco: Chinese Historical Society of America.

Yinger, M. (1994). *Ethnicity.* Albany: State University of New York Press.

Young, B. (1980). *People and Cultures of Hawaii.* Honolulu: University of Hawaii Press.

Young, K. (1968). *Negotiating with the Chinese Communists.* New York: McGraw-Hill.

Zarembka, A. (1990). *The Urban Housing Crisis.* New York: Greenwood Press.

Zelinsky, W. (1973). *The Cultural Geography of the United States.* Englewood Cliffs, NJ: Prentice-Hall.

Zimmerman, M. (1985). *How to Do Business with the Japanese.* New York: Random House.

Index

time perception, 148
and women, 128, 159
holidays
Blessing of the Waters, 135
Bodhi Day, 134
Christmas, 133, 135
Hanukkah, 133–34
Kwanzaa, 135
Las Posadas, 134–35
Ramadan, 134
Rosh Hashanah, 134
home builders, and cultural expectations, 67–68
home buying
closing, 200–201, 231–33
counteroffers, 193–94
and ethnic background of neighborhood, 162–63
explaining the process, 142, 145–46
family involvement in, 144–45
new homes, 235–41
and the "granny unit," 237
and kitchen exhausts, 237
and surveys, 238
and pooling of resources, 198
reasons for, 142–43
selection of the right home, 152–57
signs of interest in buying, 161–64
"steering" and, 164
time involved in, 148
touring process, 240
home insurance, 201
home invasion robberies, 137
home owners insurance, 201
home ownership
length of, 161
and non-Whites, 140
home selling

About the Author

Michael D. Lee has been a real estate agent and broker since 1977. During that time he has sold millions of dollars' worth of residential and commercial real estate as well as new homes and syndications.

Lee is a nationally recognized multicultural expert and consultant who appears regularly on television. He has spoken at six National Association of Realtors® conventions as well as for state and local boards of Realtors® across the country. He also speaks to new home developers throughout the United States.

Lee also conducts multicultural training in industries outside real estate, including new car sales, public transportation, financial planning, and law. He is the first Asian American in history to earn the "Certified Speaking Professional" (CSP) designation from the National Speakers Association. Lee's most popular real estate programs include: "Success with Multicultural Clients," "No-Sweat Prospecting," "How to List Buyers," and "Charging for Real Estate By-The-Hour."

Lee is often called as an expert witness in court cases where culture is an issue. He has also been an arbitrator for the American Arbitration Association. His articles on multicultural beliefs have appeared in both state and national magazines. He can be reached by calling (800) 41-SPEAK or by e-mail at *seminars@netvista.net*.

DO YOU WANT TO DO BUSINESS WITH PEOPLE FROM DIFFERENT CULTURES?

Doing business with people of diverse cultures requires knowledge and sensitivity.

MICHAEL LEE'S indispensible quarterly newsletter — CULTURAL DIFFERENCES — will provide you with a world of opportunities to do business comfortably with people from around the globe.

HERE'S JUST A SAMPLING OF THE INVALUABLE INFORMATION YOU'LL RECEIVE IN EACH ISSUE:

- ☛ Negotiating with people from other cultures
- ☛ How cultural beliefs affect business transactions
- ☛ Contracting with multicultural customers
- ☛ Differences in timing
- ☛ Personal differences
- ☛ Building rapport with people from other cultures
- ☛ Why don't they do as we do here?
- ☛ Differences in etiquette
- ☛ Cultural do's and taboos
- ☛ Getting referrals to other multicultural customers

THERE'S NOT ANOTHER PUBLICATION IN THE COUNTRY THAT CAN HELP YOU LIKE

CULTURAL DIFFERENCES!

SUBSCRIBE TODAY!
ONLY $69.95 PER YEAR
CALL (800)-41-SPEAK

CULTURAL DIFFERENCES

Helping retail and service businesses
understand multicultural customers

WHY SHOULD YOU CARE ABOUT MULTICULTURAL CUSTOMERS?

By Michael Lee

MICHAEL LEE

There are more than one million new immigrants coming into the United States every year mostly from Mexico, Latin America, Asia and the Middle East.

Add to this the millions of Americans from cultural backgrounds other than European and you have a huge potential market for your products and services.

However, people from other cultures do not buy things like Americans and have different cultural beliefs and traditions that impact the purchasing decision.

If you want to sell product or services to people from different cultures we must adjust to their way of doing business. If you don't change you will lose customers to businesses that do. Look at all of the grocery and retail stores that now cater specifically to Hispanics, Asians, Middle Easterners and African Americans.

Why do we have to adjust? Why don't they just do as Americans do? It's funny, but when people from the United States travel overseas everyone calls us by the same descriptive term, "The Ugly Americans." Why? Because when we go to France, Germany or China we expect them to adjust to us by speaking English and making us

feel at home by serving us hamburgers and french fries. Why should they since we're on their turf?

Just as it's hard for Americans to leave our 200-year-old culture at the gate when we board a transcontinental flight, it's even more difficult for someone with a culture that's thousands of years old to do the same. While people from other countries try to be as American as possible, it just takes time.

What cultural differences do we have to adjust to? First, we must be more customer-friendly and print signs and other printed matter in the language of people who frequent your store. This simple and inexpensive act says loudly, "We care."

Next, be aware of the differences in beliefs that other cultures embrace. In the United States there are very few buildings with a 13th floor because of our morbid fear that this number is bad luck. In other countries thirteen has no significance, but other numbers may be important. For instance, Asians often believe that the number "three" or "four" is unlucky. To know for sure you must ask your customers.

Yes, it's OK to ask your customers about their beliefs. Many of us shy away from discussing the subject of culture, fearing that it might make people from other cultures uncomfortable. Actually, just the